Real
Ventures

"Did We *Really* Do *That?*"

Bonnie Burgess Neely

NEWMAN SPRINGS PUBLISHING
320 Broad Street
Red Bank, NJ 07701

First originally published by Newman Springs Publishing 2022

ISBN 978-1-68498-426-8 (Paperback)
ISBN 978-1-68498-427-5 (Digital)

Printed in the United States of America

I Married "Mr. Go" (Without Knowing It)

WHEN I WAS a teen, my dream was to marry and live in a small vine-covered cottage with a happy home full of children. I was a stay-at-home type with none of my mother and sister's yearnings for travel. My dream came true. By my twenties, I was joyful with my loving husband and our three healthy children. But Bill, too, had a dream, which, I think, must have been to live out of a suitcase. Although our marriage license did not reveal it, his middle name is "Go." In our sixty years together thus far, my marriage vow "wherever you go, I will go" has taken us in various RVs over enough miles to equal more than three trips to the moon or around the equator twenty-five times!

Now I must admit the travel bug bit me during our first international trip on business to Australia and New Zealand with our two-year-old daughter. I became almost as eager for these trips as he has always been, except for one, which stands out vividly in my memory:

Bill was a cattle rancher in our early years together, and he decided it was necessary for him to fly to Mexico and Guatemala to visit various ranches and advertise his upcoming Brahman cattle sale at the Central American Brahman Convention in Guatemala City.

I said, "Fine," as I nursed our three-month-old baby and helped our six- and eight-year-olds with homework. I naturally assumed he would also place newspaper ads and mail flyers to his potential clients, as any normal person having a sale would do.

But the next day, Bill returned from his day at our ranch and ran excitedly into the house, exclaiming, "We're all going to Mexico!"

I responded, "I know you hate to leave us alone for a few weeks, but we'll be okay, and we can't afford airfare and hotels for the whole family."

"Come see what I got!" he replied, taking my hand and leading me out the door. There, in front of our house, stood a very used, very tiny RV motor home.

Dismayed and overwhelmed, I cried, "Guess what you're going to get? A *divorce*! We have never talked about camping, and you didn't even consult me about spending our money this way! How much did it cost?"

"I saw the For Sale sign as I was driving home, and I couldn't pass this up. It was only $5,000, and we can sell it when we return home, so the trip will cost very little. If I had not bought it immediately, it would have been gone."

At that moment, the children ran out, and Bill exclaimed with joyful glee, "Look, kids. We'll live in this playhouse all summer and learn to speak Spanish!"

I clutched the baby tightly to me and cried, "I *can't*! Not in Mexico! Not in June with over one-hundred-degree temperatures! Not in *this* thing!"

But by then the family vote was already three to one (and a half), and I was outnumbered. Bill was showing the youngsters how the table would convert into a bed and how we could go into the tiny, thirty-square-inch bathroom, close the "toy potty," and sit on the lid to take a shower! My tears showered onto the baby's blanket.

Being Texans, we were familiar with the *bandito* stories of travels in Mexico, but my brave cowboy assured me those things happened only in border towns.

"At least let's buy a gun for protection," I pleaded.

But no! Bill was adamant. "Guns will only get us shot!"

We compromised. We invited my bachelor brother, who was just out of the army (and I knew he had a gun), to go with us.

I thought, *In order to have the protection of two pacifist men instead of one!* For me, going into the unknown usually conjured weird black images, but these were fiery red! Bill, on the other hand, had been taught in his formative years, "The only thing to fear is fear itself."

As school drew to a close, the children and Bill grew increasingly excited, but I could not muster any enthusiasm for the trip. The East Texas thermometers were pushing 100 degrees, and I pictured their Mexican twins registering 150 degrees. He gathered tools and spare parts for the camper, "just in case," which did nothing to alleviate my imagined horrors.

I wept as I completely filled half of the few storage compartments with disposable diapers and jars of baby food. We hadn't been able to afford the extravagance of disposable diapers before, but now they were a necessity. I knew we could buy baby food in some cities south of the border, but I didn't know if the ranches we'd visit were anywhere near civilization. I thanked my lucky stars that I was nursing the baby and didn't have to worry about bottles.

In those days, few young parents were aware of the advisability of car seats; Ralph Nader's power hadn't yet made the USA safer. I vetoed the idea of our baby bed being a cardboard box with a piece of sturdy foam for a mattress, which we had used on short trips in our car when our other two children were infants. We purchased a real (probably far less comfortable) baby car bed made with an aluminum tubing frame supporting a soft plastic sling-type bassinet, which exactly fit between the two front seats of the RV (leaving *no* room to get up or around to corral two older siblings!) The bed was advertised to be ideal because it could fold away flat (a feature which was never used because we discovered a few days into the trip that there was absolutely *nowhere* to put it away when folded). We stumbled, leaped, and fell over that!!! maddening cursed bed for the entire six weeks, while in that bed, Baby Tommy slept peacefully from his third to his fifth month of life, unable to learn to turn over because that maneuver was impossible with his total body weight suspended in a hammock-like shroud.

While cramming the rest of the tiny compartments with canned goods, powdered milk, and a huge emergency first aid kit, I was thankful that summer clothes took so little room. We rationed ourselves to one nice outfit, one warm set of clothing, and four shorts sets, hoping that Mexico had laundromats. Packing to travel in an RV resembles moving because you need *everything* that you normally use in everyday life and in emergency situations, but every item must be carefully selected for size, weight, absolute necessity, versatility, and safety in motion. Then all these necessities for cooking, eating, sleeping, bathing, dressing, playing, sightseeing, or being sick (for three adults, two children, and a baby) had to be stuffed into a space about the size of one good chest of drawers. For the veteran RV camper, this becomes routine, but it was our first time, and it was an *awful* chore! My very elderly prim and proper, upper-class, uppity neighbor would come over each day during the loading process and mutter, "You'll never get it all in, dear," "Why would you *want* to travel like this?" "When will you get this *tramper* out of the driveway?" and "Oh, those poor little children!" She did wonders for my spirits!

But Bill, Pamela, and Blake were undaunted. They were *three* kids about to play in a dollhouse! And my brother Jim, who arrived from South Carolina, thankfully with only a duffel bag and a camera, added to the jubilance. Just out of college, partly a real hippie of the seventies, ignorant of the legends of *Montezuma's revenge* stomach cramps, he was ready for adventure. I gathered a little confidence when I remembered he had been an Eagle Scout and a medic in the national guard. At least we had one person along with a little camping and CPR experience. I knew my husband could handle almost any vehicle mechanical problem that might arise, and he was totally fearless! Maybe we could make it back alive after all!

Looking back from the perspective of decades, I do not know how Jim stood that summer with the six of us in a space approximately 17 by 7.5 feet with a baby bed occupying the only floor space. My children still refer to him as the "coolest uncle in the world," and why not? Each night while Bill made camper repairs and I boiled water for drinking and cooked supper, Jim took the kids to look for parrots and monkeys in the jungle, or played marbles in the sand, or had turtle races until it was time to point out constellations in the black heavens dotted with thousands of stars not visible in the city skies at home. And on rainy days, he told them ghost stories from his hammock bed.

That trip was definitely *not* uneventful. In many respects, the venture was foolhardy and naive and sometimes downright dangerous, but as with many of our adventures, we wouldn't take anything for the experiences and the memories (since we lived to tell the stories). It made our children, at very young ages, appreciate the advantages they enjoy at home and the standards of living in the United States. My brother, who had to fly home a few days early to return to work, *still likes us* (amazing!). He jokes about some of the crazy things we not-so-average travelers do. Our children grew up fascinated with learning foreign languages and two married travel agents. (I think before they could answer the question, "Will you marry me?" they must have asked, "Do you have a passport?")

When as newbies, we were heading south of the border with an infant and two kids, our friends said we were *crazy*, and I tearfully agreed as I said, "Adiós," and followed "Mr. Go" into the RV, for better or for worse. This trip became a true test of our marriage! Any seasoned sailor knows that in small spaces, the only way to stand long confinement is to have a place for everything and everything in its place. We were *not* launched with this information!

No suitcase fits in an RV, and I had done most of the vehicle packing. My husband's nickname for me has always been *Cramit*. The first few days on the road, we almost murdered each other trying to find things as kids screamed or cried for what they wanted. I'm just five feet tall, and I was the only one who knew where anything was. The whole world is designed for people to be at least five feet, five inches tall, and RVs are no exception! Whenever anyone needed something, I had to stand on the seat, hang on for dear life with one hand while searching blindly through a cabinet with the other, a kamikaze feat while traveling fifty-five miles an hour! Finally, I figured out the only way I could find anything was to throw everything onto the floor, sort through, curse my height and the stuff, and cram it all back in. My nickname became *Cramit Dammit!* That happened at least two million times in the first few days until my tall orderly men took hold of the hatch and got us organized. By then, each of us had claimed his or her own tiny space, and we learned to be neat or be *killed* on the highway curves!

My *travelholic* husband decided RV life was wonderful because there were no bathroom stops. With a schedule to keep or a destination in mind, his idea of sightseeing was to view the sights like a moving picture in fast-forward. He yelled, "Look! Isn't that great!" as we whizzed by, and the rest of us quickly looked out the back window and hollered, "What was it?" Except for getting gasoline, there were no stops for the first five hundred or so miles to the border of

Mexico. Bill kept promising us that we'd take time once we got out of Texas.

Finally, at Laredo, we were all excited and a little nervous to cross over the border into Nuevo Laredo. We changed our money at the local bank and suddenly felt rich since we got so many pesos for each US dollar. In 1975, the border town was dirty and unappealing, and as we looked back to see Texas disappearing behind us, I had the sinking feeling of a child who lost her security blanket. But Bill assured us that the interior towns of Mexico were not like that. (Of course, he had never seen the interior either!)

On the Road South

BILL HEADED STRAIGHT to San Antonio, where my best friend had moved several years before, and we spent the night in her driveway and had a very happy renewing of friendships. I was lightening up with our laughter.

Our next stop was for two nights in the border town of Laredo, Texas, to buy supplies we already found we *must* have—some tools for repairs, more diapers and baby food, gas, and most important, vehicle insurance. We exchanged dollars for pesos, thinking it would be to our advantage to do that while still in the USA.

Crossing the border into Nuevo Laredo was no problem. We forged southward on Mexico Federal Highway 85, totally ignorant of the fact that this is called by the Mexican citizens as Carretera de la Muerte, the highway of death! (Since 1964, hundreds of people each year have disappeared on that highway. By 2021, over 70,000 of those lost people have never been found!)

Our children had fought and picked on each other through the first two days of the trip, but as we traversed this scorching Mexican wasteland to Monterrey, they looked out at the miles and miles of dust and cactus as far as anyone could see. Suddenly, little brother and big sister learned to entertain themselves with coloring books and playing games together. Having only each other as playmates bonded the siblings, and the love and cooperative spirit that developed has lasted as a lifetime reward for the arduous parts of that trip.

We stopped in Monterrey for two nights at a lovely RV park, complete with local entertainers. We were all thrilled with the authentic mariachi players and singers and couples dancing in bright costumes. We could walk to the town to purchase our first souvenirs and try a few words in Spanish. Even I, the unwilling passenger, was getting into the spirit with these friendly, spirited people. I learned to stop griping because we were *on our way* and there was *no turning back*! Pure survival instinct had kicked in. We each realized it would be a *long* trip, and no one could imagine being left on the highway for bad behavior!

Now those were the days when women coveted the glamorous job of an airline stewardess. However, my height and weight, not to mention my marital status and three children, had eliminated my possibilities of applying for such a glamorous job. But stewardess I became! I prepared and served lunches on the move and cooked supper on the go, too. We couldn't waste any precious time because we had to see it *all* before it was time to appear at the ranches where Bill would promote his cattle sale. While we were traveling the superhighways of Texas and Mexico, my job wasn't too challenging. I learned to stand facing the side counter, plant my feet shoulder width apart, and sort of sway with the motion of the vehicle in order to maintain balance. It became a cooperative effort: Bill warned me of troublesome road stretches ahead, and I sat down quickly.

I served drinks in cups with lids, used a knife only on a long, straight stretch, and returned any sharp instrument immediately to the latched drawer. I opened cabinets and refrigerator with extreme caution. I devised a method of peeling the labels from canned meat and vegetables, making a slit for steam to escape, and placing several cans in a pot of water. I could hold on to this while everything heated on our little gas stove. (In retrospect, this is definitely *not* safe!) When I was ready to serve the plates, our driver would park on the side of the road to eat. The Traveling Gourmet was not with us, thank goodness, because food was plain and geared to kids' palates and, for adults, just for survival. For the most part, we couldn't afford to eat out. We also discovered why space food, invented a few years before, to be used by our first astronauts, was important: taste, nutrition, and small size. So Space Food Sticks, Tang, Vienna Sausages, and Spam kept us alive.

But not all the country south of Texas was just covering bleak desert mileage, as we had begun to fear. By the third day, we found lush green mountainous terrain with beautiful trees and streams. We made our first point-of-interest stop at the mercado in Victoria, Mexico. The children were so excited they wanted to buy all the little trinkets they found. I was more interested in taking photographs and practicing my college Spanish, which proved to be one-sided. I could speak enough to make myself understood, but I panicked when the locals jabbered back to me in *speed* Spanish. I could understand words but never fast enough to get syntax. Very frustrating!

Bill and Jim made a major purchase with the intention of giving me great peace of mind. (I had been quite concerned about our safety since travel in Mexico at that time was purported to be somewhat dangerous. I learned after we crossed the border that we were unarmed because Bill had asked Jim to leave his gun at home! My male protectors were both staunch antifirearm advocates.) My men proudly showed me the sturdy hand-carved walking sticks, which they asserted were the perfect means of armed safety for our little group of foolhardy adventurers. I never quite figured out how they intended to use these menacing tools for our protection. Did my valiant knights intend to poke an armed bandito in the stomach or bop him over the head before he had time to shoot? Or would they make a cross with the two walking sticks and hold it up as if to keep a werewolf away?

Victoria had a special waterfall we knew we wanted to see, and it was time to hike some. But the men had a better plan that delighted the children but left me behind in dismay. They rented burros to ride to the falls. Bill even hoisted little Tommy into his porta-baby backpack, and off they went. I strode along behind because I did not feel capable of staying on a burro. The falls were truly beautiful in the jungle-like mountainous scenery. We all had so much fun!

Back in the camper, we hit the road again. Everyone was starving, so I prepared sandwiches as we made S curves through the Sierra Madre Oriental Mountains. Big mistake! I should have insisted on our eating before the engine started. I was carrying a sandwich and drink when Bill suddenly hit the brakes. I was thrown forward and barely missed the baby bed but banged my head against the seat. We were fortunate that I held nothing sharp and was only a little bruised. After that, I became more selective about the roads on which I would serve, and everyone learned to squelch hunger pains carefully until we were stopped.

On the Gulf
of Mexico

W E ARRIVED IN the potentially gorgeous coastal town of Tampico. Unspoiled by riffraff or aggressive tourism, it appeared lovely to us, and we all were ready to get out of our cage for a while. We loved walking on the yellow sandy beach and playing in the ocean for the afternoon. We decided this little town was such a pleasant find we would stay the night and splurge on a restaurant meal.

We chose a typical café on the plaza. We Texans had expected tacos and enchiladas, but we saw no familiar categories on the authentic Mexican menu, so we just ordered *we-knew-not-what*. We informed the disgruntled children that Tampico had never heard of peanut butter and jelly! The crispy fried, dried-up little tasteless things rolled around some kind of meat paste (which we prayed wasn't dog or horse meat) were about as bad as they sounded. But we were hungry, so we ate them anyway. We had visited the mercado that afternoon and marveled at the sumptuous array of fresh vegetables and fruits grown locally, so we decided the salad could not hurt us, despite knowing the *cardinal rule* for travelers below the border: *if you don't peel it, don't eat it!*

The locals in the restaurant were fascinated by American tourists and were so friendly to us. Tampico had obviously not yet been discovered by Michelin! I began to lose my fear of the unknown and warm to these hospitable people. As we left, many dark-skinned hands reached out to pat the little blonde heads of our two youngsters and, to my horror, several kind locals kissed little Tommy as he slept in the backpack on his dad's shoulder. (I knew I had come a long way since our firstborn was three months old when I sprayed our sneezing *friend* with Lysol and pushed her out the door to keep germs away!)

Leaving the café, we were drawn to the central gazebo, where native musicians were beginning the wildly happy Mexican songs of a local festival. Latins do not need any special reason to have a fiesta, and I suspect this one was simply *el Sabado*, Saturday night and fun with friends. Every citizen was bedecked in his or her finest: young men all in gleaming white, young women in peasant blouses with brightly colored embroidered shawls and circular skirts over many petticoats, and most of the older men and women in all black, signifying widowhood. Couples with arms entwined, skipping side by side to the music, twirled around the plaza in the Paseo de Promenade, which surely must be their counterpart to square dancing. Our children danced around in delight, joining little native *niños*. We marveled that poor people who had toiled so hard all day in the terrific heat could have so much energy to dance away the night. We left close to midnight, and it seemed the dancing had just begun.

Thrilled with our day of immersion into this kind and beautiful culture, we returned to our camper, walking slowly on the sandy beach. With the full moon over the Gulf of Mexico, waves gently lapping the shore, strains of Latin love songs filtering through the summer night, a more romantic setting we might never find! But three kids and my brother in a seventeen-foot space were a terrific form of birth control! So was *fear*!

We nestled all snugly (too snugly) into our beds, and suddenly we realized we were all alone on this huge expanse of beach, the only *estrangeros* (wealthy gringos) in town, and we had made ourselves abundantly evident to the entire, by now inebriated, citizenry, and we were armed with two walking sticks! We three adults slept but little during that long night, our first ever without the psychological safety of a paid campsite. But when morning finally arrived, we watched the spectacular sunrise and were exhilarated by the realization that we had lived to see it! We happily concluded that the bandito stories were just Texas tall tales!

We Paid for It!

WE DECIDED TO drive early through the mountains while the children still slept. We talked softly about our memorable night. But very soon there was another reason this place became indelible in our memories. We were on our way to Veracruz, where the Spaniard Hernando Cortes landed in 1519 to begin his conquest to take Mexico from the ninth Aztec emperor, Montezuma. Bill had decided to follow the same historical route to Mexico City. The children awakened with violent stomach cramps, and in this same area where he lost his land, Montezuma took his revenge! We *all* began to feel the pangs of the restaurant excursion. Five people contending for a two-and-a-half-foot bathroom is *not* any fun! We couldn't find a campground, so we finally were forced to stop at a Mexican truck stop and make it our camp recovery station.

Veracruz was a disappointment to us in that it was a typical seaport city with a lazy downtown area, probably less appealing because of our physical state. We did a cursory drive around and wished to move on, but Montezuma was controlling all our *movements* that day! We had to stay the night, and not one of us remembers much about it except our stomach cramps.

The next day, Bill had recovered sufficiently to drive. The rest of us groaned our way through the mountains. I was thankful that at least Baby Tommy was faring well since he was getting his only nourishment from nursing. By midday, we began to feel better and could appreciate the beautiful banana groves in the hillsides. We decided the fruit was just the medicine we needed and stopped to purchase some from a little boy of Aztec heritage. Standing near the marker for entering the Tropic of Cancer, he grinned at us while he polished his big white teeth with a lemon peel for his toothbrush!

We had planned to stay in Puebla for the night, but we had gotten such an early start that day that it was early afternoon when we arrived, and everything was closed for siesta.

We never got accustomed to the fact that all of Mexico *está cerrado* (closed) daily from 1:00 to 4:00 p.m. for siesta time. By then, the locals considered it as "after lunch," but we thought it was almost suppertime and they had wasted all our shopping opportunities. (Of course, we weren't out there working in that broiling sun since early sunrise!)

We did a drive-through sightseeing tour of the industrial city and then stopped to admire the view of the majestic Popocatepetl Mountains on the far horizon with their snowcapped volcanic peaks jutting some 17,000 feet into the clouds. We couldn't communicate well enough in Spanish to ask how long the drive to Mexico City would take, but judging from the mileage on our map, we felt we might easily make it before sundown. Our campground guidebook described a camper's promised land in the huge capital city with playground and laundromat, so we voted to push onward. But we had failed to consider the Mexican highways, the S curves, and the steep altitude and bumpy roads. We would be ascending 7,382 feet into the most populous city in all North America.

With our stomachs emptied, we may have felt good again had we stayed overnight in Puebla, allowing our systems to settle. But being young, full of adventurous spirit, and unable to speak the language well enough to ask about the road ahead, we set out uninformed. As we zigzagged back and forth, climbing ever upward, we began to feel woozy and lightheaded. At first, we thought it was the aftereffects of the stomach bouts of the previous day, but then Pamela and Blake began wailing with headaches. Although none of my emergency kit contents seemed to help much, I administered juice and aspirin and rubbed little heads until the older children finally fell asleep. Jim, whose head was also pounding, remembered from his training as an army medic that these were the symptoms of altitude sickness and would pass as we grew accustomed to the thinner air. I was blessed to avoid the headache. (The men joked that *airheads* are immune!)

The mountains were impressive, but the road wound endlessly upward. We stopped just before twilight to stretch our legs and make supper. The kids' headaches were bearable after naps, although by no means gone. As nightfall came, we began to be a little nervous about continuing our journey, but there was no choice except to push ahead, and the lights of Mexico City were visible now. We could not believe how far the city stretched! Our camp guide brochure promised a fully equipped campground just a few minutes from the city center. Since we planned to stay three nights, we were determined to settle only there.

We drove several hours more, traversing miles and miles of the huge metropolis, the heart of the country. Of course, the Latin city never sleeps, but we were certainly ready to. A petrol station attendant who spoke a little English assured us that we were going in the right direction. At long last, near midnight, we located the address we had been searching for and stopped at the elaborate stone entrance and told the guard we would be staying for several days. He assigned us a good RV parking place, and we entered probably the most frightening place we had ever been!

It was an RV ghost town! We drove through acres and acres of motor-home sites and tent sites, all totally empty. Under the bright light of the nearly full moon overhead and the noises and faint glow of the teeming city of about eleven million people surrounding us, this place felt like a graveyard, and we were locked in. We almost panicked, but we *had* to stop for the night, and in twelve hours of driving, it was the only place we had seen that even allowed RV parking. There were full hookups, which we desperately needed to recharge batteries and do all the necessities of a home that travels with you. My brave men walked around (armed with their trusty hand-carved walking sticks for protection) and decided we were okay for the night, and anyway, their heads were pounding too hard from the altitude to try to make any other arrangements. I wasn't convinced of our safety when, after they thought I was asleep, they attempted to make a sort of booby-trap alarm system attached to the doors. But exhaustion took over, and we all lapsed into the *arms of Morpheus* along with our children.

When morning arrived, we awakened to brilliant sunlight and saw that the campground was indeed elaborate, if deserted! A lovely pink adobe Spanish ranch-style hacienda served as the bathhouse. In the center of this elaborate building, we discovered an atrium garden with a gurgling fountain, lush tropical greenery, and an elaborate floor of hand-painted tiles. After using our tiny bath cubicle for a week, we couldn't resist the inviting tile showers. The men went to the Señores side first and took Blake, while Pamela and I walked around carrying Baby Tommy. Pamela delighted in throwing bread crumbs to birds in the sunny atrium. When the men took over the babysitting, they returned to the camper, leaving us two girls alone at the bathhouse, which was about an empty block from our lonely RV.

We had not seen the guard or any local person since our check-in the previous night. So far as we could tell, the place was completely deserted. That should have given us peace of mind, and in the sunlight and lavish setting, nothing seemed ominous. We had just disrobed and stepped into the trickle of cool water when we heard someone walking just outside the lockless door.

I called, "Who is it?"

No answer, but the shuffling steps continued. The white-hot dagger of adrenaline stabbed in my throat as I attempted to hide my stark terror from Pamela while I suddenly hurried her out of the shower and into clothes, my imagination running wildly.

My young daughter realized I was terrified, and she, too, heard the steps getting closer. We fumbled with zippers, grabbed our towels, and cautiously opened the door a slit to peep through and survey for safe escape. Then a wave of dizzying relief swept over us when we saw the gentle Mexican maid with her mop, cleaning the already spotless, unused bathhouse. We gratefully returned to complete our showers. As we left, Pamela practiced her first, "Gracias! Buenos días," and gave the girl a few pesos.

In retrospect, we realize that campground was truly a paradise, and we should have stayed there the entire week; however, we all voted to pay our one night's bill and move on to a more populated campground in this mass of humanity we had come to see.

Adventures in Mexico City

W
E WERE PREPARING for our sightseeing venture into the city when we realized little Tommy had developed diarrhea. We were puzzled since he had only nursed and eaten from jars of Gerber baby food from home. He could not have *turista*. We gave him baby Tylenol, and in his clean diaper, he seemed to sleep without too much discomfort, so we set out to tour the National Museum of Anthropology in Chapultepec Park.

Finding a free parking place on the street beside the pay parking lot for the museum, we unloaded stroller and backpack, sandwiches, etc., for our several-hour tour. The children ran free, and it felt so good to be sightseeing as normal tourists instead of just covering mileage that day. Little Tommy slept in Bill's baby backpack the entire time.

We returned to the camper to discover a Mexican truism: paid parking is worth the fee! We had never considered that part of the fee is for the attendant to guard your possessions. We had been robbed! But although we could tell someone had been all through our locked vehicle, the only thing missing was our camera. We had taken it with us to the museum at first, only to be informed that cameras were not permitted, so we had returned to leave it in the RV. Experienced thieves must have waited for many a camera at that spot, knowing the museum rules! We were chagrinned but thankful to be safe, and the thief had not found my brother's more sophisticated camera, so we still could visually document our trip.

We headed for the special market area which caters to tourists and upper-class citizens. But we were disappointed by the maddening *está cerrada* signs reminding us it was siesta time. Our shopping had to be postponed. The older children fell asleep while we read and wrote letters, and we decided siesta might be a custom to take home with us after all! Later we shopped in the bustling Mercado de la Merced and in the wonderful *zócalo*, discovering beautiful arts and crafts made by the extremely artistic people of Mexico. These places are not to be missed! Bargaining about the prices is part of the fun, and the vendors expect this of tourists. We showed great appreciation for the lovely craftsmanship, admiring leather suits for women, handcrafted jewelry and silver pieces, patterned animal hide rugs, beautiful Indian pottery and weavings, and other treasures, but we couldn't purchase much so early in our trip.

Bright piñatas in cartoon animal shapes captivated the children, and we could not leave the Zócalo without two. Now bear in mind (*we failed to*) that we were to spend another month in the close confines of our little cage. Each piñata hung down about two feet from the ceiling of our tiny camper to become our grinning enemies for the rest of the trip!

In the Zócalo, many restaurants beckoned us with their enticing aromas and mariachi music, but our earlier experience with turista provided the resistance needed to watch our pesos. It did seem a shame to sniff those *deliciosa* simmering onions and spices while we sat on a park bench eating our picnic of Spam and canned corn!

We found an RV park, complete with people and a laundromat, and settled into the business of the night: Bill headed out with our dirty clothes and a book (the choice job!); Jim proceeded to make up all the beds, a difficult twice-daily chore. For the most part, one must lie on the bed while attempting to tuck in sheets and blankets. The exhausting task requires the urgent motivation of absolute necessity for sleep, the gyrations of every muscle in the body, and a strong four-letter vocabulary! Jim needed a helmet to protect his bumped head when making the bed over the cab, the duty which ranked next to the most hated job of each evening, second only to dealing with dump stations!

My nightly job was to oversee bath time. To shower in our little vehicle required enclosing oneself fully clothed in the thirty-inch square space, wriggling out of clothes without bending over completely (because there was not enough room to do so), throwing the clothes out a cautiously cracked doorway, and sitting on the closed toilet to use the handheld shower to get wet all over. Next one had to shut off the water to spare it since our water tank held only forty gallons. Next task was to soap all over, then quickly rinse, creating a lake on the bathroom floor and getting every surface damp. Each night I would forget to light the hot water heater fifteen minutes before my shower, and by the time I felt the cold water hit me, it was too late! I hung my towel on a high rack during the shower process, and the trick was to keep it dry. If that was successful, the towel was the *only* thing left dry in the entire room. After drying myself, I had to wipe down the whole bathroom for the next person. Then I could reach around the door and hope I had left a robe within dry reach.

The children thought the process was fun, occasionally, when more than "spit" baths were necessary. It was impossible for an adult to help them, so those showers ended up with water everywhere outside and inside the bathroom. Most of the time, I opted to have them bathe with wet paper towels, and they used medical alcohol on a paper towel for dirty feet. That method worked well, and bath time for them was fun except for a mistake one only makes once. "Yeow!" meant someone forgot and used alcohol on the wrong personal part!

Our next day in Mexico City was cool and dreary, with a misty rain falling. We didn't let that spoil our plans to drive to Teotihuacan, which was Mesoamerica's earliest urban center and stronghold of the dominant power in Mexico from AD 100–750. Stone-outlined remains of dwellings are laid out as they stood centuries before. Teotihuacan art, architecture, religious, and social structure affected all the cultures that subsequently lived in the area, including the Aztecs, who regarded those high pyramids as the "place where the gods are." We walked in awe down the avenue, going from the huge Pyramid of the Sun to the mammoth Pyramid of the Moon. We had read this was the Avenue of the Dead, where in pre-Columbian times, specially chosen children walked following the priest who led them to the top of the pyramid. These honored children were to be sacrificed to the gods on top of the vast pyramids. The enormous stones, so perfectly cut and fitted together, formed sides so steep we could not see to the top. I perched on a base stone step with Tommy while the others climbed all the way up, which required more physical strength than I could muster. Thankful that our religion did not require such a practice, I sat below, imagining how mothers and fathers in distant past eras must have felt as they waited in this place of honor while high above them, their beloved firstborn child was reverently offered up to the gods who were purported to demand this bloody sacrifice.

Jail in Mexico?

THE NEXT DAY we had planned to shop and walk around the city some more. As we searched for a place to park, Bill turned the RV onto a side street, not realizing he was going in the wrong direction on a one-way street. The sign must have said, in Spanish, Do Not Enter. There stood a policeman, who immediately came to stop us. Bill, Jim, and I could not understand his words, but we knew Bill had made a driving error, and all we could think of was the warning a friend gave us before we left the States, "Remember, according to Mexican law, anyone is *guilty until proven innocent.*"

We had visions of rotting in a Mexican jail, unable to communicate. However, Bill, acting very humble and apologetic, did a lot of jabbering in Tex-Mex while the policeman kept talking. Then Bill pulled out a large denomination American bill, and the officer pocketed it and quickly motioned us to move on. We stopped at a *pastelaría* (coffee/pastry shop) to quiet our nerves. What a scare! In a brief second, we came to full comprehension and appreciation of our US Constitution, which says everyone has the right to be presumed innocent until proven guilty.

We spent the day wandering the streets, soaking up the local culture, and people-watching. It was fun and relaxing. In the evening, we splurged on a tasty meal in a sidewalk café with a mariachi band serenading us. The kids thought it was super! Our last and most delightful stop was at the Palace of Fine Arts, where we had seats for the evening performance of the National *Baile Folklórico*. It was a thrilling time of elaborate costumes, infectious musical beat, and exciting traditional dances of Mexico by some of the country's best performers. The staging and lighting were superb. Pamela, who had taken ballet dance lessons for four years, was enthralled. Blake, our budding musician, was spellbound by the music and whirling figures. Little Tommy never even whimpered. The two hours passed far too fast. It was a night of glowing color and sound that will always remain with us as one of our happiest memories of Mexico.

Passports and Mexican Doctors

MOST OF OUR trip to this, our first major destination, had been wonderful, and we all were eager to see what lay ahead in Central America, where passports are required. Jim and Tommy were the only ones without this document. Early the next morning, we headed for the American Embassy. It amazed us to realize that this one little piece of property in the middle of Mexico City *is* the USA. We were eager to see how our officials functioned abroad. We were not, however, prepared for the long line and the wait that ensued. We found the embassy unimpressive inside, like any typical government building. We sat on uncomfortable wooden chairs for what seemed an eternity. We had no toys for the children since we had assumed the process would be merely signing papers. Bill and dear Uncle Jim took turns taking the children into the hall to play improvised games.

Little Tommy's stomach upset had grown worse. We were concerned but had thought it would surely be over by this second day. During the night, because he refused to drink boiled water from a bottle, I had been giving him Pepsi with a medicine dropper to try to settle his stomach. To keep him hydrated, I nursed him each time he fretted, and we didn't know anything else to do but watch him carefully. While I waited with him, I grew very worried as he seemed sicker. Resolving to call his doctor in Texas, I asked the embassy secretary how to make a phone call to the United States and was relieved that it was fairly easy from that building. At the campground, I had tried on a pay phone, but the coin dropped through and I was cut off before the call could be completed. My Spanish was too poor to understand the operator. Since then, I have always been sympathetic of tourists attempting to solve various problems in a foreign country.

The embassy official helped me call my pediatrician in Texas. Dr. Ed told me he himself had done a gastric residency in Mexico and reassured me that in Mexico City are some of the world's best gastroenterologists because of all the digestive tract illnesses there. I felt more at peace knowing that we could get help we could trust. The embassy recommended two doctors who spoke English and were nearby.

We finally completed the paperwork for the two passports just before siesta shutdown, but the passport process was not complete. We had to get photos made and return with them when everything reopened. We went around the corner to find the young Mexican photographer who specialized in passport pictures. Jim and Tommy's pictures were made, and the moment was captured in sepia, with little Tommy staring blankly and his mouth forming a tiny O, perhaps in response to a stomach cramp. We returned to the embassy to wait the remainder of the afternoon to attach the photos to the corresponding papers, thinking we would leave with the passports. But no! Official checks had to be run. Everything here seems to happen mañana.

Embassy officials had made a doctor's appointment for us for seven in the evening. I was impressed that the pediatrician's office was open at that hour. Because our children were usually their sickest in late afternoon, I had wished for years to find a doctor's office open past 5:00 p.m. The distinguished physician spoke perfect English with an intriguing accent. His gray hair signified experience, and his calm, confident manner won my immediate trust. He told us of his years of treating dysentery, which abounded in Mexico because of amoebae in the water. I explained that I had faithfully boiled a gallon of water each morning of our trip for forty hot, humid minutes knowing of the local water risks. As he examined Tommy, he assured me it was a little virus that would be gone soon. If not, we should return home. We received medication to give our poor baby because his fever was over 102 degrees then, and he was miserable.

Returning to the campground, we spent a sleepless night watching Tommy and eyedropper hydrating him constantly. He grew worse, and by morning, I was exhausted and very frightened. We made a quick stop at the embassy on the way out of town to pick up the completed passports, knowing we would each need one to return to the USA, and they would be good for five years.

All we wanted was to drive straight through to Texas and get our baby well. We left, determined to do just that as fast as possible. We drove hard, descending as steadfastly from the over seven-thousand-foot altitude and heading north. To our huge surprise and relief, as we descended in altitude, so did our little one's fever. By the time we were back to normal air pressure, Tommy was well! We realized he must have had an extreme case of altitude sickness. Whether the virus ran its course or our untrained guess about the altitude was correct, we were satisfied that he was fine, and we could continue our journey southward.

Burial Cave Treasures

A RRIVING IN OAXACA near the southern border of Mexico, we found an RV park, and Bill was happy to hook up everything for another fresh start. After siesta time, Jim took our kids outside to find a real turtle for each child. Then Pamela and Blake prodded their turtles for a race in the sand! They were delighted, and Bill and I were thankful for some catch-up time. I had to do the necessary *daily* chore of boiling a huge pot of water for forty minutes to be sure we had safe drinking water. The steam made the RV miserably hot, but we didn't want any more stomach problems. Jim had bought a hammock, and he hung it between two trees. Then he carried Baby Tommy out for the older kids to sway him gently. They all loved it! Later Jim enjoyed a cool evening sleeping outside in his prize purchase.

The next day, we drove to the Monte Albán Pyramids a few miles from Oaxaca. About 500 BC, Monte Albán was a large center of local civilization, which is thought to be of the Zapotec culture. The pyramids there are indicative of the largest sociopolitical and economic center that dominated much of the Oaxacan highlands. These Mesoamericans at that time were in contact with the other important and influential Teotihuacan center, which we had just seen outside Mexico City. We all loved walking around these Albán pyramids as we pondered how life here would have been so long ago. The men and our older children had the strength and determination to climb to the top of one of the huge stone monuments, but again, I chose to sit with Tommy at the base.

Of course, no locals miss an opportunity to sell trinkets to tourists. When our group was back together, we ventured beyond the fascinating history to the tents set up with handmade items, the typical tourist-tempting wares. The children and I strolled through these for over an hour and then met up with Bill, who had been taking photographs. No one knew where Jim had wandered, and it was another hour before he appeared from beyond a steep hill. He came up smiling, his rain poncho billowing behind him as he, out of breath, sprinted toward us. "Do you have any American cash, Bill, about twenty dollars?"

Bill handed him the money, and off Jim dashed again with no explanation. We watched as he slipped out of sight with a teenage Mexican boy.

I was frightened when he didn't return for some time. It was getting late, and the weather was threatening. Finally, Jim appeared and hurried us toward the RV, saying we needed to move on quickly. With no other explanation, we all scuffled into the camper and drove away. When we were a few miles down the road, Jim pulled his purchases proudly from beneath his jacket. He presented me with a necklace of gorgeous green jade beads strung on a rather dingy cotton twine. "This is to thank my sister for the wonderful trip. I hope you'll enjoy wearing these and remembering our adventures."

I was thrilled! Then he presented Bill with a most unusual carved stone statue with one leg missing. As Bill admired the piece and thanked him, Jim started to tell his exciting story of the purchases.

"I got to talking with a few local boys who could speak some English. I asked if they live around here, and they do. They were trying to sell some authentic and impressive souvenirs, but I was sure they were probably made nearby each day by smart entrepreneurs. Mexicans are so artistically talented. One boy was determined to sell me something, and he admired my rain poncho from my army days. He offered to show me a hidden place only he knew about. I was scared to follow him, not knowing what I was getting into, but I was so curious I had to go. After all, this place is centuries old, and I didn't know what I might see!

"The boy was very nervous and kept looking back over his shoulder as we hurried down the steep incline. He led me to a cave-like hole in the ground and pointed for me to go in, but I refused, so the boy indicated that if I would give him my poncho, he would get ancient pieces from the indicated grave. I agreed, and he disappeared into the opening. He finally emerged with these pieces and a statue I kept for myself. He said he and his friends had found this ancient grave, but no one was to know. He knew grave robbing was illegal, and he also was afraid the other boys would hurt him for taking a stranger there. I was happy to give him my poncho and $20. Then he hung back while I ran up the hill to find you all. These people may make these by the dozens in their own backyard and then just hide them in the hole and con some stupid tourists like me every day. But, heck, I thought these things would be interesting conversation pieces back home! Whether they're really old or not, I knew they were worth that!"

We were all just glad he got out of there alive. We reminded him he could have become the skeleton the boys show to the next tourists! On returning home a month later, I had the beads appraised, and my jeweler said he could not put a dollar valuation on them because they were the oldest and finest jade he had ever seen! The stone statue has a strange helmet and the slant-eyed face of an alien. Could we have a piece that verified some of the myths of space travelers landing there in pre-Columbian times? We like to think so!

Determined Angels in the Cactus

THE FIVE OF us had rested by being on foot and exploring for several days, and Baby Tommy was well now and sleeping soundly in his sling bed. We were happily rolling along through the beautiful scenery of the Chiapas, halfway between Mexico City and Oaxaca. Pamela and Blake were having fun at the table (which had been raised each morning to convert from their sofa bed), drawing pictures of our latest adventure. We had promised to add photos later when they were developed. In those days, there were no electronics in vehicles, so our children learned to entertain themselves and each other by being creative. They retold stories about things we had done, or which they wished or imagined we had done. Blake had also an imaginary playmate named Cowboy Bob, to whom he told many tales. Pamela, a little more grown up at nearly nine, liked talking to Jim and sometimes endlessly babbled to her patient uncle. An artist by nature, Jim gave the kids ideas of creative things to occupy them on the long drives. But this ride was not to be so long. Bill steered the suddenly wildly swerving RV to a stop as quickly as he could pull off the road. We had had a blowout. A rear tire was stripped, and the men searched for our spare. As they struggled on the mountainside to get it onto the RV, they were each thankful for the other's companionship and help.

Bill drove us slowly and carefully to the first little village to buy another tire. He found what appeared to be a garage. It at least had a gasoline pump and tools in evidence and some men in grease-streaked white attire. Bill and Jim got out to try to remember enough Spanish and hand motions to reveal our predicament. The children and I stayed in the camper.

In this tiny town, perhaps no one had ever seen an RV or even Americans, so we quickly became the object of curiosity as the fascinated villagers gathered. I began making sandwiches in our little kitchen, knowing my family would be hungry soon. The camper had a small window over the only counter space, and I was spreading mayonnaise on bread there. I looked out and saw many children of all ages gathering to peer in at us. They began holding out their hands and pleading, "Dame pan! Dame pan!" (Give me bread!) I could not see where Bill and Jim were, and I was scared by this crowd of youngsters, so I quickly pulled the shade down and locked the doors. Now, many decades later, I still carry the burden of guilt for not being able to help them. I keep remembering the Bible verse in which Jesus said, "In as much as you have fed the least of these, you have fed me."

The afternoon wore on, and still I did not see Bill and Jim, but I knew they must have found help. After a few hours, they returned to inform me that the tire repair would take a while. The local men had indicated that this small village was far from any other civilization and supplies, and this enclave in the middle of sand and cacti did not have a tire the right size, although they had searched everywhere. These innovative, creative, and kind Mexican men had determined to make the largest tire they could find fill our need. They had worked and worked to stretch the small tire over the rim of our blown tire to serve as a spare until we could reach a larger town. Yes! We could make it! When the Mexicans had succeeded in this challenging task, it was growing dark and the next town was far away, so the village police invited us to stay in front of their little adobe office overnight. We paid the many kind helpers generously and were so grateful for a place to rest and sleep soundly. We felt like Mary and Joseph in the Bible must have felt when they were given the stable for shelter.

*****

We went back to Oaxaca to spend one more night, as it would soon be too late to venture onward through the beautiful Sierra Madre Mountains of Mexico. We found the city very crowded, with an outdoor dance festival about to start in a stadium on the edge of the city. We found the only available parking, which made us pause to decide because it was unguarded on the street, but we could find no guarded parking lot. The festival was so much fun, with smiling people in elaborate, colorful native costumes from each of many different cultures of the region. Each group demonstrated its own native kind of music and dance, and it seemed to be a contest. We all loved it, and our kids twirled around happily, imitating the dancers on stage.

We were chagrinned, although not surprised, when we returned to the camper to discover again it had been ransacked, but the thief had only taken our transistor radio. We were glad we had the camera and our money with us. When bodily harm is not threatened, robberies do not create much fear, just aggravation and a little more caution.

Arriving in Guatemala

O
UR FIRST STOP as we crossed the border into Guatemala was the city of Huehuetenango, where we had no problem with the newly issued passports for Jim and Baby Tommy. Then the first order of safety was to purchase vehicle insurance. (We were not sure what the law in Guatemala was about innocence versus guilt and jail!)

We soon realized that country was completely different from its northern neighbor, and we became fascinated with the new scenery, people with colorful clothing. We fell in love with the beautiful countryside and picturesque people we saw as we began our drive through Guatemala, with its enormous volcanic mountains, peaceful pastural scenery, chickens, donkeys, and women dressed in brightly colored handwoven shawls and rippling full skirts. Men and women both wore large black hats with stiff flat brims and serviceable handmade leather shoes. Fascinated, we stopped at little villages along the way and walked around the maze of individual stalls in mercados in this country, so different from most of what we had seen in Mexico. And we bought many handcrafted items and took numerous photos.

In the lovely town of Chichicastenango, we wanted to see the huge beautiful Santo Tomás Catholic Cathedral. We saw a crowd going to the entrance, and assuming these were tourists, we joined in. We are not Catholic, so we had no idea where the procession that seemed like a parade would go. We followed in the crowd behind the priest, who was swinging the burner of incense. Unknowingly we were following and included in a solemn but joyful procession with a priest in elaborate dress leading. As we neared the nave, we realized this was a funeral. We were astonished to see a glass casket decorated with many flowers. Within was an old man's elaborately dressed body in full view right in front of us. None of our family had ever seen a dead body, so we were as fascinated as the children (who were oblivious as to why this man who appeared to be sleeping was in a glass "box"). We explained later.

He had been a special dignitary at the cathedral, and this was one of the most amazing services we had ever seen. I was astonished that we were allowed among the crowd of mourners. But the ceremony seemed celebratory. When we left the cathedral, the children excitedly talked about it for a long time.

Seeing so many local women carrying a baby on their backs wrapped in a colorful hand-woven cloth, we decided it was time for little Tommy to have a souvenir of his own. We found a weaver shop at the mercado and purchased some lovely yardage of his handmade fabric. And we bought a very sturdy red cloth about fifty inches square and decorated with many embroidered Aztec and Mayan symbols. The woman in the shop showed us how to tie Tommy securely to my back! However, although this became a treasured souvenir, I never felt he was riding safely on my back, and the next day, we returned him to the shoulder pack Bill wore while walking.

Chichicastenango is an urban cultural center whose original heritage is uncertain: Aztec or Mayan. This city has the largest market, which serves all the villages around. We were fortunate that we happened to be there when many groups of different local ethnic heritage, distinguished by the varieties of brightly colored traditional dress, had come for a festival of native dances. We loved watching the whirling figures and clapping to the lively music as our children happily pranced around in their own dances.

*****

We had read about the beautiful Lake Atitlán, where a majestic water fills the crater of an ancient volcano. This we had to see! We could drive there during siesta time, when there was nothing else to do and our children would sleep. Although it was 5,125 feet in elevation, we had no concern because Tommy had not had any more intestinal upsets, so perhaps it had been a virus in Mexico City, but that was over 2,000 feet higher than this destination. Of course, we seem to arrive at our destinations after dark always, and this time was no different because the small winding road through the mountains was long, and Bill drove slowly for safety's sake. When we were starting the road that wound up from the base of the mountain, we were in a deluge of rain. Soon we saw two men on the side of the road looking helpless. As we got closer, we realized they were probably Americans, judging from their height and clothing, which was drenched. Although we would never pick up hitchhikers in the US, we felt we *had* to help these men since the rain was so fierce. Before Bill stopped, he, Jim, and I talked among ourselves and agreed it would be okay, but I insisted the strangers must ride on the uncovered little balcony that held our generator outside on the backend of the RV. We had no other space inside, and we were vulnerable with three children.

We stopped and offered the undesirable balcony. They did not hesitate as they were just happy to get a lift to the top of the mountain. The rain pounded all the way up. When we stopped at the hotel where they were staying at the mountaintop, the men thanked us. We asked if they were tourists. They replied, "No, we are medical missionaries!" We were mortified that we had made them endure such a ride, but they laughed it off and understood. We went on to the motor-home park and settled in, thankfully, not needing to hook up in the rain.

Next day we were blessed with brilliant sunshine, and the lake down in the crater was truly magnificent! But we were still eating humble pie!

*****

The next place we visited was the beautiful Spanish Baroque city of Antigua in the central highlands of Guatemala, which is a UNESCO World Heritage Site. The name *Guatemala* can be traced to both Aztec and Mayan origin. The Aztec word meant "Land of Trees," and the Mayan word meant "Mountain of Vomiting Water." Antigua was the first capital of the country and is preserved because in 1524, it was built as the first planned city layout in Latin America, but the city was destroyed by the volcanic eruption of Volcan de Agua in 1541. Then it was rebuilt, but in 1773, it was again destroyed by the Santa Marta earthquakes, so the capital was moved to Guatemala City, a safer location in 1776, when Antigua was partially rebuilt. It was mandated that the sixteenth-century Renaissance grid pattern be preserved, and some of the original buildings were only partially reconstructed. This preservation is one of the primary reasons for the designation of *UNESCO World Heritage Site*.

A year after our visit to beautiful Antigua, it was devastated by another huge earthquake. Guatemala is in the Ring of Fire, surrounded by a horseshoe shape of volcanoes and faults, making it one of the most vulnerable places in the world. It has been devastated numerous times, including in the twenty-first century. But for tourists anywhere, ignorance is bliss, and in our naiveté, we were unaware that we could have been in a natural disaster. The next day, we arrived in the capital, Guatemala City.

We Meet a Local
Rancher Family

W E ALL SPENT the first day as tourists in Guatemala City, and we found it easy to get around and fascinating, with so much to see. Later, we went to the home of one of Bill's rancher friends, who, we hoped, would be a major purchaser of our Brahman cattle. Señor Patron invited us to park overnight in their driveway and for Bill and Jim to fly the next day with him to see his ranch and cattle. Our men were thrilled. I have always been apprehensive of small planes, but I had no voice in this matter.

The rancher's wife, Señora Rosalita, suggested that I stay with her while the men would be away. At their home, all the children could play together. I was happy to accept the invitation, knowing it would give us an opportunity to enjoy a Latin home and speak some Spanish with them.

The next morning, Senor Patron took Bill and Jim to his private plane, and the trio flew off to see the ranch near the Pacific Ocean. My children were learning to speak in Spanish more quickly than I because they were unafraid of making mistakes. It was a lovely day, and a little later, we all went shopping in the market area and ate lunch in a downtown cafe. How wonderful an experience in a foreign country!

Back at the home, the youngsters played happily together in the yard edged with glorious tropical flowers and palm trees. Rosalita spoke broken English, and I spoke broken Spanish, so we had an interesting and friendly day. But the safety of that little plane and my anxiety over being alone in this country, if my men did not return safely, lurked in the back of my mind all day. Tommy was as sweet and content as any baby could be. Pamela and Blake were so happy to be playing in a large area with toys they had never seen and trying to communicate with gestures, pointing, and laughing while learning quite a few Spanish words.

Children are so naturally friendly, and language is quickly sorted out. We hope our kids will always be open and make friends with many people, disregarding any differences. My men returned safely after a marvelous day seeing the huge cattle ranch and had lots of happy experiences to relate.

After a lovely dinner prepared and served by the housekeeper, we bade goodbye and said we hoped to host them in September at our Brahman sale. Back at the RV campground for the night, Bill and Jim had glowing reports of the large and pretty ranch. They flew over it with beautiful views of the ocean. When the rancher/pilot landed, his ranch hands met the plane and drove them all over the ranch to see the Brahman herd and other cattle on the place. Bill had learned that we had a few extra days before the convention, so he, naturally, wanted to explore another nearby country.

Jungle Terror

WHEN MY MEN perused the map to determine how long we should allow to get back to Guatemala City, he and Jim decided we would veer into Belize, a country nearby. We all were eager to see new places and say we had been in yet another country. Of course, it was twilight, as seemed to be our pattern. We were about to enter border control into Belize, but Bill saw the road that led to the village we had hoped to visit was unpaved and very rough and narrow. He decided it was not worth the risk to the RV, so he reversed, and we were back in Guatemala. I can still close my eyes and see the little houses on that dirt road beyond the border into Belize lit by warmly glowing candlelight.

Abandoning our intended explorations of that new country, we reached the border crossing to enter El Salvador, just a short distance away. This border was formed by the Río Lempa, so Jim drove our little RV onto a ferry. We were all excited but a bit apprehensive about crossing a river in twilight on a rustic-looking ferry. Bill and Jim had decided El Salvador (with no reservations, of course) would be our next great adventure, and it quickly was!

Darkness was now upon us. For the first time, we had to show all our passports, including the ones Jim and Tommy had gotten in Mexico City, so we held our breaths. The El Salvador Border Patrol Office was a small, dingy, dimly lit adobe building with two rough-looking men inside. The officer looked casually at all our passports and stamped his seal, and we were on our way out the door. However, he had another plan. He grabbed Bill's collar to stop him from leaving, and the rest of us were suddenly fearful. In awkward English, the man said, "You, this man, take," and pointed to a very rough, greasy-looking man who appeared possibly to be drunk. We started out the door again, and the officer pulled Jim back and sternly ordered, "Man, you take!"

Our men nodded and stepped outside. Our guest passenger followed slowly, and he also seemed frightened. I'm sure we foreigners looked scary to him, and the RV looked impossible.

In a soft tone, Bill instructed Jim to let the man sit in the passenger front seat and Jim to situate himself behind the stranger. Jim was to hold *both* walking sticks at the ready as Bill drove on. Our adult hearts thumped wildly, but the children were fascinatedly in awe of a stranger, and they attempted their little Spanish, "Ola!" and "Felicidad!" The man barely looked at them. He hunkered down in his seat, seemingly quite bewildered and scared.

The first village was about an hour's ride, and it grew totally dark. The little huts we passed were lighted by candles, no electricity. The soft glow in the darkness was unforgettable. Palm trees in the jungle beside the road swayed in the evening breeze, creating a soft rustling sound. As we passed through this village, the man saw his home and suddenly pointed for Bill to turn. Hand motions sufficed, but Bill was apprehensive we would not be able to turn our large vehicle around, and he could see no farther than his headlights illuminated. But he turned, hoping he could back up if necessary.

When Bill stopped at the indicated little adobe house with a straw roof, our passenger got out and bowed saying, "Gracias, gracias, gracias!" I think we all learned from that safe experience not to judge a book by its cover. People everywhere seem to be as nice in return as we are to them. Years later, we still feel we, in some way, have a friend in El Salvador!

*****

We enjoyed driving through as much of the lovely countryside and as many of the small towns in El Salvador as we could. We naive tourists were blissfully unaware that the country was on the verge of a political revolution. In the 1970s, many countries around the world experienced the growing pangs of revolution, some bloodless and some quite violent. In a country that does not speak English, it is difficult to read the local newspapers or understand radio broadcasts. Traveling in an RV, we had no electronics. Cell phones, TV in vehicles, portable computers, Wi-Fi, and GPS for personal use had not yet been invented. Futuristic in those days, only scientists and inventers had even imagined these items. We depended on ourselves, each other, maps, radio, and books for information, entertainment, and company.

We got an early start the day we were leaving the capital city San Salvador, and our drive took us by way of scenic thick jungles on each side of the road. We told the children to try to find parrots and monkeys in the trees as we drove along. They were busily drawing these animals in hopes that real ones would magically emerge and pose for their portraits.

Suddenly, Bill and I gasped simultaneously when a bullet shot across our RV hood, missing the windshield by a split second. Bill sped up as we wondered aloud what had happened. We were both shaking from the thoughts of what that second's timing could have been. The bullet would have been right through Bill's head! Terrified, we drove as fast as safely possible to the next town and stopped to find a merchant who spoke some English. We entered a general store where several were gathered around a radio, listening intently.

"Habla Ingles?" (Do you speak English?)

The manager nodded and said, "Si, Senor, un poquito." (Yes, mister, a little.)

Bill asked, "Que pasa en San Salvador?" (What is happening in San Salvador?)

Several of the local men began rapidly responding in part English, part Spanish. "Manifestación contra el gobierno! Estudiantes in San Salvador. Treinta muerta in street. Maybe more." (Student demonstration against the government. Thirty dead in the street.)

Another man admonished, "Perigroso ahora in El Salvador!" (It is dangerous now in El Salvador!)

43

We did not need a second warning. We murmured "Gracias, adiós!" and hurried out.

Bill drove the RV as quickly as possible the hundred miles to the border of Guatemala, where we had no trouble entering. With more experience and wiser now, our hindsight of many years is twenty-twenty, and we still tremble to realize that then we were ignorant of the risks we took and the dangers we, thankfully, escaped.

Guatemalan Ranchers and Convention

BACK IN THE far safer capital city of Guatemala, we again found the home of the rancher. We had high hopes of him helping Bill promote our upcoming Brahman cattle sale because this was a coveted cattle species in Central America. Brahman cattle can tolerate heat and insects well.

Jim had to pack to fly home the next day for his job. We would all miss him terribly! (I was not sure he would miss us. For a twenty-five-year-old bachelor, his confinement in our tiny quarters and the need to entertain the kids and help in every part of daily life could not have been very fulfilling! But he was a valiant, appreciative trooper and seemed to really love all we had experienced and done.) To this day, our grown children adore him, and he still likes all of us! Having him along to travel with us proved a great decision, and he joined us through the years on other journeys.

After we saw his flight depart, Bill drove our RV to a fine hotel near the convention center so we could stay there while he attended the cattle show and convention for the following two days, meeting many ranchers, seeing the local Brahmans, and promoting our sale.

The hotel management had allowed us to leave our RV parked in their lot since we were hotel guests. Next day, Bill left us at the elaborate hotel room where I had the baby's necessities and some toys and drawing pads to keep the children entertained. We even had a television (our RV did not), and the cartoons in Spanish fascinated Pamela and Blake. I had always heard that TV cartoons are the best way to learn a new language quickly. Pictures tell the story, so you don't have to struggle to understand the words. I hoped this was true for all of us, and I watched and learned eagerly along with them.

However, the two days Bill was at the cattle convention wore long, and the six- and eight-year-old grew tired of the room and the playthings I had brought. They begged to go out into the hotel hallway. I was nursing Tommy at the time and said, "Okay, but stay in this hall."

They agreed and gleefully scampered out. A few minutes later, with Tommy satisfied and in a clean diaper, we went out to see what his older siblings were doing, but to my horror, they were nowhere to be found. I loudly called their names but no answer. We got on the elevator to go in search, with a fervent prayer in my fluttering heart. As the elevator opened on the first floor, there stood my little blonde wards! They ran up to hug us and excitedly told me about the wonder of two elevators, so they could race each other up and down the ten floors of the hotel, each in his or her own lift!

I breathed a sigh of relief and smiled since they were so happy, and then I set some rules as we ate lunch in the hotel restaurant. Siesta time finally arrived, and this time I was so glad!

I wondered, *What would they have done if they got lost and could not communicate!*

Bill returned by the end of our naptime, and we were all delighted to have him back and hear all about the hundreds of cattle he perused and many ranchers he met. He felt our Brahman herd would be in high demand because of the superior quality and the way he had gentled them. (Even though this type of animal is purported to be dangerous, Bill had ours so gentle that the children could sit on their backs for photos.)

Running on Prayer

O N OUR DARING *gringos-below-the-border* adventure, we often miscalculated the distance and time necessary to cover territory in the mountainous, curving, sometimes primitive roads. A few happenings along the way made us travel in the dark to find a place to stop overnight. Highways were almost always deserted and without any lights. But my man was fearless. We all trusted that we would eventually land safely for the night, and we did.

The next morning, we were on the narrow highway through mountains returning northward to Mexico. With about twenty-five miles to go before we would stop in Puebla for lunch and to buy gas, we could see that town far below us as we wound around the mountains. But to our horror, the *ding, ding* sounded, and a red light flashed on the dashboard. A menacing arrow pointed to *E!* We were out of gas! No services or gas stations were within the next twenty-five miles or the past one hundred kilometers!

As the last bit of gas dwindled, Bill rolled onto a straight stretch and maneuvered to the shoulder of the road. While he studied what to do, I prepared and served a cold lunch. Bill suddenly lit up and exclaimed, "We have the generator!"

On the back of our little RV was a sort of outside balcony that held our generator. I knew it could not power our RV engine, so I was puzzled, but since Bill was elated, I was relieved and didn't ask questions. He got out and found his tool kit and poked his head inside to reassure us that he had everything under control. He had a piece of tube in his hand.

"I can siphon some gas from the generator!" he exclaimed with relief. It holds one and a half gallons, but I have no idea how much remains. Pray!"

And I did, fervently, while he sucked to start the siphon. He guessed he got a little over a gallon from the generator and into our RV gas tank. With me nursing our baby and the children falling asleep for their now familiar siesta, he got into the driver's seat and successfully started the motor. We thankfully descended the steep curving road for what seemed like an hour, arriving at a gas station on fumes and prayers! Thank goodness the small station was open even though it was siesta time. We were saved! We drove on toward Mexico City, which, after a while, we could see in the distance.

*****

Mexico City, in 1975, had the largest population in North America and spread out for many, many miles. As we rolled on toward Mexico City, it was growing dark. Bill thought since we had plenty of gas now, he could circle around the city and avoid Tommy's altitude sickness. He also intended to avoid the frantic city traffic the next morning as we proceeded northward. Although that had seemed possible, we drove and drove for hours, realizing how enormous this city was. After midnight, we were only about halfway around, but we were exhausted and had to sleep! Bill found a large parking lot at a shopping center that was lighted and guarded, and the attendant said he would watch out for us for the night. Necessity creates trust! But we had learned to trust that *most* people are very kind and good.

We were four and a half happy campers now that we had survived our sometimes-perilous adventures below the border, and we were headed north and *home*! We all missed Uncle Jim in these last hundreds of miles. I had learned to *love* motor coach travels, even with all our difficulties. In my heart, I had known Bill could solve any problems we might encounter, and he had proved it, but I knew I could soon breathe a sigh of relief. I had been able to accomplish my part of the road trip, keeping us well-fed, clean, and happily occupied. We had all learned so much, except Baby Tommy. Now five months old, he had never learned to turn over, and that was a gnawing concern in the back of our minds, but we knew not one of us would be able to turn from stomach to back in a bed like what he had been in for six weeks: a sling-shroud supporting all his weight! We felt assured he would learn quickly when he reached his crib at home. Thankfully, as soon as we had left the high altitude of Mexico City, he was miraculously free of his awful gastrointestinal woes, but we realized that altitude sickness could be his difficulty for life.

Because children are quick to make friends, Pamela and Blake had found playmates at each stop, fascinated with their beautiful brown skin, dark hair, and big brown eyes, and it seemed the locals were equally entranced with our little blonde blue-eyed children. We had all gotten to practice our Spanish frequently, and our kids were thrilled to be able to sort of understand another language. They caught on more rapidly than we did. We all had an appreciation for the life Americans enjoyed in comparison to the hard conditions and strength of body and spirit of many who lived to our South. Everyone we encountered was so friendly and helpful, despite the language difficulties, and it made us conscious of trying to do the same when we see strangers in our town. Our children saw what we had always tried to instill in their minds: "We are all alike. God just wrapped us in different colors like we wrap Christmas gifts."

Back to the
US Border

B EFORE LEAVING MEXICO, we wanted to stop in a few more little towns. We stopped in Saltillo, a place for rock hounds seek-
ing gemstones. We walked around as fascinated tourists, and
Bill disappeared into a jewelry store, most unusual for him to do, but
our eleventh wedding anniversary was coming up soon. I pretended
not to know where he had been, and we went on to a mercado with
the children, excited to spend some final pesos but carefully saving a
few to show their friends at school.

The next day, we drove to Nuevo Laredo and approached the
US border crossing, and we grew excited. We passed the Mexican
policía with no problem, showing our passports (which had been a
little nagging worry to us since Tommy's was issued in Mexico City,
but it turned out to be authentic).

But in 1975, US border controls were very tight because hippies
and others with hidden drugs often tried to enter America at this
crossing. Motor coach travel was not very common in those days, so
the patrol had a separate line for just RVs and vans, which were often
the hippies' mode of transportation. It was noon in mid-July, and the
temperature was 110 degrees Fahrenheit. We emerged from our tin
box and waited while the RV line being checked in front of us was at
a standstill. Pamela and Blake played in the sand, hot but happy. Bill
and I took turns holding little Tommy, and we watched in horror for
an hour and a half while the US authorities literally took the van in

front of us apart, even slitting the mattress! We thought that would happen to us next because we, too, looked like hippies. Bill was in his shorts and ratty T-shirt and had grown a beard and long scruffy hair. I had become accustomed to dressing in tight shorts and a braless halter for the long daily drives. While we waited endlessly, sweating under the broiling sun, we prepared ourselves for our now beloved RV to be torn apart.

Finally, the patrolman reached us and checked our passports, nodded, and returned them to Bill. He asked if he could search our RV, and we replied, "Of course!"

He ascended the two steps into the tiny RV and was immediately hit in the head with Pamela's favorite purchase: her big donkey piñata, which hung from the ceiling near the door. With the inspector's eyes on that, he nearly fell over the baby bed, which took up 90 percent of the floor space. He quickly climbed out of our RV. We were apprehensively holding our breaths. Stepping in front of us, the officer looked Bill in the eye (while Tommy cried loudly and Pamela and Blake had a dust battle). The man asked very seriously, "How long have you been in Mexico, mister?"

"Six weeks, sir," Bill replied.

The officer exclaimed with a wry smile and a twinkle in his eye, "Go on into the USA. If you have any drugs, you *need* them!"

Relief almost drained our energy, but we were now on our final two days of the unbelievably brave, fun, and idiotically naive trip. At last, late the next day, we drove into our driveway! Neighbors ran out to greet us in honest disbelief and happiness to welcome us vagabonds home.

Let's Invite Mom!

F OR OUR **1975** Christmas gift, Bill's widowed mother gave us half the price of a Gittings family portrait. This was a fabulous gift, as Gittings was one of the most renowned photography studios anywhere because they had made the classic celebrity photo of Sophia Loren. Bill and I were both thrilled and dismayed. We really wanted to have a large family portrait for our wall, but we had very little money to spare. How could we ever pay for the other half?

Each month his mom would ask, "Have you had the portrait made yet?"

We kept putting it off without explaining why. By summer, we thought we had saved enough, so we made the appointment for July 5. The studio was a hundred miles away from us in Dallas, Texas, so we decided to take our trusty little RV and go on July 4th to Six Flags Over Texas, a fun theme park we knew we would all enjoy. We invited Mom to accompany us to Six Flags, stay overnight in our RV, and help supervise the portrait the next day. We were trying hard to show our appreciation as well as comply with what was expected (and stop the nagging questions!).

Mom seemed happy with the idea of meeting us and staying overnight. We all had a fun day at the theme park, but we were sweltering in the July heat, almost as hot as the previous July at the Mexican border. When evening came, it was a little cooler. After dinner in a restaurant, we bedded down all cozy and cramped in our seventeen feet of space. We gave Mom the narrow sofa bed at the back. Our table turned into a double bed when we let it down at night. All three children slept there. Our appointment for the portrait was the next day at 10:00 a.m., about twenty miles away. Happy and tired after a fun day, we expected to just pass out in a good sleep in our loft bed at the top of the cab.

But our RV had other plans. The air-conditioning stopped soon after we got to bed, and no coaxing would start it again. We opened windows, but poor Mom had on long silk pajamas, and we were all burning up! It was a sleepless night of tossing and turning for us adults. Thankfully, our kids could sleep in seemingly any circumstances when they finally stopped giggling and playing, thrilled to be having a slumber party all in the same bed.

Next morning very early, after a hurried bowl of cereal, we began to get dressed. The attire for our fabulous portrait had caused much consternation. With a very tight budget, I had made the dresses that Pamela and I wore. Bill found a $2 sport coat at Goodwill. Blake had a borrowed suit from our cousin. One-and-a-half-year-old Tommy had a cute playsuit, but he had outgrown his shoes, and we could not afford another pair since it was summer!

Now dressing in the cramped quarters of the RV is never easy, but with my prompting to hurry up, finally, all the children were in tears, and I was very close! Mom kept saying, "Maybe we should cancel the appointment and schedule it for another time."

I fumed, "I will not go through this again! It would be this bad anytime. Each one of the others hates to have pictures made, but I am thrilled that we will have a family portrait from Gittings! It was a wonderful, thoughtful gift!"

Bill silently got into the driver's seat and drove as quickly as traffic would safely allow to our destination on the other side of Dallas.

We all felt better with tempers cooled, and miraculously we arrived just in time to keep the scheduled appointment. The photographer placed us in a beautiful setting, with barefoot Tommy on Bill's lap. But that eighteen-month-old little boy wanted no part of a family picture! He started crying, and tears streamed down his face. No matter how hard the photographer tried to tempt him by holding up squeaky ducks, shaking a teddy bear, coaxing, and cajoling, he just continued to cry. Mom was dismayed. Bill and I were also, but we just wanted to get through the ordeal! Tommy simmered down for just a minute or two, and the rest of us quickly put on our best faces, and the man snapped the shutter over and over. Miraculously, the photo was perfect! He was truly an experienced photographer because he had clicked the shutter between tears and fits! We treasure the portrait and the story behind it. Our little RV got us home, and Bill began to consider trading up to a larger one.

More Grandparents Aboard

MONTH LATER, MY parents came from South Carolina to visit us, and Bill offered to take them in our RV to enjoy the sights in San Antonio and to see President Johnson's ranch. My parents would sleep the two nights in a hotel, and we could park in the hotel lot. They were happy with the idea, and the trip was fun. We saw so much that was new and fascinating to all of us. The president's ranch, open to the public, was particularly interesting to Bill, who could not help comparing it to ours in Northeast Texas. Mother, Pamela, and I loved the wildflowers of many different varieties and colors in bloom all over their fields, a visual testimony to Lady Bird's slogan, Beautify America. She advocated spreading medians and borders of highways with flowers seeds that would bloom year after year on roadsides everywhere. She had chosen the project of getting rid of the ugly rusted vehicle "cemeteries" that were along many highways, and trash was thrown from cars routinely. Her campaign proved itself in the six years Johnson was in office and even now, as clubs follow Adopt-a-Highway protocol.

Back at San Antonio, we all wanted to visit SeaWorld, and we could park in its large parking lot. The theme park was great fun for us all, but when we were beginning to drive out of the lot, Bill heard a clicking noise that indicated a big problem in the RV drive shaft. He was skilled mechanically from having to overhaul trucks and tractors at our farm. He checked under the hood and could not see the problem there, so he had to get under the RV. He discovered the universal joint, which connected the driveshaft from the engine to the back wheels, had to be replaced. We had just been through the Alamo with the guide telling the history, and the boys had bought coonskin hats and toy rifles, so Blake had fun playing Davy Crockett in the parking lot with Tommy in his stroller, while Bill worked. The rest of us had no idea what a universal joint was, but my dad was surprised that Bill carried spare parts with us and had on hand what was needed. He was able to make the repair himself, thankfully, while we were still in the parking lot instead of on the shoulder of the busy city streets or the highway. His repair was perfect, and we made it the over three hundred miles home with no problems. My parents were very impressed!

Santa's Surprise

DECEMBER SCHOOL HOLIDAYS were approaching, and we joyfully prepared to drive in our trusty little RV to South Carolina to be with family for Christmas. But the task was like moving since we must take all the gifts for eight extended family members and for our children. Our little Tommy was unconcerned but just went placidly wherever we did. He had already adjusted to a life of travel. At ages seven and nine, our kids were both excited about seeing grandparents, uncles, aunt, and cousins but also concerned, "What if Santa doesn't know where we are?"

I responded, singing,

> Santa Claus is comin' to town
>
> He sees you when you're sleeping,
> He knows when you're awake.
> He knows if you've been bad or good,
> So be good for goodness' sake!
>
> So you better watch out
> You better not cry
> You better not pout
> I'm telling you why
>
> Santa Claus is comin' to town

Bill added, "Of course, Santa will know we are in South Carolina, and he will even find our RV. It will be such fun!"

Late at night, a couple of days before we left home, we had secretly wrapped the Santa gifts for our children. Our little RV had a small compartment in the back, which opened only to the outside. We carefully stowed all these very important, long-wished-for gifts there and locked the compartment, knowing the kids would not find them.

At last, school ended, and we said goodbye to our pretty little Christmas tree and made sure it was unplugged. We set out on the thousand-mile drive joyfully expectant. One important task required us to stop at a mall along the way a couple of times each day. We told the kids it was to see the holiday decorations and stretch our legs, so we wouldn't get tired. They needed no coaxing because, of course, Santa's helper was in each mall! They could tell each elf helper to remind Santa they would be in South Carolina, not Texas!

Bill stood in the Santa line with Pamela and Blake while I pushed Tommy's stroller to a toy store to find the urgently needed, most special toy Pamela had asked Santa to bring her: a Crissy doll, which Bill and I thought to be the ugliest doll ever created. But ads on children's TV shows had captivated Pamela, who had short hair. The Crissy doll had thick auburn hair, and when someone pushed the button on her stomach, her hair would grow quite long! Pamela *had* to have that doll, and since it was the hot item for little girls, we had not been able to find one anywhere. We knew this might be Pamela's last Christmas to truly believe in the magic of eight tiny reindeer and wishes coming true, so we really needed to find that doll to purchase.

Finally, at the third shopping stop along the way, I found the very last Crissy doll at the toy store. What a relief! The store wrapped it for me, and I carefully hid it among my clothes in the RV since I did not have the key to open the back compartment, which was stuffed full anyway. Later, after Santa's lap had been duly occupied by our two happy kids, who now knew the jolly old man was sure to find them in South Carolina, we drove on with no more necessary stops.

The next day, we were covering the miles on the main highway when the driver behind us began beeping his horn repeatedly. Bill checked our speedometer and saw we were going the speed limit, and nothing we could detect on the dash was wrong, but the honking continued. Finally, Bill had to pull to the shoulder of the road and get out to ask what was wrong. The man pointed to our rear compartment, which had come open, and a few presents had fallen out along the highway. We were *so* grateful to him and hoped nothing very important was missing. Bill secured the compartment tightly, and we moved on. Since it would be useless to return to try to retrieve them, we hoped someone would enjoy the gift find. We could seek other stores in South Carolina when we determined what was missing.

Grandparents, aunts, uncles, and cousins were all so happy to greet us when we arrived in Greenville three days before Christmas. We had a glorious time surrounded by so much loving, hugging, singing yuletide carols at the piano, baking holiday cookies, and playing games. Wonderful extended family togetherness was sadly rare in our lives since we lived so far away from all our relatives. But Bill had made sure we got to visit our families on both sides at least twice a year. Our RV made it easier on everyone.

On Christmas Eve, Granddaddy Jim asked Pamela and Blake if they would like to go see Santa's helper at the mall.

"Yes!" they excitedly exclaimed. "We need to be sure he knows we are here now," Blake informed him. We set out eagerly, and I stood in the Santa line with our kids. When the last child in front of us was on Santa's lap and we were very close, Pamela sneezed. To our great surprise, horror, and laughter, out flew her very loose front tooth, and it landed on Santa's shoulder! The jolly old elf laughed and presented it to me when Pamela climbed onto his lap. What a story to tell forever after. That night both the tooth fairy and Santa paid a visit to our little RV!

*****

On Christmas Eve, the family gathering was at my sister's home, and we were to sleep in our RV in her driveway after the whole family ate dinner together. Christmas stories and songs and the opening of one gift each was so much fun with everyone together. Blake's one gift he chose to open happened to be a set of walkie-talkies, and he was thrilled. He handed one to his cousin, and the two boys went to separate rooms to test the little machines. The first thing they heard was forever unforgettable to all of us! To the amazement of everyone, we all heard a male voice say, "Ho! Ho! Ho! This is old Santa, and I'm leaving the North Pole now with my reindeer to fly your way!" (We adults were almost in shock because we had *not* programmed this!)

All four of the children were ecstatically excited about this special night. They all went to the RV "playhouse" to create their own fun for a while, and we kept checking on them. But suddenly the RV horn began blowing, and we adults rushed out to determine what had happened. The four cousins, ages five to nine, were breathless with stars in their eyes.

Blake shouted "We heard Santa! We heard Santa! The reindeer were prancing and pawing on our roof! But we couldn't see them. Santa *does* know where we are!"

Later, they even spotted a red light moving across the sky and screamed, "There's Rudolph! Look!"

*****

When we started home on the last day of December, Bill decided to veer into Georgia to see President Jimmy Carter's home in Plains, Georgia, where his famous peanut farm is located. We stopped for the night hoping to get a tour, but instead, we got a virus, and all of us began throwing up! It can't be altitude sickness *this* time! We had parked near the baseball field in Plains. It was a miserable night, and we did not get out of the RV, but the children were happy to learn more about our president then in office, so they could tell their friends we were there where he grew up. Thankfully, stomach viruses are short-lived.

When we arrived home, we had a six-inch snowstorm a few days later. Our boys and a neighbor boy made a big snowman but molded it to look like a huge peanut. They decorated it with eyes and a big smile and named it with a sign that said *Jimmy Peanut*.

Venturing North

I N THE NEXT three years, since we all loved life on the road for an adventurous change, we made many short jaunts on weekends and long trips to be with grandparents. Bill was still a farmer/rancher, but he had good employees and was able to get away when he wanted to. We had fun going to nearby state parks and even camping just outside of our hometown, Paris, Texas. Since our town was small with very little entertainment, each of these excursions offered wonderful things to do and explore. Often friends would meet us for cookouts, and the kids loved playing in the woods and parks.

Now Bill was determined to trade our little RV for a slightly larger one. When Tommy was four years old, his daily playmate, Greg, had to move with his family to Ohio, and we were all dismayed. Tommy missed him so much, especially since our older children were in school and away most of each weekday. By summer, we decided to drive to Ohio in our new RV, a big, used nineteen-footer Bill had found in trade! Those two feet of extra space made it feel like a palace for the road!

We stopped at a couple of RV parks overnight along the way, but our first destination was to visit Greg's family, whom we all had missed. We could park in their driveway and sleep in our RV. We spent a happy three days with them, the boys building blockhouses, laughing, wrestling, playing outside. We cheered at Greg's swim meet and enjoyed the fun things they showed us. On the last afternoon, we all went to our first *Star Wars* movie, but about halfway through, the projector malfunctioned, and everyone had to leave with rain-check tickets for the next day. Our boys were so, so disappointed when our schedule of planned stops and a few appointments did not permit another day here, and it was months before they could see the exciting end of *Empire Strikes Back*. Of course, they were hooked for life! Who could imagine then that many years later, when Blake became a well-known composer in Los Angeles, he would have meetings at Skywalker Ranch, and he even get to meet his lifelong idol: John Williams, composer for the *Star Wars* films!

*****

Our next stop was Chicago, where none of us had ever been. Of course, we arrived in that huge city after dark, thinking traffic would be lighter (or not thinking at all). We drove around and up and down many streets in search of a place to park. We had not reserved an RV park since we did not need hookups for the night and the weather was mild. Finally, in desperation, Bill stopped a policeman and asked where we might stay.

The officer kindly said, "Just pull around the corner and you will see our police station. You are welcome to stay in our parking lot, where you will be safe."

Wow! We could hardly believe it! We certainly complied.

It was very late, and the kids should have been sleepy. We were! In this RV, Bill and I had an actual sofa bed at the back and didn't have to climb up each night over the front seats to sleep. The boys claimed that space, and Blake took the outside so his little brother would not fall out of the high bed. Pamela usually slept on the other couch bed made from the dining table, lowered at night and special cushions added. But not this time! The night at the police station was not to be missed!

All three kids climbed up the ladder to the loft bed and pulled back the curtain to watch out the little upper window. The flashing lights and sirens of the police cars coming and going beckoned them, and they pointed and exclaimed eagerly each time a prisoner was taken in handcuffs from the police car into the station. In the noise and excitement, we hardly slept, but we all had a night to talk about!

Early the next day, Bill found a parking place beside Lake Michigan where we spent the next night. From our "windows with a view," we watched the activities on land and water in this terrific city of Chicago. In late morning, we wanted to swim in the inviting lake, which appeared to be an ocean—it was so huge. But immediately we discovered our bodies could not tolerate the cold water, although the locals were enjoying this summertime sun and water. We were accustomed to swimming pools about ninety degrees from the hot summertime sun. Texas swims felt like warm baths!

On our day's shopping excursion, Tommy found a precious little stuffed monkey, which he bought with his own spending money. Junior became his adored companion for life! We drove up the east side of Lake Michigan and found the special Sleeping Bear National Park and Sand Dunes. The kids adored the huge "sandbox."

Bill and I had to make a big decision—return home or continue to explore. Since a 1,200-mile drive had not been enough, Bill decided we would venture onward for the next few weeks.

He announced, "Well, we are already up here, a thousand miles north of home. Who wants to see what we can find?"

We all eagerly agreed. RV life is *fun*! Studying the map, he planned our route up through Michigan so we could visit Blake's friend, Kurt, and his family, who had moved from Paris. Kurt's father was a choir conductor who was working with the Young Americans concert group for the summer. He had greatly encouraged Blake in his musical talent. It was fun to see our old friends in their new home. That turned out to be a great serendipity for me.

We had lunch with the Young Americans group and another of their directors, who was seated beside me at the table. Just in table conversation, Brad learned we had worked a great deal in Portugal and that I was a writer. He quizzed me about Portugal and our connections with important people there. I asked why he was so interested in that country. He replied that he was a TV producer and actor who had a children's show for Hawaii Education TV. The population of relocated Portuguese families was large in Oahu, and he was getting funds to make a children's historic tour of Portugal, their native land. He asked if I would be interested in being hired as writer. This would be my first script-writing assignment for television! I enthusiastically said, "Yes!" Although I knew nothing about script writing, I was sure I could help him with the planning of the trip for filming and the connections he needed, and I could learn about script writing as I *winged it* since I had a MA in journalism. What a glorious opportunity!

*****

One day we booked a ferry to Mackinac Island in Lake Huron, requiring a predawn passage in an angry lake that looked like the ocean. The huge waves, heavy wind in the darkness, and dense fog made me demand life jackets for Tommy and me since neither of us were good swimmers.

The captain said, "No, ma'am. The life jackets are above and are available if needed."

I argued, "But we can't swim!"

He responded, "If I give life jackets to you, it will make all the passengers afraid."

Then the foghorn blared, and I thought it meant we were in the path of an oncoming ship in the dark. I panicked and became so visibly agitated that he relented and handed me two life jackets. I wished (and of course my family wished also) that I could be the intrepid traveler they are!

Our day on Mackinac Island was fun, especially since a movie was being filmed there, and at this time in life, Blake was taking acting lessons and had dreams of being on stage and in films. We were all fascinated with a place where many people lived, but no motor vehicles (except emergency ones) were allowed on the whole island. We all loved seeing the sound stage for the shooting, and the kids even got a few autographs from actors whom they recognized. The beautiful island was quaint and seemed to give us a living picture of historic life. Many people who live there even dressed as if living in the late nineteenth century. After a fun day, we returned in daylight safely with milder weather, no fog, and more placid water. (I did not embarrass anyone then by demanding life jackets. I now knew where they were, and I could reach them.)

Add Another
Two thousand Miles,
Why Not?

THERE WAS NO stopping us now! We drove on into Canada. (Bill had packed our passports in his briefcase—just in case!). In Ottawa, Ontario, we were fascinated with the British-style Parliament House and then the impressive, colorful ceremony of Changing of the Guards at Parliament Hill. Next, Bill directed us to watch ships pass through the canal of the Rideau Waterway, the oldest continuously operated canal system in North America. It connects Lake Ontario and the Saint Lawrence River. Bill explained how the locks lifted or lowered ships smoothly and safely when water channels met at different levels, causing shallows and rapids, which cannot be safely navigated.

Next, we moved on to Montreal, Quebec, again in a deluge of rain. All was going well until Pamela climbed into the bed above us and yelled, "It's soaking wet up here! Tommy, did you wet the bed?"

"No!" our insulted four-year-old replied emphatically.

The boys moved to the back couch of the newly purchased used RV and announced it was very wet also. Bill pulled off the road and climbed onto the roof in the rain. We inspected and discovered our new RV had sprung several leaks, and yes, the whole inside and all our things were rapidly getting very wet. Now our only mission was to find a laundromat in Montreal and an RV repair place.

Alas, through the city streets we drove and drove, and it rained and rained. We could not find a laundromat, and suddenly I remembered they spoke French there. Perhaps there was a different word for *laundromat*. We parked and got out with umbrellas to try to find a local who could understand English and direct us. Seeing our bedraggled and damp family walking along and probably looking desperate, a young couple stopped and tried to understand our words. At last, they got the point and motioned for us to enter their apartment building and go to the basement to use the laundry, which was only for tenants.

We were *so grateful* and hurried to get as much of our wet bedding and garments as we could all carry. The children and I stayed for the chore while Bill drove to an auto parts store and found the necessary supplies to patch the leaks. Then he found a big bridge to park beneath and climbed on top with towels to dry the leaky places and caulk them before returning for us. By the end of the day, we hoped all the leaks were sufficiently plugged and everything inside would completely dry soon. With all our clothing and bedding dry, we ventured onward, after we showed enormous gratitude to the kind people who had helped us. We still wonder, "At home, are we so kind to strangers in trouble or too afraid to trust?"

Our trip onward proved my valiant captain's amazing mechanical ability, learned through many years as a farmer/rancher. We stayed dry and enjoyed the castle-like scenery when we toured Quebec City and tried to learn at least a bit of tourist French. The kids thought it was great to know some Spanish and French! No stopping them now! They would see the world! (A little over a decade later, each of the older two married a travel agent!)

We drove on, and the next day, we excitedly entered the Canadian side at Niagara Falls Provincial Park. We eagerly bought our tickets for the whole experience. We lined up first to go behind the falls and look through the wonder of the enormous chutes. We were each issued a black rain slick and hat, which we donned, along with the other ticket holders. Since everyone was dressed identically, we were extra vigilant about watching our children, lest we all get separated in the crowd. As we carefully proceeded on the wide pathway behind the rushing water, I found it creepy and thought how the Jews lined up to enter the gas chamber must have felt. Also, my memory wandered to the cattle we had seen marching in single file to slaughter in Dodge City, Kansas. But then I cleared my mind, holding tightly to Tommy's hand, and appreciated the beauty and wonder of this magnificent natural place.

The Canadian park and town were also beautiful, and far less spoiled by souvenir shops than the American side of the park. We couldn't resist the exciting *Maid of the Mist* boat ride on Niagara River, which took us close up to the falls. We were as excited as our children. Through the years, daredevils have chosen the terrifying experience of going around and around in the whirlpools below the powerful falls, but of course, tourist boat trips do not include that misadventure!

We learned that the first person to live through the crowd-drawing trick of daring to go over Niagara Falls in a barrel was Annie Edson Taylor, a sixty-three-year-old woman in 1901 during the nearby Pan-American Exposition at the World's Fair. She was a widowed, destitute, retired schoolteacher who thought she would make fame and money with this stunt and become *the* "maid of the mist," which would prevent her living out her life at the poorhouse. She designed her own barrel of wood with a ballast of an iron anvil to keep the barrel upright. She placed a mattress and harness inside to provide some protection for herself, and she first tested her contraption with only a cat inside. The cat survived, and she knew she would too. She did make history and became notorious, although not wealthy. Someone stole her barrel on which she had planned to stand to sell tickets for people to hear firsthand about her experience, but her formerly dynamic speaking ability fell flat. We could not imagine that stuntmen had many times competed to be the first *man* to get inside a wooden barrel and let it roll over and down the falls, but no man had succeeded, and many men died trying this idiotic stunt.

The other stunt was to attempt walking a tightrope all the way across this powerful water wonder of nature! This was first accomplished in 1859 by a Frenchman, Charles Blondin, whose tightrope was an 1,100-foot cable stretched across the Niagara Gorge at a height of 160 feet near the falls. He was a stuntman who did this successfully and made a show of it, standing on one foot once and another time lying down on the rope. He gained great fame from the performance. We had hoped to watch some of these stunts, but none was performed when we were there.

No one tried this stunt again for many years, but in 2012, daredevil Nik Wallenda was the first to walk a tightrope stretched directly in front of and very close to Niagara Falls. Although heavy fog made it impossible to see or show on camera some areas of his tightrope, his successful walk of 1,800 feet was televised worldwide.

Maine Lobsters for a Splurge

WE CONTINUED ONWARD through green forests along the Trans-Canada Highway until we reached the US border in upper Maine, and we stopped at Acadia National Park on the Atlantic coast near Bar Harbor. It is the oldest designated national park east of the Mississippi River and has preserved not only huge woodlands but also many small islands and Cadillac Mountain, the tallest (1,542 feet) mountain on the Atlantic coast of the US. Traveling in a tin box with three children for long periods can interfere with couple's privacy, so after the children were sleeping, we took refuge beneath the full moon at the picnic table in the deep woods around our RV. Such a beautiful place for a respite. We talked quietly together beneath the stars and pine trees to ensure we could make many more long journeys happily.

On our second day, we decided it was time for a meal out since Montezuma's revenge was not an issue on this trip. We went for an early lunch to a restaurant famous for the delectable Maine lobsters. We were among the first customers and ordered lobster without even checking the menu. While we eagerly awaited our lunch, a bald-headed man passed our table, and our little four-year-old called out loudly, "Mister, you forgot your hair!"

Everyone nearby, even the man of interest, giggled at this innocent concern.

While the minutes ticked by as we awaited our lunch, the waiter presented plates of beautiful big red lobsters to the table next to us. The children looked big-eyed at the meal, and suddenly Tommy screamed, "Mister, there's a big red bug on your plate! Mister, look out! There's a *big* bug on your plate!"

Our little guard helper was unstoppable, so we had to exit the restaurant and miss the meal we had eagerly looked forward to. But we laughed then and each time we recall the innocent scene of embarrassment.

*****

The next day, our driver/planner insisted we must see it *all*, so we headed down on US Highway 1 to Portland, Maine. When we found an RV park, we were delighted to learn that there would be a harness-racing event for horses and carts (sulkies) that night at the Portland racetrack nearby. Bill and his sister had owned a sulky and two little ponies to pull it when they were children on their farm in Midland, Texas. When the family sold that farm and bought the farm/ranch in East Texas, where Bill would spend twenty years working while we lived in Paris, Texas, they transported this cart and the two Shetland ponies, Misty Belle and Domino, to live there. So our kids had enjoyed the fun of riding in the two-wheel cart and learning to use the reins to guide these little ponies around our farm. Bill was as excited as the children about going to this performance in Portland. He explained to us that in harness races, there are two classes: trotters and pacers, which have separate races. All the horses want to win, but they must not break stride of either trotting or pacing and get into a run or gallop. We watched as the lead car led the carts around the ring on the warm-up before the actual race began.

Although many people gamble on the races, we did not, but Bill and the kids discussed which ones they thought would win. Bill told about when he was a child and his family went to horse races. They had guessed among themselves which would win, and they were right every race, so the people behind them commented, "You have surely won a lot of money!" But Bill's dad informed the man they were not gamblers, just making educated guesses based on the physical formations of the horses and jockeys. The couple were so angered by Mr. Neely's answer, they moved to seats far away. This cart race was a special highlight of our trip for Pamela, who had always loved horses. We could not have known then that in decades in the future, she would become a horse trainer and own and manage a horse farm. We all had fun and a great evening to remember.

History Can Be Fun!

THE NEXT STOP on our fun and educational history venture was Boston, Massachusetts, where we walked along the Paul Revere trail, with a guide telling the story of the famous midnight ride. Since our older children had already learned some of this in school, we all found the sights interesting, but we had difficulty avoiding the dog mess people had failed to pick up all along the trail, not a good advertisement for this tour!

Other famous historic point the kids loved along our route was Plymouth Rock at Pilgrim Memorial State Park in Plymouth, Massachusetts. There is no actual record that the *Mayflower* ship, carrying the first settlers to step foot in the New World of North America in 1623, landed here. Legend has designated it as the important stepping-stone where the first settlers in the New World disembarked. We also later happened upon a temporary display of replicas of the *Niña*, *Pinta*, and *Santa Maria*, famous for the 1492 voyage of discovery of the New World by Christopher Columbus. We, of course, were all familiar with the historic story, and we were delighted to step on board and explore each ship. These wooden vessels were so small as to be unbelievable for an Atlantic crossing, with horribly cramped quarters for so many people. It made us look again at how very spacious our RV is!

The favorite historic stop for our boys was at Concord/Lexington, Massachusetts. They got to participate in the mock soldier march to protect the Union from the British. In Boston Harbor, we also went through the *Old Ironsides*, a ship from Revolutionary War. We hoped that the kids were soaking up all this firsthand history and that these memories would come to them in future school history lessons.

As we made our way to upper New York State, we stopped at the beautiful Lake Champlain, where Bill wanted to show the children Fort Ticonderoga, used in the French and Indian War and the Revolutionary War. They had fun playing on the cannon and walking around within the fort. Bill had read them the book he owned when he was growing up, the children's simplified version of *The Last of the Mohicans* by James Fenimore Cooper, which is set around this fort. Lake Champlain is truly beautiful. This is also not too far from the Catskill Mountains, where Rip Van Winkle (by Washington Irving) was purported to sleep for twenty years, while missing the American Revolutionary War taking place near him. We all tried to imagine what it would feel like to sleep twenty years and then how different the world would be when you awoke. The kids took turns naming things they knew had been invented in the twentieth century.

We reminded them of the Rip Van Winkle Gardens we had discovered on another RV trip in the lower part of Louisiana on Orange Island, where an actor Joseph Jefferson, famous for playing the role of Rip Van Winkle on stage, built his home in 1869. The island and home were on the dome of a large salt mine. We had needed to stop and exercise our legs, so we had pulled our RV into this place and bought tickets to tour the beautiful flower gardens. They had been built on the salt dome. Later John Bayless Sr., maker of Tabasco sauce, bought the home and the two-thousand-acre plantation and built beautiful gardens of exotic plants within a glass conservatory. However, in 1980, the miners of the salt in the tunnels below the island made a huge mistake, and the salt dome collapsed and turned the ten-acre freshwater lake into a 1,300-foot-deep saltwater lake, but miraculously no lives were lost. It took four years to rebuild, and now a beautiful garden tour beckons visitors. We had loved the quiet and could not imagine such damage had been overcome to yield the magnificent gardens. In the museum at the visitor center, we were shown the display of a pirate's pieces of eight, which were discovered buried on this island during the reconstruction. Of course, the kids had bought pirate hats and swords and pretended to duel.

The Big Apple?

MY COLLEGE ROOMMATE and her family were living in New Jersey, with four children close to our kids' ages. We headed that way when summer came, thankful they had a driveway large enough to park our RV and stay in it. Our second day there, we all decided to go to the Big Apple, so we had a glorious day in New York. Making our way through crowded streets with a stroller for her one-year-old and the six other kids in tow, we made it to Central Park, and everyone enjoyed the fun things to do there.

We stopped for a memorable lunch at Mama Leone's Italian Restaurant. Naturally, we ordered spaghetti since most kids love it and it is not expensive. The waiter brought large portions to each of us, but our children were not accustomed to long noodles since I always break the raw spaghetti into several short pieces before cooking them. Pamela and Blake were valiantly trying to cut theirs into manageable pieces to stay on the fork, but Tommy was bewildered. The kind waiter smiled and patiently taught little Tommy to wind the noodles on his fork, and then our youngest proudly taught the rest of the children. The serenading violinist and singing waiters thrilled us since we all have a great love for music. The kids were fascinated that these musicians were right at our table. The final happy memory was the waiter bringing us delicious dessert free!

To cap off our wonderful but somewhat grueling day with seven little ones growing tired, we decided to see the city from the top of the Empire State Building. We were dismayed by the ticket price, so three adults decided to stay in the car. Bill volunteered to take the six kids up for the views while the baby stayed in the car with the rest of us, and we drove around, saving money on parking. Bill successfully got the kids on the elevator to the top and presented the tickets.

When the kids got out at the top floor of this landmark building, they ran wild but *not* in the same directions. Now terrified at the unforeseen responsibility, Bill and our older children had the unforgettable experience of gathering everyone into one spot. But two little monkeys were among them, and Bill was almost panicked and overwhelmed by the job of preventing the three-year-old and four-year-old little boys from trying to climb the guard fence to peer down at the tiny cars and people 1,250 feet below.

"We just want to see the big apple, and we don't see it anywhere!" they innocently cried in unison.

Bill held each one up and then, as quickly as possible, he herded the group to the exit, with all heads counted and still intact! On the down elevator, Pamela and Blake tried to explain that *Big Apple* is just a nickname for Manhattan. Many decades later, the responsibility still makes Bill's heart thump!

As school would be starting the fall semester soon, it was time to journey homeward with many wonderful ventures in our memories. It took about a week of more happy stops and explorations in parks and mountain trails to cover the remaining 1,500 miles of our over 3,000-mile journey. Bill liked to choose "blue highways" (asphalt two lanes) for varied routes, less traffic, and different sites to view. He studied the state maps each night to decide which way to go. He had always loved to drive, but he had to be tired because I was not brave enough to take over the steering wheel, and I was plenty busy with children's needs, entertainment, and meals.

Branded!

WE MADE IT! And we *all* loved the adventures and had fun telling friends and relatives about our escapades. Pamela and Blake had plenty of material for the annual first-week-of-school writing assignment, "What I Did This Summer." Hopefully, they would not have to read it aloud in class since most of our small-town citizens had not ever been far out of our little Texas town. Little four-year-old Tommy had more of a tale because he had somehow rolled over Blake in the high bed over the cab and fallen to the floor in the night, hitting his head on the passenger seat. I had butterfly Band-Aids, and it bled a lot, but we were able to patch him up and quell his tears. Although he did not require stitches, he has the scar on his forehead and tells the tale even as a grown man. He had also another accident he still enjoys relating.

As he was putting on pajama bottoms one winter night, he backed up against our RV heater and got a burn on his rear end from the hot grill. The next week, we were with Bill's mother, and when she saw the mark, she thought we had spanked him with a kitchen spatula! We assured her we would never do such a thing! At that time in the United States, there was a highly publicized campaign to stop child abuse, and anyone who spanked a child in public could have the child taken away by the authorities! Tommy had never been spanked! I was writing a book about child abuse at that time, so our family discussed the topic often at home, thankful none of us had experienced it.

At that period of our lives, I was also writing a weekly syndicated newspaper column about fun things to do with children. Readers would send me ideas to write about, and I first tested these on my children to see if I could recommend them. Knowing the new law about not spanking children in public, one woman had written me that the best way to discipline a naughty child in public was to quietly pinch him or her to make the bad behavior stop. Tommy and I were in a grocery store check-out lane one day at noon when we were both hungry. We had to wait in front of the candy stand, and he began to beg and then cry loudly for candy. I told him. "No candy. We'll be home soon to eat lunch."

I thought of the new suggestion from the reader, so I quietly and lightly pinched him to stop his tantrum. Suddenly, right in front of the newsstand which held my column, he screamed, "My mom just did child abuse to me!"

How to Embarrass Young Teens

IT WAS NEARING time for spring break for the children and college professor Bill, so our youngsters excitedly begged for an RV trip. We loved Bill's idea of heading for Washington, DC. I told the children we must contact our Texas state senator John Tower for passes to tour the Capitol and White House. Pamela and Blake each wrote a letter asking for a meeting and for the passes, and I put these in the envelope with mine and mailed it. The trip up to the District of Columbia from our Texas home was fun, and we found cherry trees in full blossom.

We found parking for our little RV along the mall and walked the kinks out of our legs by going to the various impressive monuments there. What a beautiful city our capital is! Knowing April is a popular time for tourists, Bill had had reserved an RV park ahead of time across the Potomac River in Virginia, just a few miles outside the city. We were able to go to nearby Mount Vernon, the stately Georgian-style home of George and Martha Washington. Originally constructed of wood in 1734 for Washington's father, the mansion was rebuilt when it became George's, who lived there until his death in 1799. About a century later, a philanthropic organization restored it because of its historical importance. Pamela and I loved the gardens, where Tommy could run about.

The next day at his office, Mr. Tower was very cordial to us, welcoming his constituents. He presented the children with the tour tickets for us all and asked them what they were learning in school about our government. They felt very big and important.

On the steps to the Capitol, Tommy's umbrella stroller bit the dust. It simply fell apart, and he was excited to be free! In Statuary Hall, our tour guide told us this was formerly where the House of Representatives met. We all gazed in wonder at the beautiful domed ceiling so far above us. The guide then demonstrated the secret echo chamber in one spot of the huge room. In the marble floor is a metal plaque marking the place where John Quincy Adams had a desk when he was a member of the House for eighteen years. Adams would sit staring at the floor, and no one knew he could hear even whispers from across the room. The guide explained that many times through the years, lawmakers looking at the floor had surreptitiously eavesdropped on another group who were talking quietly of secret plans. Few secrets could be kept in this great hall. No one knows whether this was a planned feature of the room or whether it was an accident of the beautiful architecture when the Capitol was built in 1855–56. As we continued the tour, Pamela and Blake had fun testing the echo-chamber effect when they frequently dropped back and took turns standing by the plaque and listening while the other across the room whispered something. Even Tommy tried the game.

Our tour guide took us to the very high upper balcony to look both up at the dome and down at the Great Hall and feel how enormous the building is. We held on to Tommy's hand, knowing he was such a monkey, he might try to climb the rail!

We felt awe when we went into the solemn and beautiful Senate Chamber. To our surprise, the guide cautioned us to be quiet and ushered us into the House of Representatives, which was in session. He told the children in the group of the opportunity to be an intern as a summer job when they are older. Blake's eyes lit up, and we could see his mind jumping to that fascinating job.

*****

The next day, we awoke to a huge deluge of rain. Luckily that day's plan was to visit the Smithsonian Institution museums. We knew this would be a highlight for Tommy, so Pamela and Blake told him excitedly we would see dinosaurs. Tommy could already identify and name many of these prehistoric creatures in books. He was born an artist and had already won a ribbon at our local art fair in Paris, Texas, for his drawing of a dinosaur! We were lucky to find a parking spot large enough for our RV close to the museum entrance, but we had not packed raingear. We thought of running for the door, but the downpour was too hard. So I quickly devised raincoats for the children from three large trash bags. Each child had a hat, so these bags would cover their bodies. Of course, the older children rebelled, but I persisted, knowing it would be a long day if we were in wet clothes. Bill and I shared an umbrella.

At the enormous Smithsonian Institute, we first chose the Natural History building. We hurried to the room with the dinosaur skeletons. The children were all so in awe they forgot their trash bags were still covering them as they peered up at the giant skeleton. Then a family, who lived next door to us in Texas, entered the room via another hallway and cheerfully greeted us; however, we were all a little embarrassed over the rain sacks, and Blake quickly wriggled out of his first. Humiliated, he whispered to Pamela, "I hope they don't tell anyone at home!" The Smithsonian had plenty for each of us to find fascinating and fun, so we spent the entire day in wonder.

The next day also presented drenching rain. We drove around the city, and in late morning, we could not believe Bill again found a parking place large enough for our RV on the street about a block from the White House, where we were scheduled for the 2:00 p.m. tour. We ate sandwiches in the RV, and the children changed into their best clothes. We saw the rain had let up to a slight drizzle, so we were *all* glad no trash sacks were necessary! Bill and I would have been embarrassed to pull out those large brown protectors again. As we stepped out of the RV onto the sidewalk, another family who lived a block from us in Paris walked up and joined us. Their two girls were the age of Pamela and Blake, and eleven-year-old Blake had a crush on Shannon, an adorable little blonde fourth grader who was in his class at school. We knew Blake was so relieved he was not in a sack, so we thought he could live through the embarrassment of RV travel when the other family were staying in a grand hotel.

When we neared the White House door for the tour, we saw President Carter emerge from the front entrance. With his big friendly smile on his face, he waved to everyone. The Marine One helicopter was waiting for him. He boarded and flew away. What a thrill! We had seen the president in person. Our White House tour was so impressive, and Pamela and I loved seeing the beautiful furnishings. Our little artist Tommy commented on many of the huge paintings and asked about the historic scenes depicted. The guide told us many interesting facts about life in the White House and about how it had been built on a swamp.

We were all excited to be there in Washington, and this venture would make school history classes much more meaningful. We thought little four-year-old Tommy would be oblivious to all that we were doing and hearing, but he was very good on the tour. A month later, back at home, I was watering our garden in the sun, and Tommy was holding the hose. Trying to impress on his little mind spiritual gratitude to God, I asked, "Tommy, who gives us these beautiful flowers?"

He promptly answered, "Jimmy Carter!"

After the White House tour, Bill led us to see some of the important buildings in this center of Washington. He pointed out the Department of Agriculture and told the children his mom and dad had met there when they both worked in that building in their young adult years. Bill had been born in Washington, DC, and he was baptized in New York Avenue Presbyterian Church, so we walked over to see that sanctuary. Peter Marshall, then chaplain of the United States Senate and minister of that congregation, had baptized Bill. We were all duly impressed, as Pamela and I had read the book, *A Man Called Peter*, by Catherine Marshall. I told the children they had all been baptized in the same heirloom gown Bill had worn at his baptism.

We wanted to see the Library of Congress, which is on Capitol Hill and is the largest library in the world, housed in three buildings. We found we could walk into the Thomas Jefferson building, and since our children loved going each week to our little city library in Paris, Texas, they thought this would be fun. When we walked into the magnificent building, we gasped at its Gilded Age opulence. Then we learned it houses not only books but also photographs, recordings, maps, and a lot more. The three library buildings contain over 170 million items, including all that have a United States copyright.

Blake Returns to DC

WE COULD NEVER have imagined that a decade later, when Blake was chosen to represent his high school at a conference in Washington, he would be again in the Library of Congress as part of his tour then. By then my first book was published. However, mischievous as he was, slipped away alone from a guided tour that looked down on the library, and Blake quietly followed an employee downstairs and entered the main floor of the library, closed to the public. As he looked up to wave to his tour group, he was approached by a librarian. When he explained that he wanted to see his mom's new book, she frowned and said that was not possible and escorted him out."

In another daring venture on that high school trip, bold Blake had called the White House several times, identifying himself and asking to speak to First Lady Barbara Bush. George Hubert Bush was president then. Mrs. Bush's assistant asked his connection to the First Lady, and he explained that his grandmother lived across the street from the Bush family home in Midland, Texas and that she and the First Lady were good friends. She was very nice and told him politely she would give his message to Mrs. Bush, who might find a minute to call him back.

Later that evening, Blake's high school tour group were hosted at the home of an ambassador. As the ambassador was welcoming the students, a staff member interrupted to say that there was a phone call from the white house. And it was for Blake! He went proudly to the phone was politely told, "The first lady is unable to visit with you, but gives her regards to dorothy and please let us know if there is anything you need during your stay in Washington." With a sly grin, Blake returned to his group who wanted to know why the White House was calling him!

We all wanted to tour the United States Department of the Treasury, which is in control of how and where our money is printed. We were disappointed that a Mint was not in DC. The kids had hoped to see coins minted and get to take home samples! Coins were only minted in Philadelphia, our country's first capital city; Denver, Colorado; San Francisco, California; and West Point, New York. But then, to our delight, we learned we could tour the Bureau of Engraving, where our paper money (Federal Reserve Notes) is printed. This was a first experience for all of us. It was not possible to comprehend that we were watching millions of dollars being printed and stacked uncut on trolleys to ride to their destination, where they are cut apart to become actual money!

Blake, Tommy, and Pamela asked the guide in unison, "Do we get samples from our tour?"

The guide laughed and responded, "We have a gift shop where you can buy all kinds of our national currency, old and new."

We couldn't wait to go there, where we learned about the popular hobby of collecting coins, which become more valuable through the decades, especially if they are printed incorrectly or no longer made, such as the $2 bill, which was discontinued for some years. The kids thought they would perhaps become numismatists and study and collect money. What a great hobby (if one could afford it!).

We passed the FBI building, and the rest of the family walked around outside while I went in. On our drive to Washington, when we stopped in a little town, I saw a man I was sure I had seen recently on wanted posters in post offices. I wanted to be a good citizen and report it. Bill was embarrassed because he was sure it was not the same man. I filled out the form to report such a sighting, and the administrator thanked me. I told him we were unsure but thought it was worth checking.

All too soon, we had to begin our drive back to Texas to be ready for school on Monday morning. Our last stop, not too far from the RV park in Virginia, was Arlington Cemetery. We all wanted to see the carefully guarded Tomb of the Unknown Soldier. Bill, a history enthusiast, explained to the children that this tomb stood for all the soldiers who died in all the wars in which Americans had given their lives, and the names of many of them are unknown. The solemn respect of the soldiers and the ceremonial conduct was reverent and impressive.

Bill drove our RV next to Charlottesville, Virginia, where we stopped to tour Monticello, the home of Thomas Jefferson, where we saw many of his amazing inventions. Blake and Pamela were especially fascinated with the enormous clock on the second floor beside the banister. The clock's pendulum hung down two stories to keep accurate time and to serve as a calendar.

Intending for our children to experience as many of the historical places of importance as possible, we made another stop at Appomattox Courthouse in Virginia to see where Robert E. Lee, general of the Confederacy, surrendered to Ulysses Grant, the Union general, to end the Civil War on April 9, 1865. We were happy to find that we had arrived at a special time when men in the official uniforms of a century ago were performing a reenactment. We returned home thoroughly saturated with American history, and school became more interesting because of our education through experience, thanks to our little RV and our tireless driver/historian.

From Our Paris
to Yours

BY THE TIME Pamela was entering high school and Blake was in middle school, we were planning another RV trip. Pamela loudly rebelled. "No! Why would I want to ride in a space smaller than my own bathroom with my whole family? No one else I know travels that way, and it is embarrassing! I hate being without a phone or TV or even my records to listen to. Please, *no more!*"

So we honored her wishes, sold the little RV, and we bought a motorboat so we could have family outings on the lake not far from our home. This provided a lot of outdoor fun with our family and friends: picnics, swimming, skiing, barbecues, fishing, and just enjoying the big lake as we rode around. There were tent sites. Bill and I missed our RV wandering, but we were not ready to pack up necessities for sleeping out.

As Pamela enjoyed her teen years, our boat provided a good way to entertain boyfriends we wanted to get to know. Blake and Tommy sometimes invited a friend, and tubing behind the boat was their favorite fun with great laughter and upsets into the water.

Bill had worked in Europe for a while and had yearned to see more of the enticing continent. He had an idea that might even appeal to our teenagers. Excitedly he asked me, "Do you want to go to France?"

"Of course," I replied, "but what about the kids?"

"Oh, we'll *all* go. We can rent an RV. Since we made it through Central America, Europe should be easier."

"That would be great!" I agreed. We crossed our fingers about Pamela's reaction to the idea.

When Bill informed the children of his plan, puzzled eight-year-old Tommy asked, "But how do we get an RV across the ocean?"

"We'll rent one over there when we arrive," Bill responded confidently. "Since we live in Paris, Texas, let's fly to Paris, France!"

I watched the thrill on all three faces, especially Pamela's. Bill had already been looking at the maps he had of Europe. Without Internet in those days, he had to go to the library to research, but he could not find any RV rentals in France. He called an RV dealership in Dallas. The man he talked to said he would inquire and let Bill know. A few days later, he informed Bill that he could not find an RV to rent in France but could reserve one for us in Amsterdam and have it delivered to Paris for the date we request. So it was settled!

*****

In early June, as soon as school had ended, we left. We didn't delay because, fortunately, Bill had learned that many places in France are closed during July, which is the entire country's summer holiday. We drove to Dallas and flew to New York City, changed planes, and arrived in *the other* Paris in time to watch sunrise as our plane landed. The kids excitedly said, "Look, there's the Eiffel Tower!"

We had made sure we all knew key words in French, like "Cas d'urgence!" (emergency); "Aide!" (help); "Je suis malade" (I'm sick); "Trouve ma mère et mon père s'il te plait" (please find my mother and father); "Je suis perdu!" (I'm lost); "Ou sont les toilettes?" (where's the bathroom?); and "Feu!" (fire!).

Although we hoped not to need these phrases, we all had practiced them many times before coming to France, hoping our pronunciation at least resembled French so we could make ourselves understood in an emergency.

We did need these words on our first night in Paris. At the quaint and picturesque old inn we chose, Bill and the boys were assigned a room upstairs, while Pamela and I were on the first floor. In the middle of the night, the alarm sounded, and we heard the words "Cas d'urgence! Feu!" Thank goodness we saw Bill and the boys running down the stairs as we hurried out of our room, and it turned out to be a false alarm. Everyone was okay, but after that, we insisted on being in adjoining rooms in hotels.

It was the first visit to France for all of us, and we were very enthusiastic. Bill had planned three days to do the sights in Paris before we got the rented RV. Naturally, our favorite place was the Eiffel Tower, and the children proudly informed several other English-speaking tourists that we were also from Paris. "Our Paris, in Texas, has the second largest Eiffel Tower in the world, and it has a big, red cowboy hat on top of it!"

We stopped for lunch at a little sidewalk café whose specialty was fish, so we ordered that. Our children had more grown-up palates now since we had traveled so much. But all our appetites were quelched when the little whole fish filled each of our four plates with their dead eyes staring up at us! We each quickly beheaded our fishes, wrapping the removal in a paper napkin. Remembering the lobster event years earlier, we were glad for Tommy's simpler meal of mashed potatoes and peas. Then we all had a problem with deboning the fish since we were only accustomed to fillets or fish sticks at home.

Later we found croque monsieurs more enticing (grilled ham-and-cheese sandwiches). Those became our staples for those Parisienne days, but when we got into the RV a few days later, no one complained about RV food. We all found our visit to a local supermarket to be very enlightening but, alas, no peanut butter! Europeans prefer Nutella, made from hazelnuts mixed with chocolate, so that would have to do. During those three days on foot, our favorite midafternoon rest stops were at the street cafes, where we could order exquisite pastries and café au lait for Bill, Pamela, and me, and the boys liked Laranjada.

We were all enthralled with the majesty of Notre Dame Cathedral and found it hard to believe that this gigantic monument had been built without machines centuries ago. When we walked around the outside, Bill pointed out the stabilizing flying buttresses.

Both boys seemed to hear only *butt* and doubled over in laughter at the word. Later we discovered the magnificent Petite Chapelle and entered while a beautiful concert was in progress. All of us love music, and this reverent performance in the quiet beauty of blue stained glass all around and above was so moving as never to be forgotten.

We all wanted to go to Cathedral Saint-Louis-des-Invalides, Napoleon's tomb. Bill, whose minor in college was history, related Napoleonic French history as we walked toward the monument. In the huge room with marble floor, we waited for our turn in line to go up to the ornate caskets of Napoleon and his wife, Josephine, which brought to my mind the tales of his devoted love for her. Pamela, who loves horses, was especially interested in the statue of Napoleon Bonaparte mounted on his horse, and then at nearby Musee de l'Armee, we saw *le Vizir*, his favorite horse, preserved perfectly by expert taxidermy.

In the afternoon, when we needed rest for our aching feet, our boat ride on the Seine River was relaxing. We loved seeing the city from the water since we had walked beside this river through Paris for a long way. Then I told the children that most cities were built on rivers because before cars were invented, boats were the main form of transportation besides horses. However, the horror to all of us was that these rivers were also open sewers, and chamber pots were emptied into them, often poured out of upper windows of homes.

"Yuck!" everyone exclaimed, thankful we lived in modern, more sanitary times!

*****

Returning to the center of Paris, we walked the famous shopping street, Champs-Élysées, peering into the fabulous store windows, where fashion is impressive and women's clothing very sexy. American modesty does not seem to exist here, and even billboard ads were sometimes portraying nudes. After dark, the lights glittered everywhere, and we spotted a restaurant that appealed to us, but it was across this very wide street, and traffic was heavy. When the light changed, indicating we could cross, Bill, Pamela, and Tommy went ahead immediately. Blake and I delayed a moment to look at something behind us and then started across, not realizing the crossing light was about to end. Cars were preparing to go when we got to the middle of the thoroughfare. I yelled for Blake to run with me, but as I reached the other side safely, I looked back in horror to see our ten-year-old boy in the center of the Champs-Elysees with traffic zooming all around him! It was a nightmare, but thank God, the driver in the lane where Blake was frozen in terror remained stopped and ignored the horns blaring behind his car. He had seen in his rear mirror the extreme danger of scores of motorcycles in a group that were approaching at tremendous speed. We screamed at Blake to wait while our hearts nearly thumped out of our bodies. Thank God, the motorcycles passed, the light changed to permit safe crossing, and Blake returned to our enveloping hugs. We are forever grateful, and we all are more careful of street crossings, especially in foreign places where we cannot read the signals.

European Caravan
Tour Begins

T HE RV ARRIVED from Amsterdam, and we headed out with a
road map of France, which we obtained from the visitor center. We stopped at a petrol station to fill with gas and got a
disappointing response from the attendant, who could not understand a word of Bill's French. Pamela, now in high school, had studied enough French to feel confident, so she tried, but we quickly
learned that French with a Paris, Texas, accent is unintelligible in
Paris, France! As we drove out of the city, Bill decided he and Pamela
must write French to communicate our needs. We had bought a little English-French dictionary to prepare ourselves with emergency
vocabulary prior to our arrival. I assured them it was probably just
the people they had tried to talk to, and we would get by with hand
gestures. The boys got into the game of creating those gestures, and
we were having fun with our first local problem to solve.

Bill had studied library books and maps to plan our route
through the French countryside. He saw a few mentions of campgrounds, so he felt we would have no problems. Before Tommy was
born, Pamela and Blake, at ages eight and five, had gone with us on
Bill's extended business trip to Portugal and had attended a Portuguese
day care center for a couple of weeks. There they had learned a small
Portuguese vocabulary to communicate with the other children. We
also remembered experiences in the Central American countries and
the fun challenge of trying to communicate in Spanish. For Tommy,

this was a first, but he quickly got into the spirit of it, and Pamela and Blake taught him a few French words. We all eagerly looked forward to this new challenge. Pamela and Bill were confident with their French vocabulary, and the little dictionary assured us of some communication and comprehension.

Bill ably maneuvered us through the traffic of Paris. We were near the end of our first hours of getting accustomed to this RV, or *caravan*, as they call it in Europe. It was about the size our first two RVs had been and felt similar. However, we found there were some limiting features we had not considered and a reason no one had not been able to find us an RV to rent in France. Many of the towns in France are walled, and the entrances are too low or too narrow for an RV to go through! This limited our explorations to some extent, but we were still seeing a lot and enjoying the trip.

Bill and I appreciated the lush countryside as we left Paris, while the children amused themselves with drawing, reading, and writing letters to friends back home. But we were embarrassed at billboards depicting naked couples in ads, especially for perfume. The boys stopped drawing and appreciated each sign with a giggle. Our first stop was at Chartres, where we visited the beautiful cathedral with magnificent stained-glass windows. Then we drove on to Orleans to see the region of Jeanne d'Arc. All the children were impressed with the story of a woman soldier impersonating a man and valiantly fighting the English to save France, but she was burned at the stake. A statue of her in her soldier outfit and on her horse was in the city center.

By then, it was late afternoon and time to move on. We were hoping to find an RV park, but no luck. We did not need hookups for this first night on the road, and weather was not so hot, so we knew we could open the windows and be comfortable. As we drove along, Cowboy Bill had an idea: maybe we could pay a farmer to let us sleep overnight somewhere on his place. We began to watch for a suitable farm.

Pretty soon, we found a nice-looking farmhouse, and Bill and Pamela went to knock on the door and try their French, accompanied by hand motions. The rest of us stood beside the RV so the couple could see we did not look like thieves but just a family of tourists from the USA. The man nodded with a friendly smile, and Bill gave him some *francs*. The farmer showed us where to park beside a lovely wheat field, and Bill foresaw no problems since the sky did not look cloudy, so hopefully we would not get stuck. We were grateful to be able to watch the sunset and have a quiet place to bed down. I prepared our supper in the unfamiliar little kitchen and had difficulty figuring out the stove. But we managed, and all had wet paper towel baths and bedded down early. Tommy now had a hammock bed strung across the RV beneath the upper bunk bed. When the kids were dreaming and I was about to fall asleep, Bill began to wheeze and cough. He thought he must be allergic to the wheat and tree pollen, and our open windows did not help. At first, we thought his symptoms would end, but they grew worse, and his eyes were itching horribly. He began to have what we thought was an asthma attack. I gave him Benadryl, the only allergy medicine I had, and it was the red liquid for children. Bill progressively grew worse and decided to open the bottle of Bordeaux wine he had bought that day, and he drank a couple of glasses. His coughing eased, and he started to fall asleep but was still wheezing badly. I closed the windows and watched him most of the night, trying to figure out from our vocabulary book how to say, "I am afraid my husband is dying! Call the doctor!" But we all awoke at daylight and decided not to try fields again! Bill seemed better and improved as the day progressed. He insisted he was fine and wanted to do the driving.

We drove southward beside the Loire River and stopped at the castle Chaumont-sur-Loire. On the tour of the enormous structure with many pointed towers, we learned it had been built in the AD ninth century. The boys imagined knights and sword fights, while Pamela and I noticed how bare and cold the dank stone walls were. This was certainly not what we and Disney had imagined the castle of Cinderella's Prince Charming to be! Then the guide told us the princesses had little lapdogs to keep their hands warm and larger dogs to warm their feet.

As we drove on later, I was fascinated to go through the area of Limoges, famous for the delicate porcelain china. One of my grandmother's most treasured possessions was her Limoges china. We toured the famous porcelain factory, and Pamela bought a small piece. But along the roadways, each of the other inviting-looking walled towns we were lured to enter presented an insurmountable problem of the low-arch entrance, blocking us completely.

Finally, we came to the lovely castle at Carcassonne, a huge fortress with double walls and lots of towers, so impressive! The thing our boys were most fascinated with were the dungeons on the lowest level, which were used during the Spanish Inquisition in the Middle Ages to imprison religious heretics. The guide explained the horrible torture devices, and there were no knights in shining armor to save those people from cruel deaths. We all loved perusing the many souvenirs at the gift shop, and the boys couldn't resist buying toy swords. Pamela was tempted to buy a tiara for her long blonde hair, but she decided to save her money until later in our adventures.

I Can't Remember Where!

T WAS THE end of the week, and we had learned that banks were closed on the weekend. We simply *had* to get some travelers' checks cashed and buy groceries. (ATMs and debit cards were things of the future.) We were all out of clean clothes and had not been able to find an RV park or a laundromat. Finally, Bill came to a village whose stone wall entrance had no arch and was just wide enough to maneuver our RV through. Pamela and I bundled up all the dirty clothes, towels, and sheets, ready to disembark when we found the washateria. Bill let us out and said he and the boys would go for groceries, money, and find other things to do for a couple of hours and then return for us. Our travel prospects were looking brighter!

We found enough empty machines to wash and dry everything. Several hours later, with everything fresh and folded in our sacks, we went outside about to await our boys. But they didn't arrive. An hour went by; it was twilight, and we were both concerned. It grew dark as another hour went by. I was trying to hide my panic from Pamela, but she began crying, "Mom, something terrible has happened. What are we going to do?"

I tried to reassure her, but I was not convincing. We stood there for what seemed like forever longer, searching every street movement with hope. Then, about 8:30 p.m., the little RV appeared, and we both cried with relief!

We hurried inside with our load of clothes and saw that the boys, and even Bill, were in tears.

"What happened?" Pamela and I asked in unison. "Did you have a wreck?"

"Daddy lost you!" Tommy exclaimed loudly.

Blake confirmed the predicament, and Bill explained through tears of relief. They had driven through many twists and turns in the totally unfamiliar territory and, without realizing it, had gotten into another town without a wall. They had been so busy with their chores they had never thought to try to remember the French street signs and names. Bill, who is usually so good with directions, became very disoriented and befuddled with the language and couldn't remember the name of the town or street where they had left us! They had driven around in circles so many times they had to stop for more petrol and couldn't even ask directions to return to us. Even if they had known enough French, they had no idea the town's name and could not guess at it on the map. Finally, they recognized a few sights and began to search each street and at last saw us!

As I recall this now humorous incident, I always begin to sing the country song, "He may ride forever beneath the streets of Boston...the man who never returned."

Exhausted from our experiences and hungry, we were very fortunate to find a campground just a little farther on. We pulled in but discovered campgrounds in France are built only for tent campers, and hence no RV could be rented in this country. The people were nice enough to let us park overnight at the campground, but to our dismay, there was no sanitation dump. But we could fill our water tank with fresh water. All the tour books and information about traveling in France had assured us that we did not have to boil drinking water here, as had been necessary in Central America!

Alcoholics All and Bonga-Bongas

HROUGH YEARS OF RV travel, we knew how to conserve water and always paid special attention to the waste tank capacity. I had quickly learned that soap suds require a lot of water to expel, so I kept surfaces clean with rubbing alcohol, as in hospitals. It was perfect: killed all germs, left no suds or residue, and required no rinsing, so it was our best option for cleaning the camper or our dirty feet. But of course, we could not bring this liquid on the international flight, so we had to buy it locally. In France, it was only available in pharmacies, so in the nearby town the next day, I went in and requested five bottles of rubbing alcohol. I wanted to have enough to last us through our trip since I knew stops near stores were often difficult with nowhere for a large vehicle to park. The pharmacist looked at me like I was a criminal, and I was helpless to explain that I clean with it. He said the limit was one bottle per person. He obviously had to guard against alcoholics drinking it in desperation! I bought one and thanked him. Returning to the caravan, I told everyone to get out and go buy one bottle of rubbing alcohol. To our surprise, even six-year-old Tommy was allowed to return to the RV with his bottle! Years later when Blake was grown, he made the statement that whenever he smelled alcohol, he thought of his mom. I just hope he explained he meant rubbing alcohol, so his friends don't think I'm a derelict drunk!

During our third week in France, we drove south to the famous Mediterranean beaches and selected Saint-Tropez, which we had seen in a movie. We found an RV park, Plage des Tahiti, which had much-needed hookups for electricity and fresh water, and the park had a sewage dump. We decided to stay for several days.

The placid sea was so inviting! Pamela got her book and sun-screen and enjoyed stretching out on a beach towel. The boys were thrilled to be free and ran toward the beautiful blue-green water. Bill and I got beach mats and sunglasses and headed for a rest on the sandy shore while we watched for the boys' safety. After a while, they came running breathlessly up to us. Thirteen-year-old Blake had a huge grin and said, "This beach is great! The girls are *topless!*"

Six-year-old Tommy, in disdain, exclaimed while cupping his hands up and down at his chest, "I don't understand the big deal over *bonga-bongas!*"

We took it easy and enjoyed the fun coastal area for several days. On the third day, we drove out through Cannes, the home of the most prestigious film festival in the world, but we didn't see any movie stars. Fascinated with foreign money, the kids wanted to acquire some more. When they realized we were close to Italy, they begged for us to drive across that border, so Bill headed for San Remo, where they each exchanged one US dollar and returned to the RV thrilled with how rich they had become, since 1,651 Italian lire equaled one US dollar. We all could say we had been to Italy (without confessing it was only for a couple of hours!)

We returned to the French coast for one more night and then drove north to Grasse, France, where Pamela and I wanted to visit the famed *parfumeries.* On the winding little mountain road over-looking the French Riviera, there was no place to park, so Bill let us girls out to run into the factory to see how perfume is made and perhaps purchase a potion as our favorite souvenir. Scents are known to trigger memory. The factory director was very polite as he ushered us through the building, which looked like a scientific laboratory. Exquisite fragrances of many different flowers filled the air, and the attendant invited us to dab our arms with various selections, explaining that body chemistry determines the final effects of a perfume someone wears. How we wished we could buy some little bottles to take home, but they were far more expensive than we had anticipated. Although she was aware we were not able to buy, the attendant continued to be very cordial, and we were grateful that she spoke good English to us. We left without purchasing any but with more informed appreciation for perfumes.

Bill found a less difficult highway and headed for Geneva, Switzerland. We spotted a good place to park and headed to tour the fairytale-looking Chateau de Chillon on an island at Montreux near Lake Geneva, not knowing that many years later, Pamela would marry a man whose family had a home in the mountains here. The boys again enjoyed pretending to be knights, and Pamela dreamed of being a princess. Lake Geneva is so placid and beautiful, with the picturesque mountains surrounding it, and we loved walking around and looking into store windows, finding prices far higher in all the Swiss shops than in United States stores.

The scenery in the high mountains beckoned because it reminded us of Heidi in our favorite children's storybook. We drove upward to the town of Gruyeres, where we dined outside at a cheese factory and had the local favorite meal of dipping bread in a crock of cheeses melting over little candles. It was such a perfect experience, and we all loved it. Next, we rode a gondola to a glacier, high in these *Alps*. Tommy had long since outgrown his altitude sickness, and we all loved to ski, so a gondola ride was a real thrill since we only had previously experienced ski lifts in the United States. Of course, before leaving this pristine and exquisite country, the children exchanged some US dollars for Swiss francs to add to their collections, but they got far fewer coins than in Italy.

Is This English or Not?

AT CALAIS, FRANCE, we returned our rented RV and took the speedy hovercraft across the English Channel to Dover. (The building of the Chunnel under the English Channel was yet years in the future.) We all liked the thrill of going so fast as to be almost flying over the water as our craft hovered close to the waves. Fun and exciting!

In England, it was a relief to get to speak English and be understood everywhere, but the English pronunciation of locals required some puzzling deciphering on our part. We immediately learned we had to watch out for how to cross the street since driving in Britain is on the "wrong" side of the road (opposite the United States). We had never really thought about the way we cross a street in America. We realized, at home, an oncoming car passing closest to us would come from the left, posing the most danger. With traffic now opposite, we had to remind each other to look to the right before crossing a street. Even the pedestrian crosswalks in many places had the words "Look Right" painted on them in bold letters.

We rented a van in Dover and drove to Oxford, where we were leaving Bill for a three-week graduate course at the university. We helped him take his things to his third-floor dorm room in the ancient majestic Worcester College, one of the colleges on the Oxford University campus. His room was sparse, and his single bed was a shock to us. It had a crisscross of ropes, perhaps centuries old, to serve as springs for his thin mattress! We got him settled and his bed made and then Tommy discovered under the bed a big rope with a knot on one end. "Dad, look at this!" All students had already been informed about this when they signed up for the course, so Bill explained, "This is the fire escape to climb down from dorm room windows."

"Cool! That would be fun!" Tommy, who had always loved heights and climbing, immediately wanted to try this challenge and swing out the window on the rope. Bill laughed as he prevented Tommy's plan. I could not let my imagination jump to that scenario, so we ushered the kids down the steep wooden staircases. We drove to meet my sister and brother, who would make an adventurous van excursion with the children and me for the next three weeks while Bill fulfilled his dream of attending literature classes at Oxford.

Search for Ancestors,
if the Van Survives Us

THE REST OF us were heading northward to enjoy exploring the beautiful countryside of England. My brother, thankfully, took over the driving since I was not about to attempt it on the wrong side of the narrow little roads with neat hedgerows on each side. At one place, we stopped to ask a farmer by the road, "Sir, can you tell us how to get to York?"

In a droll manner, he replied, "You take the York Road, of course!" and he moved on.

Jim muttered under his breath, "Duh! If we knew where that was, of course we would take it!"

At our third petrol stop, Blake wanted to help Jim fill the tank. Jim went in and paid and signaled Blake to start the pump. A station attendant was standing at the next pump watching, and when it was full, Blake announced he was finished. Jim came to return the nozzle to the pump, but he discovered Blake had filled the tank with diesel fuel and our rental van had a gas engine! We didn't know what to do and had visions of having to purchase a ruined rental van. Blake and Jim both were chagrinned. The station attendant provided a syphon to empty the diesel, but he gave us no refund. Then we had to pay for the gas to fill up again. We crossed our fingers, and the engine did start and did not give any problems later.

We arrived after dark to the town of Dunbar, Scotland, on the North Sea. *Dunbar* was the surname prominent in our ancient ancestry, so we were very curious. We found a lovely small hotel right by the ocean and checked in for the night, the boys and Jim in one room and Pamela and I and my sister, Pam, in the other. We didn't see any hotel guests but assumed they were all out eating since the dining room of the hotel was closed until breakfast. We left to enjoy a restaurant recommended in the tourist guide and returned about 10:00 p.m., entered the small hotel lobby, and saw no attendant, so we went to our rooms. It seemed the hotel was empty because all the rooms were dark when we had looked up from the parking lot, and we just assumed people here went to bed early. But it felt creepy!

We finally found our room numbers in the dark hallway and settled in. The hotel rooms did not have private baths but one for ladies and one for men on each floor. Our room was clean. We looked out the window, and the full moon illuminated a graveyard close by and then the billowing waves of the North Sea and the mouth of the Firth of Forth beyond. We were all uneasy as the wind grew high.

Pamela commented, "This is the perfect setting for a ghost movie or a murder mystery!"

We girls went into the bathroom together. Each stall was closed, and from one came the flushing sound, but no one came out, and we looked for feet underneath, and there were none! We were scared and hurried to finish and return to our room. But it was a sleepless night as we scared each other with our whispered thoughts and imaginings. We had heard of hotel ghosts in Britain! We hoped they were friendly Caspers if we met some. Maybe we already had encountered a female ghost in the bathroom.

The next day, the boys had a scary tale to tell also. They had decided to explore the hotel with flashlights to see how many rooms were occupied. On the top floor, they heard a single weird strain of guitar music from one room, and it did not sound like a radio. They called out, thinking it might be the manager, but no one answered. They knocked, but no answer. Then they tried the door handle, which was unlocked, but no one was within. But the music was coming from there and continued as they closed the door. They hurried back to their room and stayed awake all night. We all heard footsteps on the wooden floors during the night.

The next morning at breakfast, even the waitress seemed creepy, but our imaginations had gone wild. We asked where the other guests were, saying we heard footsteps frequently during the night.

She replied, "The men who stay here come only on the weekend because they work the oil rigs in the North Sea during the week, so we never have guests during the week."

We realized the silver teapot on the buffet had the name Dunbar engraved on it. My sister explained our ancestry and asked if, by any chance, she could purchase the vessel. The lady was happy to sell it to her. When we quizzed our host about ghosts, she quickly vanished into the kitchen, refusing to elaborate.

Pam happily exclaimed, "I'll just take the ghost home with me in this teapot! I know our ancestors were contacting us in the night!"

There was a large graveyard right next to our parking lot, and bravely we looked for Dunbar gravestones, but we quickly gave up since they were not readily apparent. We got away as fast as we could!

Counting Coins

W E LOVED THE English and Scottish scenery, the little villages and shops, and saw all the tourist sights we could
find along our circuitous route. We ventured over to Wales
to tour the huge castle there and to experience the strange-sounding
Welsh Celtic language, which we could not understand at all. The
kids also collected United Kingdom coins, as many different denom-
inations as they could get, which later became our lifesaver!

By our last night on the road before we met Bill, we had all
almost run out of money and travelers' checks, even though we had
stayed in very small cheap places. It became a final quest to find the
cheapest place possible to sleep that evening. We had made sandwiches of cheese and bread from a little general store and were thankful water in Great Britain was free and potable. Sleeping became the
problem. We had heard that some pubs have cheap rooms for rent.
Jim went into several pubs, asking, and he finally found one that
looked okay and had a vacant room. He asked the price, and we went
up to peruse the one room and some questionable-looking furnishings, wondering if we were perhaps staying in a brothel! We had to
pool our money to see if we could stay, and the children's coin collection saved the night for us! We barely had enough, but we would be
in Oxford tomorrow, so we would make it! (And none of us got lice
or worse from that room. At least we didn't hear any ghosts!) But Bill
had nearly become one.

When we met Bill at Oxford, he told how much he loved his
three weeks there of learning in one-on-one conferences with the

dons (professors). We bought a painting from an artist who was in the lovely garden, creating a scenic watercolor painting of his dorm setting. We all went out for a dinner celebration in London before departing Europe the following day. While we were at the restaurant, Bill related his harrowing tale:

He was returning from the library late one night when he had to climb the ancient three flights of wooden stairs in the deserted hallway and felt a stifling sensation; he couldn't breathe and collapsed. He lay on the stairs and saw his life pass before him. Gasping for air, he saw the *great dark void* he had read about and knew he was dying. He was not able to call for help. He had always had severe allergies, but we had never thought to beware of the ancient buildings filled with dust, mold, and mildew, not to mention the pollen in season. He finally revived enough to make it to bed and slept, believing he would not wake up, but the night air revived him, and he got allergy medicine to help him make it the rest of the term.

Frightened at the realization that no one could have contacted us if he had died, we celebrated our reunion a little too much! (This was years before cell phones.) The children still tease us about punting drunk on the Thames River since we normally do not drink alcoholic beverages.

Stars, Stars Everywhere

WITHOUT AN RV in the years when our teenagers had rebelled against traveling "in a vehicle the size of my bathroom with my whole family and without TV, phone, or music!" according to Pamela, our travels were more normal. The summer after our European adventure, we flew to California, rented a van, and stayed in a Holiday Inn located at Vine and Hollywood Streets, a prime location to see all the craziness of the famous city. We could not believe the hippie foot traffic along the sidewalks in those days, the crazy costumes some people wore to stay in character. The risqué lingerie fashions shown in shop windows and on billboards were almost as X-rated as those in France. Our mouths dropped open involuntarily at some of the sights we saw!

The children were eager to see movie stars, and the first morning, Bill realized we were driving behind an open convertible which Rod Stewart, the British rock star, was driving. Later, Blake spotted another open convertible with Eddie Murphy as driver. We bought a star map and followed the directions to mansions of most famous stars, several in the same neighborhood. On one street, we waved to Jimmy Stewart, who was walking his dog. We stopped in front of Rock Hudson's edifice with numerous statues in the garden and were amused at a figurine that looked like two tourists peering over his property wall. We could never have imagined that about thirty years later, our sons would be living in this city and accustomed to seeing movie stars on streets anywhere.

We drove to the Griffith Observatory at the top of the mountain, where we could look out on the vast city and also enjoy the lectures and star projections at the planetarium. Universal Studios was a terrific tour, but we passed Jaws, who jumped out of the water beside our little train car and scared us all. Pamela never liked to be in the ocean after that. Tommy was thrilled and timid when he was selected from the tourists to act in a mock film pretending to be asleep. In a scene from *ET* with children on bikes riding into the sky, we learned about a green-screen background for the magic effect.

Later, we drove to Escondido to go to a safari park, a drive-through zoo with many African animals that came up close to our car. I was a little alarmed when the chimps began to climb all over our van and looked quite menacing. The kids delighted in feeding the zebras, which were poking their heads through our open windows. They seemed to know that bags of their food were sold to visitors at the entrance. We also had to go to the San Diego Zoo, which was known at that time to be one of the best zoos in America. It was truly amazing, and the animals seemed to have good clean habitats. On to Anaheim, where Disneyland was a *must*, and it was a special Mickey anniversary, so the park was quite crowded. Tommy, our budding artist, was fascinated when we got to do the backstage tour to see how the characters were designed. Who could believe back then that both Blake, as a musician, and Tommy, as an artist, would one day work for Disney Studios! And we would have a granddaughter born on Mickey Mouse's birthday! But "when you wish upon a star, your dreams come true!"

Let's Fool Big Sis!

PAMELA WAS IN her sophomore year at college when our boys, fourteen and eight, were planning our summer vacation, which we hoped would include her. We all had missed her during school months. Bill suggested we make our first trip through the Great American West and travel all the way to Las Vegas! We were all eager for this adventure, although we had had no RV for six years. Bill enticed Pamela's enthusiasm by asking if she would join the family trip to Las Vegas. A bit reluctantly, she acquiesced for a family vacation, knowing we no longer owned an RV. This was not her choice for summer holidays, but Bill assured her it would only be for a couple of weeks. She could keep her dorm apartment since we would return in plenty of time for her second semester summer classes. She also reminded us that her boyfriend was coming from far away to visit us at summer's end for her twentieth birthday. We promised we would be home well before then.

Bill and the boys were excited because they had formulated the brilliant idea to purchase tents and make it a new kind of camping vacation. I was not so happy with the prospects of sleeping on the ground, but with their excitement, they convinced me, and they made an expensive trip to the camping outfitter store, returning with so much gear I knew we would have to purchase a rooftop luggage carrier for our van.

I warned everyone that Pamela might rebel and cancel out of our trip. Blake said, "Let's fool her. Let's not tell her we are tent camping!"

Knowing how important and special this was to the boys, Bill and I agreed, so we told Pamela, "Pack light because all you'll need are jeans and good walking shoes. It's vacation time everywhere, so we won't need to dress up!"

At her university campus, we added her suitcase to all our stuff in the back of the van. She never noticed or asked about the luggage rack on top, and she was in a sundress and low heels—our young adult daughter! We were all very happy to be together again. At our first gas stop in West Texas the kids played imaginary photo op for *GQ Magazine* and took pictures of each other posing, even Pamela! We laughed and had such a good time together all day and checked into a nice motel for the night.

The next morning at breakfast Pamela asked, "What is our destination for tonight?"

Bill responded, "Silverton, Colorado. It's an old mining town with silver mines in the mountains." (The idea of a hotel with silver accoutrements probably danced in Pamela's mind.) We drove all day toward the campground Bill had reserved on the lovely Animas River, unbeknown to our college sophisticate.

When we checked in at the campground, Pamela was visibly shocked and not at all happy about the surprise. The boys were ecstatic! We set up the new tents, with Bill's and mine a two-person pup tent. For our three kids, Bill had purchased a larger igloo tent, three new sleeping bags, and foam mats to go beneath them. With lanterns, a hibachi grill, and necessary utensils, we were all set to barbecue burgers for supper, and the stars were just coming out. Four of us thought it was glorious, but one thought it a nightmare she was far too mature to endure! I could empathize with her as I remembered my trepidations on our first night in our little RV years before.

Pamela headed to the bathhouse to shower and to shampoo her long beautiful naturally blonde hair. We thought that would improve her mood after the long drive, but in a little while, we heard a loud cry of "Oh no!" Alarmed, I ran to see what had happened and found my wet-haired furious daughter, who pointed to the sign that said, "No hair dryers. Power supply not strong enough." I had to hide my inward chuckle as I helped her wrap a towel around her head and sit by the campfire to dry her tresses, as women had done for centuries before hair dryers were invented.

The boys were having so much fun chuckling together at the joke on big sister, and we all enjoyed the s'mores we made on the fire. Pamela's mood improved as she got warm, and we all reminisced our RV days.

"The tents will be a new experience and fun, if we all *make* it fun!" I announced, and the boys headed for the igloo.

A little later, we went to our tent, and Pamela, who mumbled under her angry breath, "You are all just trying to kill me before my boyfriend comes!" reluctantly joined her brothers in the waterproof abode. Within a brief time, there was laughter from the igloo, and we figured the boys had won her over, knowing they could make anyone laugh. The three have always been close and enjoyed each other. Everything went quiet, and we were dozing off to sleep when we heard our car door slam. Bill ran out to see what was going on.

He returned, looking dismayed. "She says it is raining inside the tent and she is too old to sleep with her brothers. I told her she could remain in the van all night. I looked in on the boys and got her sleeping bag for her. Sure enough, the moisture from their hot breaths was truly creating mist within, so I left the igloo partially unzipped. Actual rain is not expected, and Pamela locked herself in the van."

The next day, we found an outdoor supply store and bought Pamela her own tent. She was right. We had not realized how very grown up she had become, and she did not need to share the boys' tent. That day was thrilling for all three boys. We had all heard about many happy adventures Bill had related after his three annual men-only getaway. He and his best childhood friend trailered their motorbikes behind the RV to ride jeep trails on Colorado mountainsides. Bill said we had to experience this fun now, so he rented a Jeep.

We all squashed in, and the bumpy drive began, cutting across the steepest part of the mountainside on a very narrow, barely visible Jeep trail, which looked like a goat path. At first it was fun, but then we reached the steepest part of the mountainside to traverse. We felt the Jeep must be hanging on by only two wheels and would turn over and dump us down the mountainside at any moment. Pamela and I first begged and then *demanded* to be let out! Walking would be much safer, and then we could go for help if, or when, the boys rolled down the mountain. But they had a very fun ride and later returned to give us a lift back to town. We didn't feel we had missed anything we wanted to experience!

Since we had a lot of fun seeing everything at the historic Old West town of Silverton and peered into some of the abandoned silver mines, we stayed a second night, with Pamela a little more satisfied in her own quarters but still mumbling "I hate camping!" The breathtaking magic of the black night sky sprinkled with millions of sparkling diamonds was more wondrous than any of us had ever imagined, so we lingered a long time in the firelight.

The next day, everyone was happier as we drove on to Lake Powell, where Bill had reserved a site at the only campground in the area. We were dismayed when it looked like a crowded asphalt parking lot with campsites very close together, but it was the only thing available. That night was a different story! The kids had their two tents, which seemed to have solved the problems, so we tried to sleep in ours. In the middle of the night, the boys cried out. They had been awakened and really scared because they heard the nearby howls of coyotes. We now heard them too and were searching to see how close they were. We had been careful not to have any food at the tents, knowing it would attract wild animals from miles away, but the other close tent campers may not have been so wise. We told the boys to get into the van to finish the night, and we would get Pamela and join them there.

I tried to awaken our daughter, but she was sleeping soundly, and I couldn't rouse her. I was puzzled, but she felt a normal temperature and was breathing regularly; I hoped she was just recovering from lack of sleep in the previous nights. I went to the van to join the others, and we wondered what to do. The coyote howls sounded closer and closer, and all four of us kept our noses pressed to the windows, watching for Pamela's safety, with the boys creating horror stories of what could happen. Bill knew we could jump out and scare coyotes away if necessary. He had dealt with them at our farm and knew they would only bother small animals. I had read that coyotes would not attack a person unless they felt threatened first, so I hoped that information was accurate. The scary night sounds finally faded into the distance after what seemed like hours. No one but Pamela slept that night.

Just before dawn, I walked over to the small hotel nearby and said I wanted to reserve the very first vacated room, and I would pay any amount. They said they did not expect an empty one, but I sat in the lobby waiting and praying for someone to leave, and it happened! We got a room for one night and promised to leave the next morning.

When Pamela finally awoke and learned we were vacating the tents and packing them away, she confessed that she had put herself to sleep by taking two migraine pills, even though she had no headache. She just needed sleep and not to feel the hard ground and hard circumstances!

Bill rented a large boat for us to enjoy a wonderful day on Lake Powell, a huge lake, and the water level was high that year from lots of rain. Our day and the photos were wonderful. The water was beautiful, and the coves of the lake had shallow caves, big holes, and arches of sandstone to explore. We all loved it, and Pamela admitted it was worth the torture she had endured to get here.

The Grand Canyon Beckons

O UR EXPENSIVE TENTS and gear had cost, not saved, us any money, and we stowed them permanently on top of the van and drove to the Grand Canyon. Although we could not get reservations to take the Colorado River boat trip, no one was sorry because that would be nearly a week of rustic camping. We were quite fortunate to get a hotel and could *all* really enjoy our visit to this natural wonder of the world. We hiked and explored many of the trails, but *not* the one down into the canyon, which required a much higher level of fitness than any of us could claim. The rim trails were beautiful, and we loved perusing the gift shops and admiring the handmade objects from talented craftspeople of the local tribes: *Havasupai, Hualapai, Navajo, Hopi, Paiute* and *Zuni*.

In the afternoon, I was tired and begged off. I sat on the porch of the big lodge while Bill took the kids on another trail to peer down into the amazing canyon depths. I was reading my book when an older woman came up the stairs to the porch in a state of panic and loudly announced, "There is a little boy on the narrow ledge beyond the huge boulder that juts out on the cliff over the canyon, and they are trying to get him back safely! Pray!"

I said a prayer and continued reading. In a few minutes, Bill and the three kids returned, so we could head for dinner in the lodge restaurant.

In a very excited tone, Blake exclaimed, "You won't believe what happened!"

"What?" I asked.

Then he, Bill, and Pamela began at once, "You know how Tommy likes to climb trees?"

"Of course. Tommy, did you find a great tree to climb?" I asked our ten-year-old.

He shook his head, looking sheepish.

"Mom, before anyone realized it, he walked alone out on this ledge over the Grand Canyon!" Blake announced.

Pamela added, "It was only about ten inches wide, and no one could follow him."

Bill reported, "I thought if we tried to get to him, he might look back at us and fall, so we held our breaths and prayed, knowing he has always been an agile little monkey who loves heights. But it was the scare of my life!"

Blake added, "The ledge went all the way around the huge cliff overlook, and he made it to the other side grinning. He was so proud of himself!"

I was shaking when I said, "Tommy, you know you did wrong, and it was very, very dangerous. Did you know that everyone at this hotel was praying for your safety since a woman rushed back to tell everyone she had seen a boy out there on the edge, but no one could go out for him? The guards made everyone stay back. You were breaking a law!"

I swept our chagrinned little boy into a huge bear hug with tears of relief streaming down all our faces and thank-you prayers in our hearts.

*****

Our next stop was Las Vegas, which all of us were eager to experience, although we were not gamblers. We checked in at Caesars Palace, a great change from tents! We loved the swimming pool and the beautiful fountains as we cooled off after our day's drive. We walked through the magnificent shopping mall inside, with the ceiling painted like the blue sky, since some people stayed inside a casino hotel for days and never went outside! Later, on the Strip, we had to see inside each of the amazing casino hotels, whose architecture and innovations baffled and impressed each of us. The amazing buildings were copies of famous places around the world. Architects must have had fun trying to outdo each other.

After dinner at a casino buffet, Bill handed each of the kids a $10 bill and said, "Since no one under twenty-one is allowed in the gambling part, you can tell us which game you want us to play with your money. You can watch from the big windows and doorways of the casino."

The eyes of all three lit up, and we could see their wonder and excitement.

Bill continued, "But when your $10 is gone, it's gone! No more! The most important thing to learn about gambling is that *no one wins*! We always set a limit that would be about equal to the price of a movie."

I added, "We won't stay long because we were both taught when we were children that gambling is bad for anyone and can be addictive, so you are better off never to start! Some people actually can't stop gambling, and some even lose everything they own, including their home and car. This will be fun and a great lesson we hope you always remember."

When we went into the casino, our kids had disappeared for a few minutes, and we assumed they were in the restrooms. After we found the slot machines where Bill would play poker with his $10, we looked up and saw Pamela, dressed in her beautiful sundress and heels, and Blake, dressed in a suit, being herded out by the bouncer guard. They were dismayed because they had thought their best attire would convince people they were twenty-one years old.

Bill walked over and asked where they each wanted the $10 placed.

Pamela responded, "Wheel of fortune," which she could watch from where she stood. She chose the number 1,000 marker on the wheel's lighted face, and we all watched as the big wheel went round and round. Naturally, it stopped on fifty, and her money was gone.

Blake chose craps because he knew that was a forbidden word and thought it was funny. He picked a number, and the dice were cast, but he, too, quickly joined the losers. Bill and I inwardly hoped the antigambling lessons were a great $20 investment.

Tommy was watching from a glass viewing area. We went over and asked where we should place his bet. He proudly announced, "I already won!" as he patted his pocket.

Bewildered, we asked, "Did you find a slot machine in the snack bar?"

He replied with a grin, "No! My money stays in my pocket, so I *won!*"

Wow! The saying "A little child shall lead them" proved very pertinent. We hoped he would always be so wise.

Empty-Nest Excitement

MPTY NEST WAS upon us. Our two older children were married and living about as far away from our Texas home as possible within the United States. They were not trying to escape us, but Blake, a composer, had a great job in Los Angeles with Disney Records and his wife with American Express. Pamela married an American Express manager who lived in New Jersey, so she continued her American Express employment in a different New Jersey office. Tommy was in college in Tulsa, Oklahoma. Bill, who had sold our ranch/farm and had been teaching part time at Paris Junior College, decided to take the semester off for travel.

Since we lived in the middle of the United States and our children on two coasts and in the middle, what better excuse for buying another RV! We found the perfect one in midsummer as we prepared for Tommy to return to college the next month. We could even use it for moving some of his stuff, so we decided on a twenty-eight-foot class A Dutchman for the road, reasoning that if we cover enough miles and sleep in it enough nights, we can break even instead of using the dollars on hotel and plane costs. See the country and see our children! What a great excuse!

In late August, just after we got Tommy settled in Tulsa, Pamela called to say, "Come soon. The doctor says our baby is due any day!"

We were so excited to become grandparents and had the perfect vehicle to get there. We packed and drove over 1,500 miles, arriving in mid-September, but we could not find an RV park nearby. Eric's parents lived on a rural farm, and they were in Europe for the summer. They had graciously told Eric and Pamela we could park on their farm for this very important visit, sorry that they could not be there in time for the birth.

Pamela, at nearly nine months pregnant, rested, and we enjoyed being with her while Eric worked each day. By the weekend, we knew they needed some private time before baby arrived, so we decided to tour New England to see the gorgeous fall leaves, which we had only seen in calendar photos. By then mobile phones had been invented, and we actually had one, a huge contraption which worked in some places. We crossed our fingers that it would work when the important call came, and we knew we could return within a day of their phone announcement.

The doctor had been premature in his declaration in late August that the baby would soon be there, but we were happy to see the beautiful autumn. The leaves were truly as brilliantly colored as the calendar photos we had seen. Pumpkin patches and cornfield mazes were advertised throughout New England, and we loved sampling cider at various apple orchards. We spent a lazy, happy two weeks of anticipation seeing so many places we had never been before. When we returned to New Jersey near the end of September, we parked again at the parents' farm. On Saturday afternoon, our son-in-law Eric, who knew Bill loved car races, informed us that there would be an IndyCar Race the next day about an hour away at Nazareth, Pennsylvania, and he had learned we could park our RV within the track and watch the entire race, with choice views from the top of our motor coach. Bill was thrilled to do this, so we left that evening to get set up for the next day's race.

We were truly in the center of the track and were awakened to the exciting roar of the engines. We took our phone, folding chairs, sunscreen, sunglasses, and hats to the top of our RV when we climbed the ladder on the backend. It was so much fun to see the cars fly around us, encircling the track every thirteen seconds, according to my watch! After about an hour, I realized with huge chagrin, "If they call us, we cannot hear the phone." And we couldn't get out! We would be stuck there until the race ended! After several hours, the noise and the race were over, and we climbed down and headed back to our daughter's home. We teased Eric about positioning his in-laws exactly where he wanted us: out of the way for the big delivery time! He responded that there was, indeed, a tunnel to get out of center field if we had needed to.

When Pamela went into labor, we waited at our RV, with Eric promising to call us as soon as the baby was born, or sooner if we were needed. We anxiously waited in our RV, with nothing to do except read, but we couldn't concentrate. Eric had told us that when he had been at the farm a month before, he had lost his wedding ring when he got out of the swimming pool there. We decided to spend our time looking for it, so we rented a metal detector. We amused ourselves for several hours with the goal of finding the lost ring. And we did! We returned the metal detector to the rental agency and gift wrapped the ring in a box we bought. We had it for baby Alex to give as a birth gift to his dad. Finally, the call came, and we eagerly rushed to the hospital. We were all so proud of the precious and perfect little boy who had made them parents and us grandparents for the first time! When infant Alex presented the gift box to Eric, he and Pamela were delighted we had found his wedding ring.

This new RV had provided us the trip of a lifetime! Now, as grandparents, we returned home by way of Tulsa to see our youngest happily settled in college life. About six weeks later, we drove to South Carolina, enjoying the beautiful Appalachian and Blue Ridge Mountains and stopping in state parks. In my hometown of Greenville, South Carolina, we were so happy to give my parents the treat of taking them to see their first great-grandchild. My dad had suffered many strokes and could only walk slowly with a cane and could not talk. My mother, his caregiver, really needed a happy change of scene, and they were very excited. Our RV was the perfect way to take them since Daddy could stretch out on the sofa and Mother could rest in the comfortable lounge chair for the drives, which we tried to make restful each day.

Bill took a longer route for sightseeing. Daddy enjoyed the wheelchair ride along the handicap pathway to Natural Bridge in

Virginia. Mother was game for any adventure and found every sight so interesting. At night, they stayed in a hotel, which permitted us to park in their parking lot. The next day, Mom wanted to go to Luray Caverns, which she had loved as a child and wanted me to see. While Mother and I strolled with a guide among the stalactites and stalagmites through the amazing pathways inside Luray Caverns, she related seeing it in her college years. Bill pushed Dad's wheelchair through the antique car museum on-site, so we each had a lovely day.

When we made it to New Jersey, we were all thrilled to see the precious little boy, now about five weeks old. After several days in New Jersey, the four generations celebrated my birthday. Thankful for our RV, we returned Mother and Daddy to their South Carolina home safely. The fall leaves were still in full color, and we were back home in Texas before very cold weather set in.

Hiding at a Truck Stop

WE SETTLED IN for a few days in our Paris, and then wanderlust set in again. Since it would not be winter in California, we eagerly headed to see our son and his wife there. We had learned that since our previous RV days ten years before, truck stops allowed RVs to park overnight free. On long journeys, when we had miles to cover and were not particularly interested in seeing various points of interest along the way, Bill preferred driving late at night with less traffic, so we left home in late afternoon. Our first stop was about midnight in Oklahoma City at a large truck stop. We didn't see any other RVs, so Bill drove to the farthest row and found a place to back in and "hide" between two huge semis.

We pulled down our shades so no one could peer inside. Bill was in the shower, and I was in my robe on the couch reading when someone knocked on the door. It alarmed me, and I asked, "Who is it, and what do you want?"

"It is the police guard, ma'am. Can you please open the door so I can ask you a question?"

I reluctantly obeyed after peeping out and seeing his uniform.

He tipped his hat as he looked me over, stopping with my white hair. "Are you traveling alone?" he queried, and I responded, "No, my husband is in the shower."

A bit awkwardly, he said, "You look like a very nice person, but we have a lot of trouble back here with hookers in RVs, so I'm going to have to ask you all to move to the front of the truck stop to the designated RV parking area."

I assured him we would, and he thanked me and left, while I inwardly asked, *Do you think I'm too old or too unattractive to be one of those women?*

Our night was pleasant, and we slept well, using the roaring diesel engines on the trucks, which stayed on all night, as our sleep sound. We hit the road again in early morning to beat Oklahoma City traffic. As we moved on west, we found a very small roadside city park with a few RV sites for that second night. There were only three RVs, but the wayside park was lighted, and it appeared safe. After midnight, a knock on the front door alarmed both of us.

I begged Bill not to answer it. "He may have a gun!"

But Bill asked through closed window and locked door, "What do you want?"

The man, who looked a bit disheveled, begged for money for gas, giving a convincing sob story about trying to drive his car two hundred miles to see his daughter, who was hospitalized. Reluctantly, Bill pulled out a $20 bill and handed it through a slit opening in the window. The man thanked Bill and left.

I said, "Yeah, I know you were thinking, just like I was, 'What if it were us trying to get to our daughter?'"

But we both felt like we had been conned, and we were frightened and felt vulnerable the rest of the night. We moved our vehicle to park next to another RV and had a somewhat restless night. The next morning, the little park looked pretty in the sunlight, and we walked around to see what had made it a wayside point of interest. But it just seemed like a place to break long miles of driving where there were few towns. After that, we only stayed in guarded places.

Thanksgiving Joy

W**E HAVE MADE** many trips to Los Angeles through the years and stayed in all the different RV parks there. Our favorite for the views and the peaceful settings is Malibu Beach RV Park, set on a cliff that is beautifully landscaped with flowers and palm trees and unobstructed views of the gorgeous golden sunsets over the Pacific Ocean. We could walk to the public beach and pass in front of the mansions along the private beach. However, when we got our larger RVs and had to transverse Los Angeles from east to west, it became difficult, and our children lived long drives from there.

We found another RV park we really liked, Dockweiler RV Park near Manhattan Beach. We loved the ease of getting to the harbor or skating on the sidewalk along the beaches and seeing the amazing throngs of tourists and locals enjoying all the beach activities there.

When our children bought homes in another part of LA, we began to stay at Balboa Park in the campground there, now named Hollywood RV Park, which was near their home. Balboa was a lovely municipal park to walk in each morning and enjoy the wildlife on the large lake there. We could even play golf when we chose to or rent boats.

But in recent years, we chose to stay at the beautiful oasis setting of Stagecoach RV Park in Banning, California. It was a little over an hour from our son's home, and we could unhook our tow vehicle and not have to take the RV into the city traffic. The peaceful campground is a respite for our children to visit on the way to Joshua Tree National Park, past the grove of enormous solar windmills.

Our most joyful trip to LA was in mid-November, when our daughter-in-law wanted us to be at the birth to greet their first baby. It was so exciting to count the hours in the waiting room of the maternity floor of the hospital and have our son come out and announce, "It's a girl, your first granddaughter!" We were so happy to be there when they came home with their precious little girl, and we stayed to help a few days and yet had our own space to retreat to when they needed their own family time. What a blessing our RV has been on so many occasions.

We headed home on the day before Thanksgiving since no one was wanting a huge feast on such an exciting week. On Turkey Day in Las Cruces, New Mexico, we stopped to eat lunch at a huge truck stop that we knew had good home-cooked food. It seemed strange to eat Thanksgiving dinner there, but I was thankful not to have to cook it! The meal was delicious, and many other travelers enjoyed the same. On our way back to the RV, I found a beautiful diamond-and-sapphire gold ring on the asphalt. I returned to leave a message with their management of how to contact us if anyone were asking about it. No one ever called, so I presented our first grand-daughter, Jordan, with this ring on her sixteenth birthday and told her the story of her first few days of life.

Grandson and Canada

THE NEXT SPRING, our second grandson was born in New Jersey, so we got our RV ready for the trip north as soon as my professor husband was free for the summer. We had missed this birth, and he was an adorable two-month-old baby when we first got to hold him. It was so dear to see this sweet family of four and watch big brother pat and love on little baby brother. We spent a glorious few days with the young family in their new home and played with our adorable almost-two-year-old grandson in the big backyard. How we wished we could live nearby and be with them more often, but then we would be across the continent from our other children, so we were very thankful we had learned the freedom of travel our RV provides. We were able to park in our daughter's driveway, so we enjoyed every minute. The big tree overhead provided perfect shade; however, it later posed a problem.

Almost every RV park has an exit sign saying, "Did you close your stairs? Did you pull your TV antenna down? Did you remember your wife?" When it was time to leave and travel on, we were sad and forgot to do the checklist for getting on the road. We drove away wondering why our family and some neighbors were waving so intensely and calling to us. We thought they were saying goodbye, and we knew the neighbors were fascinated by the RV since big vehicles were not popular in crowded New England's narrow roads. RV parks were few, and old bridges were low. When we stopped for gas, oh no! We realized we had forgotten to lower our TV antenna. This was 1995 and the first RV we had owned with a TV. We had left the antenna behind in the tree branch!

We drove a couple of days before we found a place that could install another antenna for us. While we awaited the repair in the lounge of the garage, Bill studied his maps to decide our destination. He said, "We are already this far north, why not Canada!" When our RV was again like new and all inspected for other problems, we headed toward the friendly border, glad we always packed our passports.

We knew Canadian border agents would check us carefully, so without being asked, we said, "We have no guns. We don't believe in them."

Immediately, having seen our Wild West Texas license plates, the officer ordered us to abandon our vehicle. She proceeded to go through every nook and compartment, then let us pass on into the beautiful Eastern Townships region of Quebec, where we found a little village with an RV park and hooked up for the weekend. It was late Saturday evening, so we had to wait to get groceries the next day. We were almost out of food, since this was an unplanned venture, but we had bread and peanut butter. Next day, we awoke to a deluge of rain and learned that all of Quebec was closed on Sundays. We could not get food or services anywhere, but, thankfully, we were not starving, and this time we had no leaks.

We loved the explorations of this beautiful province and stopped in many provincial parks, visited museums, and were always fascinated tourists. However, when we stopped in one park overnight, eagerly hoping to find good trails through the woods, we started to get out of the RV and were literally accosted by swarms of huge mosquitos! Dismayed, we headed to an outfitter store and bought a double-netted running suit and a veiled hat for me and a fisherman's hat with protective netting for Bill, whom the mosquitos don't usually bother. We returned to the campsite to hike around the lake, and although we felt and looked ridiculous, we loved the scenery and got no bites!

The next morning, I looked out of our RV and saw a large bear cub investigating our campsite. I grabbed my camera and went out to follow it around, taking pictures. Bill was alarmed and wisely ordered me back to safety. But the little live teddy bear looked so harmless!

Whistle Stop!

I N THE MIDDLE of Canada, we arrived at Cochrane, Ontario, well known for their Cochrane Polar Bear Habitat. We were entranced watching several huge bears carefully tended within large cages. When a polar bear was found injured in the wild, it was brought there to be nursed back to health.

At Cochrane, we boarded one of the only two whistle-stop trains left in Canada. Because we were journalists, the visitor center manager wanted us to write about this historic service, and we were happy to do so. We rode the train to James Bay, where the Hudson's Bay Company was founded in 1670, the oldest incorporated joint-stock merchandising company in the English-speaking world.

Huge trees on each side of the tracks formed vast forests of evergreens and maples, and we saw no civilization anywhere along the way. The train stopped several times when a lone fisherman or a cyclist couple whistled and waved so they could get aboard with canoes and bikes after a day of outdoor exploration. At one of these stops, the conductor invited Bill and me to come help drive the train. Bill was thrilled to work the controls while I took notes and pictures. Seeing the *cow catcher* on the front of the engine, I asked, "Is that for bears and moose? I guess they could turn the train over."

To our surprise, the engineer responded, "Yes and no. We can look ahead and see those large animals in time to stop or scare them away with our horn, but the most dangerous things that can derail the train are wet leaves or caterpillars because they make the tracks slick!"

When we reached James Bay, part of the Hudson Bay, we enjoyed our first water taxi ride to Moose Factory Island, where we stayed overnight in Cree Village Ecolodge, a totally green hotel, built, owned, and managed by the Cree People. In the 1800s, the peaceful and friendly Cree, native First People who have lived there in this extreme north for over six thousand years, welcomed settlers, and provided furs to the Hudson's Bay Company. At the Ecolodge, the total power was from solar and wind energy. Delicious fresh food in the restaurant was locally grown and prepared. The lodge decorations and linens were made by the Cree people. It was a lovely and comfortable stay overnight. We were happy to know the environment was not being damaged in any way. The building was cooled by a system of pipes that ran under the cold lake water and in pipes beneath the lodge floors.

Since we were journalists, the manager next morning gave us a tour, which was a little more than we had expected, but we learned a lot. In the basement, we perused the waterless sewer system. There were huge mounds of soil supplied with red worms, which digested the human waste. Periodically the dirt was turned by pitchfork so paper products would dissolve in the humid soil. Although it was unsettling but amazing to see, there was absolutely no odor and proved very sanitary.

On our return train ride, the conductor showed us the mail car, where mail was stowed to be distributed regularly in these most remote areas on Central Canada. We met a nice old man who shared our journey. He pulled the whistle cord, and the train stopped at his little wooden shack, literally in the middle of nowhere. He told us he had lived there in the forest all his life, and since he lived alone his home was always open to bears and dogs. About twenty dogs met him, yapping for the bag of restaurant scraps he had carried from the city. We could hardly believe this was the twentieth century.

*****

When we returned to Cochrane, we continued our RV travels westward. It was midsummer, and Canada was experiencing the worst heat wave ever recorded. In the afternoon, I drove about 150 miles on a straight highway to give Bill a rest, but as we approached the edge of a town in central Saskatchewan and stopped for a red light, the RV engine gave signs of trouble. I was able to maneuver our coach into a nearby parking lot in front of some houses and turned it off. When Bill tried to restart it, the engine would not start. We called AAA for help, but they said it would be at least the next morning before they could get to us because there were similar problems all over the area due to the extreme heat.

In that gas-powered RV, our engine was partially on the outside and partially inside between the driver and passenger seat beneath a carpet over the hump in the floor. Bill got out and began to tinker under the hood while I walked our little dog. As I was returning, two men in grease-stained white outfits passed me with a cheerful "hello." When they saw our RV, they went to Bill and asked if they could help.

"We work at a garage and are just on our way home for the night," one said.

Bill gratefully thanked them. One got under our vehicle with Bill and the other got into the RV with me and removed the engine cover. They worked for a couple of hours with no luck, and as it grew dark, everyone had to give up.

They pointed to the house in front of us and said, "You are right in front of our home, and you are welcome to stay here overnight."

Bill thanked them profusely and pulled large bills from his wallet to pay them, but the men refused the money, saying they enjoy helping people. When they would not accept payment, I grabbed two of our business cards with our address, phone numbers, and website listings beneath our names.

I said, "With all you have done to help us, the least we can do is to invite you to stay with us when you travel to the United States. We'll be happy to host you and show you around."

The two men looked at each other as they pocketed the cards. Then one sheepishly responded, "Thank you, ma'am, but I don't think that will ever happen. You see, we just got out of prison and can never leave Canada!"

I was a little apprehensive that night since we were *sitting ducks*. I wondered what prison buddies they would pass our information on to!

Rushing Home before Email

WE HAD MADE it all the way across and up and down Canada, enjoying the cool freshness of forests, lakes, rivers, mountains, and the vastness of nature. As we returned toward home, we stopped in Buffalo, Wyoming, at the museum and were thrilled to see what we realized was truly an example of the first RV in North America, a completely outfitted covered wagon! Thankful we journey in this century, we peered inside to see a few clothes, blankets, some firewood, bedding, utensils, and models of food that would have been staples for the pioneers' excruciating journeys west.

Next, we drove on to Cincinnati, Ohio, where Bill received a rare call on our huge mobile phone. Our realtor at home said he had sold a piece of property for us, and Bill must sign the papers as soon as possible. In those days of early 1990s, electronics were new and mostly used only in big businesses and universities. Although we had heard of emailing, it was still a mystery to most people, and Zoom and FaceTime were not yet even in the minds of the creators. Many products and conveniences we take for granted today were nonexistent in those days. Electronic signatures did not become legal until President Clinton signed such a bill in June 2000. We had to rush home or lose our land sale!

With only a few stops for gasoline, we drove straight to our home in Paris, Texas. It took us two days, but we made it in time. While Bill took care of business, I went to Walmart for groceries. My loaded cart required some time for the cash register clerk to complete, and there were ten people behind me in line. She entered my credit card, and a message popped up for her to have me call Visa management immediately. I was puzzled since I knew our Visa bill was paid, and we were not overdrawn at the bank. I had to leave my groceries there with the cashier waiting bewilderedly while I went to use the phone at the service desk. The long line of shoppers wanting to check out were none too happy, and I was embarrassed. I called Visa, and the consultant said, "Ma'am, we think your card has been stolen because today there were charges on it for gasoline in Joplin, Missouri, another in Tulsa, Oklahoma, and another in Los Angeles, California."

I laughed at the coincidence and replied, "Thank you for checking for our safety, but those are all correct. We were traveling in Missouri, and our college kids in California and Oklahoma also use our credit card, and I guess we all needed gas today."

I returned to the cash register. My groceries were in my basket ready to go, and the clerk was already checking the next person's items. But for a moment, I learned how humiliating and sad it must be to have a credit card denied when one can do nothing about it.

For the months of our long journey that summer, we had felt safer because we were carrying a mobile phone with us, an early model that was about twelve inches by five inches in size, and heavy! We had arranged mobile phone service and found out how to make calls before we left home, but rates were expensive, so we only made a call on it if we could not find a pay phone to check in with our family every two weeks of travel. We kept our phone on and charged in case someone needed to call us in an emergency. But during our entire two months in Canada, we had only used our mobile phone for three brief calls, since pay phones along the way were convenient.

A few weeks after we returned home, our mobile phone bill arrived, and we nearly fainted! The charges were over $1,000 for our trip across Canada. I called the phone company to explain we needed a correction for our bill, which surely had an error. But the answer was very disappointing and alarming: "You kept your phone on all across Canada, and you were charged every time you entered a different cell tower area." I was furious and told them they had never explained that to me before we left, even though I had asked them all about the travel dos and don'ts. They refused to remove the charges until they learned I was a travel journalist and could easily publish a damaging feature against this mobile phone company. All the charges were finally dropped, and we changed mobile phone providers for good!

The next year, we traded our RV when we learned most motor coaches begin, after sixty-five thousand miles, to need frequent expensive repairs, and we had already eighty thousand miles on our odometer.

On to the Yukon

THE NEXT SUMMER break, we had our new motor home and headed for a conference in Vancouver, British Columbia. We were over halfway there when we received a phone call that the conference was cancelled. Disappointed but undaunted, we realized, "We have a new RV and are already at the top of the continental USA. We have been in all the other states, so let's go on to Alaska! We won't be this close again! What a serendipity!"

Soon we were driving through British Columbia, one of the most beautiful places we had seen in North America. We took our time stopping to appreciate many exquisite places there. Next, we were on the Alcan Highway, which took us through the vast Yukon. Suddenly I remembered and exclaimed out loud, "Bill, I own some land in the Yukon!"

Surprised, he responded that he had never heard me mention that.

"Well, I wasn't even sure where the Yukon was when I was six years old and *Sergeant Preston of the Yukon*, on television, asked all his little friends to send a quarter and the cereal box top, and he would give each child one square inch of his valuable Yukon Territory! Of course, I sent my quarter and box top!"

Partially across the Yukon, which appeared uninhabited since we saw only thick forests and lovely lakes, we stopped at the very rare service station. While Bill was getting gasoline, I looked at the sky and saw clouds building and asked the attendant, "What is the weather prediction?"

He responded, "How would I know? We don't get newspapers or TV or radio reception here!"

I could hardly believe what I heard. How could this place be so remote? But the scenery all around were beautiful. I could not imagine living so far from life as I know it. One would have to be so self-sufficient and brave.

We drove on, and by the end of the day, we reached civilization in the town of Dawson City, Yukon, and found a place to park for the night near the river we would cross by ferry into Alaska tomorrow. We learned that RVs were welcome to park overnight free at wide bare ground on roadside shoulders where we saw others who had settled in for the night. Apparently, these places were considered safe. Bill was quite tired, so we were happy to find such a spot.

Next morning, when we went into the town of Dawson City, I made my way to the courthouse nearby and said, "You will probably think I'm crazy, and it's okay to laugh, but I am supposed to own one square inch of the Yukon, and I wanted to inquire where it might be!"

The friendly official smiled knowingly. "You are one of Sergeant Preston's faithful kids! And yes, your deed was good for many years, and you *did* own a square inch of that forest out the window behind us until last year. General Mills stopped paying the taxes, and the land reverted to the Yukon Territory ownership!"

I was thrilled and stunned when he gave me a copy of my now useless deed. Bill and I could hardly believe it, but what a great story!

Alaskan Adventures

FTER A FEW nights in Dawson City, we drove our RV onto a small ferry to cross the Yukon River and drove into Alaska on the Top of the World Highway. At the town of Chicken, Alaska, we officially reentered the USA. A border patrolman there was so astute. Without looking at our passports or the RV license plate, the officer said, "I think you must be from South Carolina, and your husband sounds like a Texan. How close am I?"

We were amazed at his accuracy for both of us. I asked, "But how did you know? Is that on our passports?"

"No," he responded, "we see so many people that it became my hobby to try to detect accents accurately."

"Well, you are incredible!" I said.

Then I asked about the name of the little entrance town. "Why is it named Chicken?"

The friendly officer said, "The official state bird of Alaska is the Ptarmigan, and the gold miners in the 1890s who founded our town ate a lot of ptarmigan grouse, which look like chickens. They decided to name the town for these tasty little fowls, but they could not spell ptarmigan, so they named the town Chicken since those little birds look a bit like chickens. You would enjoy a little book about the first schoolteacher in this remote place, which is for sale in the shop there."

We drove on into our northernmost state, Alaska! We could hardly believe we were in this place of stories and dreams, and we had wonderful explorations there for two weeks! One memorable place was the fish ladders, which First Peoples had installed to help the salmon up the waterfalls to spawn farther upstream. After visiting a museum with an old gold mine and smelting equipment, we wanted to seek our fortune at panning for gold. We rented the sieves and proceeded to go to the stream where gold nuggets had been found in recent years. I quickly grew tired of the squatting position, which was very hard on our bodies, so I set my equipment aside and just watched.

I saw many salmon slowly swimming downstream to die after spawning, and I commented to the local vendor nearby, "It looks like I could just reach down and catch one."

He replied, "Yes, you can, and there is no reason not to. Go ahead."

I placed my hands easily around the body of a large salmon, which Bill estimated to weigh about twenty pounds, and lifted it out of the water. Perhaps I should have kept it for dinner, but I could not bear the thought of killing and eating it, so I released him to his natural cycle.

On the ground near the stream, Bill found a prize: a large green rock with a brilliant gold stripe through it. We kept it for a souvenir of Alaska. When we returned home, it was analyzed and certified to be valuable jade with a vein of true gold running through it. We had it cut for a pair of treasured bookends.

One evening, we signed up for a potlatch dinner with the local First Peoples tribe. This was a festive evening with demonstrations of indigenous dances, explanations of their brightly colored art in wall hangings, and the totem pole. The meal of salmon, basted with honey and grilled on a fire, was delicious. All the local people were so welcoming and showed us their unique traditions and ways of life, which we thoroughly appreciated and enjoyed—a memorable evening!

We traveled the Alaska Highway using the necessary *Milepost* Alaska book, which describes the passages and points of interest everywhere. We stayed on one main road that took travelers through the most important accessible towns. The capital city of Juneau was only accessible by boat or plane, and we were disappointed not to get there.

The highway in Alaska is asphalt, and the permafrost ground freezes so severely the surface breaks. On the asphalt highway, gravel places, bumps, and holes are inevitable. But the scenery of snow-capped mountains, gorgeous lakes, quaint historic settlements, and the vast Pacific Ocean more than compensate for the often-rough roadway. We were glad our vehicle and tires were sound.

I could vividly remember the flag ceremony at my junior high school when I was an eighth grader and Alaska and Hawaii were welcomed by Congress as our newest states. We lowered the flag with forty-eight stars and proudly saluted the new US flag with fifty stars. Of course, most people since then had always wanted to visit Alaska and see the land of midnight sun and twenty-four-hour darkness, and now we could scarcely believe we were here! We reserved a ferry to return us and our RV to British Columbia, which would cut out hundreds of miles of driving the Lower 48 when we journeyed by land back to Texas and give us a few extra days in Alaska before Bill had to return to teach at Paris Junior College.

At the Begich-Boggs Visitor Center, we learned a lot from the ranger's lecture about glaciers. Then we watched a beautiful film about glaciers in Alaska. When the film ended in the darkened room, the screen went up, and the curtains behind it opened. There in front of us outside the big bay window was a huge glacier sparkling in the sunlight. It was so beautiful we all gasped in surprise. We were eager to see more glaciers, so we booked a boat tour to go to the one she recommended. We rode out into the arm of the ocean and watched the sad but impressive sight of the huge glacier calving, which means shedding huge chunks of snow and ice that had been frozen there for thousands of years.

We were able to pull our RV onto part of the wharf to spend the night before and after a day on a water excursion on the Pacific shore at Seward. We were eager to see orcas, the great black-and-white killer whales of SeaWorld fame. And the trip also gave us fabulous views of glaciers, some of which were calving in the summer sun. In Alaska, we often saw huge bald eagles, a rare sight for those of us from the Lower 48.

Several times in our first few days there, we saw a strange family group. The father led the group on a bicycle with two children following on their bikes. The mother was on her bike with a young child riding in a small tow cart attached behind. They seemed to cover the same mileage we did, and they had camping equipment with them. It made us wonder at their bravery, but the traffic speed limits along this highway was low, and every driver carefully regarded the group's safety. We spoke to them in a rest stop once, and they explained this was a long-anticipated educational adventure for them. We lost sight of them for several days, and then we read in a newspaper that one of the children had been hit by a car. It made us so sad as we wondered which little one was injured or killed.

Beware! Bears!

WE PREFER NATURAL settings to cities, and mountains are always our favorite refuges. We had been in grizzly and black bear country now for a while and kept hoping for up-close photos, even though we had been warned on many RV trips how to observe bear safety. Never feed a bear because "a fed bear is a dead bear." I had special memories of my childhood when our days at Cherokee Indian Reservation in the Blue Ridge Mountains were thrilling because little brown bear cubs were chained at several street corners where cars were allowed to stop and passengers could feed the cubs! I guess in those days, naturalists had not realized this only caused bears to become addicted to people's food, which was so easy to find in campgrounds, so bears became menaces.

From the highway many miles away, we had seen the great Mount Denali, formerly named Mount McKinley, with its snow-covered peaks gleaming in the sunlight. It is the highest peak in the United States at 20,308 feet. We decided to settle at Denali National Park Campground for a few days. When we checked in, the ranger gave us two sheets that said, "REQUIRED TO READ BEFORE ENTERING THE PARK."

After we set up our RV, we sat and read the instructions for how to protect ourselves if a bear was nearby. First, decide if it is a brown, black, or grizzly bear (the one with a hump on its back), then act accordingly:

- If it is a brown bear, look it in the eyes and speak softly while backing away slowly. (But to me, black bears appeared to be the same color as the brown bears.)
- If it is a grizzly, raise your arms and appear as big and loud as possible and do *not* look it in the eye. Make a lot of noise as you back away but do *not* run. It will think you are prey and will chase you. If it does chase you, drop to the ground and roll into a ball to protect your vital organs and play dead. (But who would have the time or the foresight to determine which way to act?)

However, duly informed, I asked the ranger to recommend a good path for us to hike.

He said, "I can only recommend one path right now because we are plagued with bear closures. There is a father bear on a rampage to find his cubs, and the mother bear is protecting them, so it is very dangerous."

I asked in alarm, "Bear closures? Do you mean they have mauled people who have to be sewn up?"

He chuckled. "No, I mean trails are closed to prevent that." He said we should take the park bus the next day, take water and a picnic, and tell the bus driver to let us out at a particular creek and to return to pick us up several hours later.

The next day, we got on the bus with Bill's backpack holding food and water, and mine held emergency items, cell phone, camera, and film. The bus took visitors on the road to Denali Visitor Center since no one was allowed to drive there. We wanted to hike that day and planned to go that total distance to the great Denali in the bus the next day. The driver let us depart at the creek, and we expected others to get off also, but when we looked back, the bus was driving away and we were left alone. The area was a vast prairie to the edge of the dense woods far beyond. The driver had told us to follow along the creek so we would not get lost. However, bordering the creek on both sides was a dense natural hedge of tall berry bushes.

As we walked along, we did what the instructions had advised us, "Talk softly and calmly the entire time you are walking so you will not surprise a bear. If he knows you are around, he is not likely to attack." So we kept saying, "Whoa, bear! We are here, bear. Do not fear, bear," until we were bored with the phrase, so we sang some songs softly. Then suddenly, we remembered that berries, which were ripe on all these bushes, were at the top of a bear's favorite food list! And here we were totally alone and miles from civilization! We tried our cell phone, but it didn't work. What would we do if harm came?

Since we were doing everything the ranger had told us to do, we decided worry would not help. By then we had hiked about a mile. We climbed to the top of a little knoll and sat in the grass to enjoy our picnic. We have found that peanut butter and jelly keeps well when we are hiking, so that is our typical fare. As we enjoyed that, we were careful not to drop crumbs. We heard a little squeaky sound and looked to a nearby little mound in the grass and up popped a precious little "parka," an Arctic ground squirrel, who was talking to another nearby, and we realized we were on top of their warren of burrows belowground. Then we remembered with fright: these were the very favorite food prey of bears! We packed quickly and headed back to the road, following the clear gurgling creek as our pathway guide. We waited awhile for the bus, but it arrived as the schedule indicated, and we were thankful not to be forgotten.

Inuit Games

WHEN WE VENTURED up to Fairbanks, we found a little museum with a fascinating display of a handcrafted miniature layout of all the villages and towns along the Yukon River. The patience required to create this perfect dollhouse-sized replica was remarkable. A university there was having a demonstration of indigenous games, similar to a local Olympic tournament. The young adult Inuit boys were dressed in skins and beads, some with painted features. The emcee explained that the games were to show that the ancient skills of survival in this frigid land were being preserved by these young people who learned them. The boys seemed to be having fun, but the skills demonstrated were very strenuous. The tribes had made thrilling games to teach children how to skin animals, build igloos, create fur garments, fight animals, and many other activities that demanded repetition and strong bodies to learn. The actual animals and equipment, which would have been used in real-life work, were not present. The skills were acted out as contests I found very interesting. I have continued to be impressed that the native culture is carefully being preserved to provide life's necessities for items that cannot be purchased.

From Fairbanks, we drove to the town of North Pole, Alaska, which, of course, offered envelopes with the return address of Santa Claus, North Pole, and had the North Pole cancellation seal on it. Parents could buy these and insert a "letter from Santa" and keep them until December to give a child as if it had arrived in the mail. We did not find Santa on his throne, since it was lunchtime, and no children were present. We strolled around the outside of the castle-like building and had the fantastic good luck to see Santa at his back fence dressed still in his red velvet pants lined in white fur, black boots, white undershirt and suspenders, feeding his reindeer by hand! What a sight to remember and make even an adults' Christmas fantasy believable!

The midnight sun of Alaska was no myth. We found it fascinating to look out our window at around 3:00 a.m. and see the sun setting, although a yellow-pink glow remained the rest of the night, making it difficult to sleep for those of us not accustomed to it. But it was great to experience, and I hoped someday also to get to experience the twenty-four-hour darkness in winter, when the sunlight enters the lowest latitude of the earth. Another very memorable sight we had was the beautiful fuchsia-colored fireweed thick on the ground beneath a forest that had been decimated by fire. We learned that the seeds of this flower can only sprout if warmed by fire! They provided lush beauty in a vast area of devastation, with charred black broken trunks of trees standing among them.

The date for us to leave by ferry to Port Rupert, British Columbia, came all too soon. We arrived in Anchorage the day before and went to pick up our tickets for the eagerly anticipated ferry ride on the Pacific Ocean. But it was not to be for us! The fishermen at Prince Rupert were on strike and had created a barrier that prevented any ferry from passing through, so all ferries were cancelled for the foreseeable future. We could not wait because Bill's classes would start again, and the trip back to Texas would take a minimum of ten days of hard driving. We had to forge ahead by land without delay.

Before we left, we stopped to get a prescription filled at a drugstore, and when the pharmacist saw my doctor was in Paris, Texas, he said, "I am so glad you are not dead!"

I was astonished, and he quickly explained it was very unusual to have a woman from Paris, Texas, hiking in British Columbia, but one had been there last week and was killed by a bear at Liard River Hot Springs Provincial Park, where we had stayed overnight two weeks before. We felt sick at heart to learn that her son had also been badly mauled when he tried to save his mother.

On one of our hikes in British Columbia a couple of weeks before, we had set out on a trail through the dense woods and realized we were the only ones on this path, but we went ahead chatting and taking pictures. Suddenly, a large mother bear and her two cubs crossed our path in front and very close to us. I was so thrilled I could think of nothing but grabbing my camera, but Bill had wisely caught my arm and quietly and quickly pulled me to retreat back up the path.

When we returned home, we discovered that one of our best friends, who was very kindhearted, had found a way to get the boy returned to Texas, and he took care of him for months as he recuperated.

Monsters

THE TIME CAME for another summer trip to California to see
our children. We stopped the second evening for gas at a large
truck stop in Phoenix, Arizona. We had stayed several times in
their welcome RV parking places. This time, we intended to move on
after Bill filled the tank with gas. But when he got back into the RV,
the automatic stairs would not come in, and it is not possible to ride
down a highway with them sticking out dangerously. Bill can usually
repair anything, but it was very hot, and he had already driven about
four hundred miles that day. He tried and tried to make the stairs
retract, but they would not. I realized we were across the street from
a big truck repair center. I walked over and intended to use my white
hair as my best persuasion.

I first stopped at each repair bay and made a compliment to the
mechanic who was working. Finally, as there was no one in the office,
I asked one of the mechanics working on a huge semi if we could pull
our RV over to get help.

He said, "No, ma'am, that won't be necessary. I'm through here,
and I'll get my toolbox and come over there to do it!" He was skilled,
and it only took a few minutes for him to have us ready to ride safely.
People are so nice everywhere!

With our sons living in California, we made many trips there in
our RV. On our first RV trip, we had not anticipated a border inspection station. That was not common when traveling from one state to
another within the United States, but more like country to country,
which we had experienced in Europe.

We were entering California from Arizona, where we had bought a lot of the beautiful fruit grown there. When the California border patrolman asked, "Do you have any fruit and vegetables?" we replied, "Yes," not anticipating any problem.

"Well, you must pull over and park right beside our inspection station and dispose of all your fresh produce."

I was astonished and asked, "You mean throw it away?"

He replied, "Yes, or you can eat it right here. We must protect our crops from fruit flies and other insects."

Bill parked in the indicated spot beside two other RVs. I began to prepare the largest fruit salad we had ever eaten while I boiled potatoes and carrots and fried onions to keep for dinner. Cooked produce posed no threat. We ate all the fruit, and Bill placed the peelings into the large trash can on the asphalt drive, and we were waved on into California.

I kept puzzling over the incident as we drove. "House flies and fruit flies certainly don't know that line in the road is something they cannot cross. This doesn't make sense. And that open trash bin the state provides just invites the flies."

We made many subsequent trips to California, remembering not to enter with produce. A few years later, we drove on northward, laden with delicious California citrus and strawberries. We reached Washington State, where we spent a week in the beautiful state and national parks. It was Rainier cherry time, and again we bought several pounds of the juicy delights grown locally. Then we traveled on to Canada, and border patrol made us consume or throw away our delicious cherries. We were not far into British Columbia when we started seeing roadside stands selling cherries. It was then I realized the answer to the question that had puzzled me for several trips to California: The fruit flies were not the real problem. Each state and province wisely protected its own local agricultural industry sales!

A few years later, on yet another entry into California, we had learned to have an empty produce drawer in our refrigerator and make our fresh food purchases locally. We were taking housewarming gifts for our son's new home. When we were stopped at the inspection station, we honestly answered, "No, sir, we don't have any fresh fruit or vegetables," and we went on to our favorite RV campground in Los Angeles. We parked and unloaded our gifts to have more room in our RV, which had been cramped all the way out. Because I knew our son had loved the huge indoor atrium and its beautiful plants in our home where he grew up, I had, in early spring, potted some for this trip and left them outdoors in our yard to grow until our visit in June. These plants were in large pots, which had taken all the floor space beside our RV bed, requiring us to jump in and out of the bed during the week of driving west. I placed these pots outside the RV beneath a tree to take for the housewarming the next day, envisioning his joy over the nostalgic gift.

That next morning, I began moving the potted plants to our car to take to our kids. I was painfully stung several times by little black ants. Thinking they were only part of the RV park, we drove away. But then I realized the ants were in our pots, so we stopped for ant spray and made sure they were all killed. We waited another day to be sure before we took the plants to their new home. Our son and daughter-in-law were delighted with the heirloom greenery and placed them in special spots to enhance their new home.

I thought of the incident no more, and another year passed. That June, we drove to Los Angeles to our same RV campground, and they designated the same spot for us because of the size of our rig. We settled in, and I set up our lawn chairs to rest awhile. I had not been in the chair more than fifteen minutes when I felt stinging pain and looked down to see my ankle being enveloped with little black monsters! To my horror, I realized perhaps we had unknowingly introduced the Texas plague to Los Angeles! Suddenly, I realized why border agriculture inspection is necessary. We had not intentionally lied. The guard the previous year had asked if we had any fresh fruits or vegetables. We had just not considered that the potted plants we were transporting were also produce. We bought ant poison for yards and tried valiantly to get rid of the little black pests permanently at the camp. That was decades ago, but it still makes us so chagrinned that our unthinking error could have lasting bad consequences in California.

It Fixes Anything!

WE WERE PREPARED for my sister and her husband to meet us in Las Vegas and share our large RV space for ten days. We were excited about showing them the many incredibly different national parks of Utah. So that we didn't have to waste hiking and exploring time on shopping, I had planned and purchased ten days' worth of groceries, and miraculously our large refrigerator held all the cold and frozen items. We parked across the street from the airport, and I drove our tow car to meet their plane. We happily got them settled in our RV and the car reattached to the tow bar. Bill drove out of the parking lot to enter the busy city street, hoping to make it to the desert highway and miss rush-hour traffic.

We were all laughing and talking when suddenly Bill hit a bump in the road, and to our horror, the refrigerator door just fell off! This predicament was unheard of, and some cold groceries started to roll across the floor, but miraculously no jars broke. Bill maneuvered the big rig to a parking lot as quickly as possible so that the men could try to figure out what to do.

Sis and I removed the items that had remained in the door's compartments and placed into bags what we could not cram into the icebox shelves. The men held the door and diligently tried over and over to make the hinges fit together again, but they were broken.

When Bill and I were planning the route to everywhere we wanted to take our special guests, we had realized most of the places we would stay were miles from grocery stores. I have always lived by the Girl Scout motto: Be Prepared. But this time, I had taken it too far! What would we do for ten days with no cold food? And all these groceries would go to waste! We were chagrinned but also laughing at the ridiculous situation!

All four brains were ticking, searching for a solution to what seemed an impossible problem, when Bill suddenly exclaimed, "I've got it!"

Since I knew he could handle most mechanical difficulties, I thought he had found something in the RV book that told him how to fix the refrigerator. But he went outside to the storage compartment for his toolbox and returned with a large roll of duct tape. He and Harry carefully and efficiently constructed eight makeshift hinges from the tape and tested the door while we all crossed our fingers. It stayed!

Sis and I hesitantly replaced the items that had to fit on the door, fearing that the extra weight would pull the door off its new hinges, but it held!

"Hooray!" we all shouted in joy and disbelief, satisfied that the problem was solved (hopefully).

Bill was about to start the engine when I realized one slight curve in the road and the refrigerator door would fly open. The men devised duct tape locks up and down the handle side of the door, and we were on the road again, slowly at first.

To our amazement, the "hinges" held the entire ten days, and the "locks" proved to be easy to unstick and then stick back into place as we needed items from within the refrigerator.

We learned, yes, the ads are true: duct tape can do *anything*!

*****

We spent the next week visiting several of the wonderful Utah national parks. At Bryce Canyon, my sister and I wanted to hike to the bottom and walk through the red hoodoo formations. Bill volunteered to carry our backpack of water, coats, etc., heavier than one person should wear on a long hike. But Bill is strong. When we started back up on the steep climb, Bill went ahead of us so he could drive the car to pick us up. He made the climb a lot faster than we could, and the car was about three-fourths mile away. He knew we were tired, but he did not admit how exhausted and in pain he was. His back had given him trouble in the past, but it was really hurting by the time he reached the top. He never let on that he was in pain for the next two days. That night turned very cold, and we awoke the next morning to nature's beauty we had hoped Pam and Harry would get to see—snow in the night had decorated each of the thousands of majestic red spires in Bryce Canyon like white icing on cakes. It was spectacular with the golden sun rising and making each snowcap sparkle like the candles on a frosted cake!

When our sightseeing days were nearly up, we drove back to Las Vegas, where Pam and Harry had reserved a hotel room for the final night. We were to meet them for dinner. Bill lay down for a nap, and when he awoke, his back was in too much pain to go, so I went ahead without him for a last night with our guests to enjoy the casinos and the Strip, although none of us were gamblers or drinkers! We had a nice evening, but my thoughts were constantly on Bill.

The next morning, Bill literally could not get out of bed. Pam and Harry got a car service to the airport while I called Bill's orthopedist in Texas. He prescribed a strong painkiller that made Bill sleep, so I had to drive us home to Texas. About a month later, Bill had to have back surgery. The heavy backpack and strenuous hike had exacerbated the problem that had been there in his back for a long time and had finally made the surgery necessary.

Don't Leave Home without It!

WE WERE HEADED to the wedding of my college roommate's daughter on the Rappahannock River in Virginia, hoping to arrive in late afternoon. However, our diesel engine had other intentions. On a very deserted road in the rain, this new RV suddenly died. We had plenty of fuel, and all the gauges looked right except one. The red arrow on the engine temperature gauge had suddenly gone to its maximum indication, and Bill could not figure out why. Praying we were in mobile phone range, I called AAA to please send help. Fortunately, they agreed to send a repairman right away.

We were about fifty-two miles from any services, so we waited over an hour for the welcome help to arrive. On that motor coach, the engine was located beneath the queen-size bed in the back. The man showed his ID and entered our home on the road. He lifted the heavy bed and studied the engine for a long while. Then he told Bill, who was watching intently, "The fan belt is broken. It needs a new one!"

The worker went to his truck but was disappointed to say he did not have the right one. He phoned his garage to send one out, and in another hour, the second man arrived with the belt. Together they worked hard in the cramped quarters where a *push diesel engine* is housed and finally got our RV running. But they told us it needed more work that could only be done at the garage. They asked us to follow them in the now early evening darkness on the empty country

157

road. An hour later, we arrived at the garage that AAA uses in that area, and they began work to make certain the engine had no other problems. It grew very late, and before they left for their homes, they told us we could stay overnight in their parking lot.

We have been saved by reliable AAA several times. Most RV sales have a roadside assistance program that comes with the new vehicle, and we strongly advise everyone not to get on the road without a similar membership. When you have a home on the road, bumping over many terrains and roads, there is always something that happens, whether it is as tiny as a bolt coming loose, locking yourself out of the RV, a flat tire, a dead engine, or many more possibilities! We quickly learned to be prepared for the worst, hope for the best, and roll with the punches!

We have owned gas-powered RVs, which, in the early days, proved very hot because part of the engine was beneath a big hump in the carpet between the driver and passenger seats and also created an obstacle for moving out of the front area. Then we changed to diesel-powered RVs because diesel fuel in those days was much cheaper, but the engine noise was very objectionable to anyone outside the vehicle. And the two different RVs we had with *push engines* beneath the bed were nearly impossible for even the best mechanic to work on. Garages for semitrucks are long distances apart and often require long waits for appointments. In our small town, there was only one special mechanic, Bart Hadley, who knew how to change the oil in our RV main engine and the generator engine, which had to be done before each long trip. We were very blessed that he was also a friend and neighbor and would come to our home to help solve any difficult situation that arose.

We have selected our more recent RVs with gas engines, and luckily gas is now cheaper than diesel. The hump in the middle for the engine is not a problem in new models. Class C motor coaches are more like a pickup truck, with front motor, airbags, and side doors. For just a couple, we prefer class C, with the bed over the driver's area, because this style of RV is safer in an accident and cooler with the cab roof overhanging the front window enough to provide shade. Most class C motor coaches have twin or queen bed in the back. Class A motor homes are great if you want space for extra people. This type of vehicle is like a bus and provides great landscape viewing in front, but the huge glass also made temperatures elevate. Since we are fair complexioned and sunburn easily, this was not our best choice. I always felt a little threatened being right in front of the huge windshield, with no engine between me and the road. It seemed that in a wreck, I would be thrown through the windshield, despite seat belt protection.

Wonders of Nature

S INCE NATIONAL PARKS are our favorite places to stay and explore all the wonders of nature, we wanted to share our experience at Yellowstone, the very first national park to be designated such in the whole world. President Ulysses S. Grant signed the paper to create it in 1874. Not far away is the Grand Teton National Park. Bill found an ideal RV campground about halfway between each of the two parks, knowing the traffic in each is very tedious. We met my sister, Pam, and her husband, Harry, in Jackson Hole, Wyoming, and had a nice day taking photos beneath the famous arch of antlers. I could enjoy this unique landmark arch since deer don't have to be killed to get the antlers. They shed these each year. Walking around in this old Western town was lots of fun, and we found some good cowboy restaurants.

The next day, we began searching for the favorite scenic places and best hikes we could find in Yellowstone. We were slowly driving through a mountainous road when we came to a traffic jam. Many cars were beside the road, with a lot of people out with their cameras and park rangers holding everyone back. The wonderful attraction was a mother bear and her little cub hungrily gathering berries in the woods on the opposite side of the road. Everyone who grew up hugging a teddy bear has the unconscious thought that bears are cuddly and cute, so rangers must be vigilant to keep tourists at a safe distance. It was a thrill to take pictures of these creatures in their natural habitat.

Our next stop was at the majestic Yellowstone River in the Grand Canyon of Yellowstone, so beautifully depicted in the *Four Seasons* paintings by Thomas Moran, which we had seen in an art museum. We carefully walked down the long iron stairway to get close and take pictures of the very steep Yellowstone Falls and of the river in the deep canyon, which truly was made of natural yellow stones, whose color comes from rusting iron in them, not sulfur.

At Hayden Valley, we had another thrill. We spotted some gray wolves, which had been considered endangered for years and had been removed from Yellowstone because farmers and ranchers in surrounding areas were shooting these wild animals blamed for killing their domestic livestock. After being away for years, the grays had been reintroduced into Yellowstone not too long before we arrived. It was rare to see a pair walking across the meadow, and we took pictures of them as they got closer to the parking lot.

A little later in a different parking lot, we watched a small herd of enormous buffalo as they crossed the road, stopping traffic. Again, people tried to get out of the protection of their cars to get good pictures. But these animals are big enough to turn a car over if they decided to stampede or to get rough. Even though they look like big shaggy cattle, they are dangerous. Again, rangers were trying to herd people to safety back in their cars. We had remained in our car in the parking lot, glad not to be in the street, and to our surprise and anxious delight, a pair of buffalo approached our car, and one rubbed against the driver's side mirror. Bill would not let us roll down the window to get better pictures. He was keenly aware of the potential dangers since he had herded cattle for most of his life. But the events of the day were very exciting.

The last two days we were there, we drove over to see the Grand Tetons National Park. From across the lake, where we had hiked in the early morning, the twin peaks reached high into the sky and created beautiful photos with the colored fall leaves. Pam, who was an experienced hiker, had selected a trail ascending one of the Teton Mountains for us to climb. And what a steep climb it was! The trail had several resting places, which were flat ledges overlooking the majestic lake below. Two of us decided we had climbed far enough by the second rest stop, so we sat for a while and watched nature and other people as we waited for our other two climbers. Our trip together was glorious, and we hated when it was time to take them back to the airport to return home.

Could Mark Twain Make Laughter of This?

WE DROVE THROUGH Missouri on our way from the Grand Tetons en route to Florida to meet our grandson's plane and have him enjoy RV life for his seventeenth birthday. Bill and I were both English majors in college, and one of our favorite authors was Samuel Langhorne Clemens, known as Mark Twain. Hannibal, Missouri, was Twain's hometown and the setting for *The Adventures of Tom Sawyer* and *The Adventures of Huckleberry Finn*. We were happy to settle at the KOA Campground there for a few days.

Our new thirty-six-foot Monaco diesel RV was our first with hydraulic slide-outs. It was so easy to push a button and automatically expand the inside space by two feet in width. Soon we were set up with this extra space and all hooked up to the campground facilities of water, electricity, sewer, and cable TV. This RV also had push buttons for the four steel legs that extended beneath the RV to keep it level for a good night's sleep. Magic! So Bill pushed those buttons on this new toy. We took a long walk around the little harbor town on the Mississippi River. We recognized some of the old buildings described in Twain's books and followed the popular tour through Tom's home, Becky's home, and the schoolhouse described in the books. That night, we took a dinner cruise on the peaceful Mississippi River. It was a storybook evening watching the sun set on the water.

Before checking out on that Saturday afternoon, we had tickets to see inside the local cave vividly described in the books. We prepared the inside of the RV for the road, to be ready to leave as soon as our tour ended, and Bill unhooked and stowed all the outside connections. On his signal, I pushed the button to raise the automatic levelers and bring in the big slide-out, which extended the thirty-four-foot length of our RV behind the driver's seat. But no movement occurred! Bill checked the battery power and the gasoline level. RVs have built-in guards to protect against a driver's forgetfulness, and no warning signs were apparent. We had devised a way of reminding ourselves to lower the TV antenna. We wound a colored pipe cleaner onto the steering wheel whenever the antenna was up and took the reminder off as we stowed the antenna.

We had driven our other RVs 70,000 to 80,000 miles with few major problems and then traded before major breakdowns might start occurring. This RV was only a year old and had 11,005 miles on it, so it should not be giving problems. Bill studied the book that came with it and could not figure out what he was doing wrong. Since it was early morning on Saturday, we could not find anyone to call for help. Bill was feeling hopeless, so I left to ask the RV park management to call a repairman. I explained to the KOA manager that our situation was *urgent.* We were literally *nailed to the ground!* And we were on a tight schedule to make it to Florida to meet our grandson's plane. We could not wait until Monday for repairs. We simply *had* to move on. But he told me it would be difficult to find help on a Saturday because most garages in the little town of Hannibal were closed, but he would call a mechanic he knew.

While we were waiting, we discussed how easy automatic slide-out and leveler legs had sounded when we bought this RV. I had asked if the RV had a hand crank in case the automatic features did not work. The salesperson assured me the automatic features would not give any problems, but I had been skeptical. We had never had slide-outs, and to level our other RVs, Bill had to drive carefully onto big square risers under the wheels, as needed. These squares looked like giant Legos. Then we would see if a penny would roll down the aisle inside to determine when we were level. (We finally learned to keep a carpenter's level inside the RV.)

I could miss our tour, but my professor husband had counted on it since he teaches the Twain books in his college classes. But Bill insisted he would stay to help the repairman and I should go on tour alone. Just as I was leaving, the help appeared with a large toolbox and set about to solve our predicament. While I was having fun reliving the familiar scenes of the Tom Sawyer adventures, Bill got under the RV with Andrew, the mechanic. They had to bleed each hydraulic lift to get the levelers to retract, to "unnail us" from the ground. This required hours, and as each of the four "legs" was completely drained, Bill was able to jack it up into its place in the bottom of the RV, hoping each spring would hold it in position, so we could travel safely.

When I returned, they were still under our coach, so I called a Monaco repair center, but the closest one was in Saint Louis, and they had no appointments available for over a week. The only other Monaco repair place in the Southeast was in Orlando, Florida. How fortuitous, since that was our destination to meet our grandson, but it was 1,110 miles away. We made an appointment with those experts for the repairs, and we prayed we could make it safely with no more disasters. We both feared the levelers or slide-out opening along the highway; what a horror!

Andrew worked for nearly eight hours before he and Bill together were finally able to physically push the large and heavy RV slide into its closed position and manually put the inside latch in place. We thanked the kind mechanic for giving us his expertise and his Saturday and paid him a big bonus. Then we headed toward Florida. But there was still a major problem.

I was checking our warranty, knowing we were just over the one-year limit but hoping the "or 12,000 miles" clause would work to get our RV completely safe without costing a fortune. We didn't dare try the automatic features for levelers and slide-out for the two nights on the road and were very thankful to find Walmart parking lots fairly level and ready to accommodate us. We finally arrived in Orlando at the repair center. We showed them the warranty, but alas, our speedometer read 12,018 miles. Surely, Monaco would honor the warranty, considering our great difficulties when a new RV should never have malfunctioned like this. However, the very nice management at the RV center there told us the bad news. Monaco had gone out of business and was in receivership, and that was probably the reason we had gotten stuck with a "*lemon.*" It was the reason Monaco would not allow the extra few miles and stand behind the warranty.

We were able to spend the night there at the garage, and the mechanics tried to determine if our RV could be fixed, but it could not. We asked if we could trade it for one of the beautiful new ones they had for sale. They kindly agreed, knowing that with enough time, there would be some way they could salvage ours. We happily selected a wonderful new Winnebago RV thirty-four feet long with a gas engine. While owning two diesels, we had discovered that diesel engines cannot be worked on in just any garage but usually only in truck centers, which are not plentiful across North America. We moved into the new RV in their parking lot and special ordered some built-in cabinets that we wanted them to make and install for us. We left the new rig in place while we went to meet our grandson's plane.

Harry Potter and Snakes!

WHILE OUR CUSTOM cabinets in the new RV were being made, we left for a few days to stay in a hotel with our grandson and visit his choices of all the tourist attractions of Orlando, especially the new Wizarding World of Harry Potter at Universal Resort, which had opened just in time for Alex's seventeenth birthday celebration. Alex had been a Potter fan since he was six and had even tried out for the movie character starring role because at age twelve, he looked exactly like the images of Harry. Alex and Bill and I had devoured all the books by J. K. Rowling. We all thought Universal had done a fantastic job of creating the Wizarding World of Harry Potter, where we spent a delightful day. Alex happily bought an official Harry Potter robe for his souvenir.

For our naturalist grandson, who loved studying snakes, frogs, and the like, we visited Gatorland wildlife park, where we watched the workers feed raw chicken to the numerous alligators in their little lake. Alex talked me into wearing a live boa constrictor around my shoulders while holding a living baby alligator in my lap for a photo op. Of course, he was eager to do the same, but Bill could hardly watch! Snakes make him squeamish. We had planned our days with our grandson to include a special place in Saint Cloud, Florida, we knew he would love. It was the Reptile World Serpentarium, not always open to the general public, but I had been granted permission for us to interview herpetologist George Van Horn and Rosa, his wife, the owners. I would write magazine articles about this facility where they milk venomous snakes to make serum for inoculations to save a life when a person is snake bitten.

We found the scientific displays informative in the little science center, and soon we went to the seating in front of the large glass window to watch the milking process. Since he and I did not fear snakes, Alex wanted so much to be the photographer for the article, so he could go inside with me to watch the process up close. However, because Alex was seventeen, not yet an adult, he was not allowed to enter. Van Horn beckoned Bill and me to follow him into the enclosure where numerous boxes with air holes were stacked on shelves around the room. Snakes are the one thing Bill is very afraid of since he grew up in West Texas where rattlesnakes are a common danger, so he was not a cheerful photographer, but we could see Alex beyond the glass eagerly holding his camera ready also.

The scientist set up four crystal goblets on the table next to the window and pointed to me to stand in the approximately two-foot-wide space between the table and the glass window, but I said I preferred to stay on the wide floor space on the entrance side of the table. First, Rosa very carefully handed George a long rattlesnake to milk, and she continued to hold the heavy back end of the snake as he placed the head of the serpent at the goblet, forcing his mouth open and pushing its fangs into the glass rim to strike, and he collected the venom. Then his wife placed the snake back into his box and took down another container. She explained that if she had not held the tail end, the snake would have wound itself around George's arm to strike him.

We shuddered as she removed the second deadly snake, a cottonmouth moccasin, and they repeated the milking process as Bill and Alex took pictures and I took notes. The third snake was a very small but extremely dangerous coral snake. To our surprise, George used a syringe to feed baby food into the snake's mouth until its sides swelled. Then holding both ends of the little snake, he carefully pressed its mouth down on the clean goblet, collecting the venom in the same process as with the other two serpents.

Bill had been ready to get out of the room from the minute he entered, especially after he realized each of the many wood boxes with air holes around the room contained a living venomous snake. But there was one snake yet to milk. I was very close to the big table where the venom was collected. A large open trash can was nearby, and Bill was close to the door now, videoing the process. The largest snake was pulled from his box, a white king cobra about twelve feet long. Rosa held the end of the huge, heavy serpent tightly while her husband reached for its head, but suddenly the snake heaved himself free, landed on the table, and then lurched to the floor right at my feet!

Bill panicked and dropped the camera, which was secured by the neck strap, and I calmly stepped back, bumping the trash can, which crashed over loudly. Since we had recently been in India and watched the snake charmers make cobras dance to their pipe music, I was not particularly alarmed because in the back of my mind, it seemed huge but harmless. George and Rosa quickly captured the beast and milked it and then carefully stowed it away. George then showed us his stub of a finger. Years before, when he had been milking a king cobra with a class of elementary-age schoolchildren watching from the seating outside the window, the snake bit him and the children clapped, thinking it was like a TV drama. He was rushed to the hospital, where he lost half his finger and was near death for a long time. Bill was already out the door and with Alex, while I asked questions as a journalist should! We couldn't believe *we did that*!

Other Uses for Our Motor Coach

TOM HAD GRADUATED from Tulsa University in Oklahoma and taught art in a junior college there for a year. Now it was time for him to begin his master of fine arts degree at San Francisco Art Institute. It fell to us to find an apartment for him because his classes in California would begin just after his teaching in Tulsa ended. We loaded our big RV and tow car with as much of his stuff and furniture as we could take. The inside of our coach looked comical as we made our way across country, with chairs and a table stacked on our sofa, his futon on top of our bed during the days of driving, boxes of dishes and books, etc., in our storage compartments, and his clothing and suitcases in the trunk of our car. Our miniature schnauzer, Trina, was bewildered to seek her spot in our crowded vehicle, but we were glad we didn't have to hire a moving van and we could be of help to Tom.

We settled our RV at Candlestick Park for the couple of weeks we had to be there. In the evenings, we could see the ball games with a short walk from our RV, so it was another pleasant adventure. At that time in San Francisco, to rent an apartment, you were required to present your income tax return, a letter of recommendation for the tenant, and three months' rent cash in advance. We were armed with all that and knew we needed to find living quarters near Tom's school. But the task proved to be daunting! At the first apartment we chose, the manager declared we could not rent for our son; he had to be present, and they had to approve him, the tenant. For a different apartment, we had to make an appointment with a realtor, stand in line for an hour, rush in amid about twenty other searchers, walk through the intended rental, and then make a bid. After seeing it with rats and open pipes, we backed out of the bidding and still have that woeful image in our minds, thankful we live in a small town. The next place we found advertised was a six-hundred-square-foot studio condo for sale that sounded and looked ideal. We calculated that it was inexpensive enough to offset the two years' outrageous apartment rental prices, but then we learned it was in an earthquake zone and the tall cliff behind it would likely be a mudslide. No thanks!

Discouraged and tired after a week of this, we were taking a stroll along the wharf and found what we thought would be a perfect thrill for our twenty-four-year-old bachelor son: a yacht with a nice cabin for living quarters, with a parking lot for his car, and in walking distance to his school. We thought it would be perfect, since it was for sale for a quite reasonable price and slippage rental was cheap compared to apartment rent. And when he graduated two years later, we could start a different form of travels in an "RV" on the water! When we called him, excited over the plan, he flatly refused to live on a boat for the next two years!

We resorted to having a few relaxing days as tourists in the huge city of San Francisco and get to know the place our son was moving to, not knowing a single person. It was a great city to visit, but it seemed very difficult to live here. We were greatly challenged by the steep hills you must climb to walk around the city. We kept looking at apartment ads and affordable sales for places to live but with no luck. We climbed one day to the top of Nob Hill and found a miraculous answer to my prayers. We saw a place where a woman was putting a For Rent sign in the window. We were delighted and asked if we could see it. This tiny studio apartment with a parking garage was perfect and the right price. We had also learned that theft and crime was not frequent at the top of this high hill because it was such a difficult climb! The lady had not advertised the little apartment yet, and she removed the placard when we signed the contract. We were so relieved, and when Tom arrived the next day, he was very happy with it. It was located halfway between his school and the studio the school had assigned for him.

However, driving a large RV into San Francisco in all the traffic and high hills looked impossible. How could we unload it here at the top of Nob Hill? After we puzzled over this problem, we asked the apartment manager what to do. She advised us to rent a small truck for the move, and we did. Evidently city drivers were accustomed to trucks which had to double park for unloading, and while we and Tom unloaded quickly, the cars moved around us, and no horns sounded.

The apartment problem was solved, and we spent several happy days with Tom learning the many points of interest and great restaurants in his new city. Blake joined us for a couple of days to see Tom's new abode. We walked across the Golden Gate Bridge and had a wonderful time exploring, but our little fourteen-year-old dog suddenly got very sick.

We found a veterinarian, who advised us to put her down. Bill held our precious companion, and with tears in our eyes, we held her as the vet put her out of her misery. He advised us of a beautiful dog cemetery and crematorium, and we agreed for him to scatter her ashes in this peaceful farm for her final resting place. We were so upset. It was so hard to leave our little dog and our son in this place where we knew no one.

A few days later, while choking back tears, we said long good-byes to Tom as we left for Texas, where Bill's teaching year was to begin the next week. We were so sad, and the grief made Bill physically sick and unable to drive, so I took over the wheel with his careful guidance. It was a large RV, and we were towing a car. We advise all RV couples for both people to learn how to drive the vehicle and how to manage in campgrounds. It *can* and probably *will* become necessary for one or the other to take over sometimes.

I was not comfortable being the driver for the big RV, so Bill suggested we take the road that goes straight through Yosemite National Park for the views, even though we had no time to stop and hike, since his teaching deadline was approaching. It was truly a beautiful drive, with tall trees and high mountains all around us.

The road was not difficult since we went slowly, and our vehicle size was within all the limits. We did not attempt any of the tunnels. We planned to return another time for a longer stay to really explore this majestic place, made famous through Ansel Adams's black-and-white photo images and the thrilling writings of John Muir. We saw that finding a parking place for an RV would be very difficult, and in later years, the national park service provided bus service within many of the popular national parks to eliminate parking problems, save the environment, and solve a lot of other problems, which growing numbers of tourists had caused.

I saw signs for Mono Lake Tufa State Natural Reserve at Lee Vining, California, and we decided to go there for the night and see this most unusual place we had read about. The tufa towers of the lake are magnificent castle-like spires of calcium carbonate rock which create picturesque islands in the lake. There we learned the lake is in an endorheic basin, which means there are no outlets for the water to leave. Mono Lake formed about 760,000 years ago and has a far greater salt content than the ocean. Some people want to swim in the lake, to feel the magical uplift of the salt making it impossible to sink, but that held no temptation for us. I was fascinated by the little brine shrimp, whose official name is *Artemia monica*, a species found nowhere else on earth. These were all around the water's edge, and there are trillions of these living in this lake where they feed on the plankton algae, which gave an eerie green cast to the lake water in summer. This was a very interesting park to visit and had nice camping facilities, for which we were grateful, helping to take our minds off leaving San Francisco.

I was sufficiently rested to continue as driver; however, at one point, I exclaimed in consternation, "There is a car that just won't back off. It is following me too closely!"

Bill laughed, reminding me it was our own car we were towing!

Native Americans and Dinosaurs

I WAS DRIVING THROUGH New Mexico and needed a rest. I turned into a small side road where I saw a sign saying Dinosaur. I was able to park on the wide dirt road at the homestead of a Mexican family, who were sitting in folding chairs under a cloth canopy with a table of souvenirs in front of them. Bill did not feel well enough to get out, so I walked over to ask about the dinosaur. In heavily accented English, they answered, "We will show you the dinosaur bones we found on our land."

I bought a ticket, and a pretty little brown girl about nine years old took my hand and began to lead me across the dry, parched land. We walked out of sight of our RV, and the little one pointed to the ground just ahead. "See!"

I had thought I might see one or two bones that they would claim were from a dinosaur (just a gig to make a little money). But there in front of us lay the almost complete skeleton of a huge ancient, extinct animal, which truly appeared to be a T. rex! I was amazed and thrilled to see this, still buried but with enough soil carefully removed to reveal the authenticity of the beast's skeleton. I was sorry Bill and our dinosaur-enthusiasts son and grandson had missed this incredible find! This family had wisely kept the find intact, and I hoped they could claim ownership since it was on their own land. This proved one of the main reasons we love traveling by RV—because it enables us to explore out-of-the-way places that are fascinating adventures and meet many different kind people.

I drove for a couple of days. When we were only going forward and Bill was directing our route, I was fine. (I have no sense of direction, and he has innate GPS embedded in his brain, and these were the days before Wi-Fi and GPS were available.) But I could not back our RV, nor could I park it or perform the hookups. (I have learned that some skills are better *not* to learn, or they become my job, like mowing the lawn!)

I liked having the privilege of turning off the main road if I saw a sign that pointed to something interesting, as I did when I saw the Window Rock sign in Arizona near the New Mexico border. We drove into the little town to see the unusual natural window formation and take a walk. The huge circular hole in the large sandstone mountain truly created a window to peer out at the sky. In 1936, this place was designated by the commissioner of Indian Affairs as the seat of Navajo Central Agency. It had been a ceremonial place with the name meaning "center of the world." The Navajo people chose the name Window Rock for this special landmark.

We always enjoy times to explore in the Native American places and like to speak with the people we find in each. The Navajo were friendly to us and proudly showed us many of their special craft items for sale. A young boy of about eleven years had a beautiful painting he had made on a flat rock. He was very happy when we bought it, and we have always enjoyed remembering his big smile as we gaze at his art on our bookshelf now years later.

Bill loves to read, and he teaches literature in college, so he was drawn to the grandfather statue, a small male clay figure holding a child on his lap and reading a book to him. Bill bought it, and it became our first in a small collection of grandmother and grandfather statues reading to grandchildren, as we so enjoyed doing as our children and grandchildren grew. I found the Navajo beadwork to be of very high quality and bought several pieces of jewelry. This was a special stop to give us more knowledge about Native Americans having their own form of government even within the United States.

Bill had to take over the driving in the twists and dangerous curves of some of the mountain roads we had to pass through in the Southwest, but as long as we stayed on Interstate Highway 10 and 20, I could drive because the road was wide, flat, and an easy drive, except for high traffic. Going through New Mexico, we stopped when I was tired and spent the night at a wonderful campground we found quite by accident in Valley of Fires recreation area in the Tularosa Valley. This long valley is covered in many miles with gray and black basalt lava from the *Malpais* (badlands) flow about five thousand years ago. In some places, the lava is 165 feet thick and covers over forty miles. The lava is interspersed with many kinds of cacti, yucca, cholla, mesquite, and creosote bushes. A paved trail led through the landscape and gave us a good walk to stretch our legs and watch the brilliant pink to orange glow of the sun setting in the big western sky. That was an unexpectedly memorable evening within a totally strange landscape.

Bill had many fond childhood memories of places in New Mexico and Texas, but since we had to hurry home on this trip, he promised to tell me the tales the next time we could travel through there. When we reached Midland, Texas, where Bill had grown up and had many friends but no longer any family, we had to stop for the night. Usually, we planned ahead and visited friends and parked in their driveways, but this time we had to push on through and not stop to visit, so we parked in the Walmart parking lot. I wanted to touch base with some friends there, but Bill vetoed the idea, saying it would be quite an embarrassment to let his sophisticated buddies know we were sleeping in our vehicle at Walmart! (Only RVers understand this!)

July Fourth in Long Island

NEW IN-LAWS IN the family invited us to come to their summer home in Long Island. Looking forward to that, we asked if the roads and driveway could accommodate an RV towing a car, in total about the size of a semitruck. They assured us it was fine. En route, we stopped for a visit with our daughter and her family in New Jersey. Pamela and Eric gave us a very thoughtful and perfect surprise gift just as we were saying goodbye: a GPS for big trucks. This would be great in helping us avoid places unsuitable for our vehicle's height, width, and weight. However, since we were leaving right then, they did not have time to show us how to use it. Eric is an electronic genius, but we are new-gadget idiots! We thought we could figure it out as we traveled, so we said goodbye because it was Friday, July 3, and we knew holiday traffic would be horrendous. He told us the best route to take to avoid New York City, and we were off.

When we got to the bypass he had recommended for avoiding the city, there was a Detour sign, and we were forced to go through Brooklyn! We kept watching for an End of Detour sign, but there was none. We continued eastward on Atlantic Avenue and suddenly found ourselves beneath the track of the subway train that emerged from underground in Brooklyn. Bill stopped, and I got out to be sure the top of the RV and air conditioner would not scrape it. Our Texas license plates were clearly visible, and so was my white hair when I carefully stepped out into the street to indicate our problem and stop traffic so we could move into another lane. I found New Yorkers were *very* nice and helpful. Cars stopped courteously to let us out (dispelling the myth that Yankees are rude).

It was about 4:00 p.m., and workers were eager to get the holiday weekend started, so many people were leaving work early. The small stores on each side of Atlantic Avenue were putting up Closed signs, and suddenly a young man hurried across the street amid the dense traffic, running right in front of the car just in front of us. Our lane was stopped for a red traffic light, but he did not see that the opposite side of the street had cars turning rapidly into it from a side street. He ran directly in front of a turning car, which was going fast. It hit him, threw him into the air, and he landed just in front of our RV. Many police and witnesses emerged, and all traffic stopped until the body was removed by an ambulance. What a sad, dreadful memory!

By the time the traffic began again slowly, we had read the map and knew we *had* to turn left to get to Long Island, or we would be at the end of Atlantic Avenue, which we guessed would be a very wet ending at the ocean. But every cross street had a sign saying, No Buses Allowed. Since we were the size of a bus, we assumed we could not go safely under those bridges or on those streets. Finally, after anxious miles, we were able to turn and were on the wide highway to Long Island. Open space and the lovely vineyards along the road gave us peaceful scenery to calm our rattled nerves as we continued our drive. We were looking forward to seeing the famous Long Island and celebrating with friends and family.

*****

We followed the directions we had received of how to get to their address, but the last few miles were on a narrow two-lane road. Ed, our host, had told us he had trimmed all the bushes so we could make it to their address safely, and they had a large place for us to park for the three nights. They informed us there were no other neighbors on their street. Finally, the street marker appeared, but alas, it was a one-lane road, and a telephone pole was just at the corner where we had to make a right-angle turn to enter it. *Not possible* with a thirty-five-foot RV towing a car! It was now twilight. I got out to stop any traffic that might appear, but fortunately none came. With great effort, Bill unhooked the tow car, which had almost jackknifed in the attempted turn, and that would have made unhooking impossible. I backed the car away while he carefully maneuvered the turn by pulling up and back, up and back, until the RV could go straight forward. He headed into the narrow half-mile stretch to their home. Driving the car, I followed, cringing as I saw our new RV was being scraped by tall, dense greenery on each side of the road. We thought since most New York City residents do not even drive, they probably could not imagine the size of their visitors' vehicle. They had gone to great work to trim the hedge to accommodate us, but it was not quite enough, although we certainly appreciated their effort and did not tell them our difficulties.

When we arrived, they ran out to welcome us and indicated the place we should park. They had cleared a very wide flat place in their drive for us, but it was, unfortunately, also a right angle turn, which was impossible from the one-lane road. Undaunted, they offered for us to pull straight ahead onto their green grass. We hated to risk harming their lovely lawn, but they were so gracious, and I pulled the car into the driveway parking space reserved for us while Bill drove the RV straight onto the grass.

Their summer house was so attractive, and they were such thoughtful hosts, making us feel right at home and entertaining us in fun ways: frequent swims in their pool, a famous vineyard tour and tasting experience, a day at the ocean, and delicious meals. They treated us like family, and that was very special for us. We loved walking on the wooded trails near their home and shopping in the elite little Long Island stores. As we visited and played "getting to know you," we learned that only the parents knew how to drive, and the college son and his visitors were all practicing for their driver's test the following week. Everyone was fascinated with our RV and the idea of driving such a large vehicle so far. They were having difficulties managing the tricks of driving a car!

180

We spent the nights in our RV, but for Bill, the three nights were nearly sleepless. He lay awake trying to figure out how on earth he would be able to turn the RV around to head out because he felt it would be impossible to back that narrow half mile.

The morning for us to depart arrived. Everyone came out to bid us a safe trip. Bill had to start the procedure of dodging trees while going forward and backward, forward and backward, a few feet at a time to turn our RV around 180 degrees. It became a fascinating show for the onlookers, who were incredulous at Bill's skill. (Bill was amazed at his predicament and very uncomfortable and self-conscious at being the person of interest!) Not only were there lots of tall trees to avoid, one of the men warned, "Watch out for the gopher holes. They are huge and very, very deep!"

I bade goodbye and drove the car to the two-lane road beyond and waited for Bill. After over an hour, he finally arrived, made the right-angle turn with difficulty, and parked on the small highway to attach our car. We made it! By comparison, Manhattan traffic seemed a piece of cake on our return!

We Did It!

WE HAVE BEEN so fortunate to get to travel in our RV to every state except Hawaii because Bill's teaching career and our empty nest gave us the opportunities. Among our favorite places are the Pacific Northwest national parks and in Canada, the provincial parks. We drove from Texas toward Washington State on highways we had not traversed before. When we were in the wide grassy plains of Nebraska, we stopped for the night at a tiny town. To exercise a bit, we walked to town just after dinner when daylight was long. What a fun thing we encountered—a bed race!

We learned this was an age-old summer festival, and since we lived in a small town, we understood locals must create their own entertainment. This was not to be missed! A woman was resting on pillows in each bed with blankets pulled up, and her husband was pushing the bed from behind. The race was on the Main Street through town, and the spectators cheered wildly for their favorites. We suppose we will never see such an event again!

On our way farther northwest, we stopped in a beautiful park at the base of a mountain in Wyoming and decided to get some walking miles in for a nice change. The lake in the park was so pretty, with ducks floating along and flowering shrubs decorating the edge. We strolled peacefully around the flat paved walkway, starting at three in the afternoon. In years of hiking in the mountains, we have learned always to take food, water, coats, hats, sunglasses, raingear, flashlights, first aid, and a whistle in our backpacks. We had been told by rangers those high mountains create their own weather, and it can change suddenly from bright sun to snow and high winds, so we always went well prepared with a heavy backpack. But this hike was different. It was such a flat little park that it never occurred to us to take any gear.

The walkway curved around a tall boulder and began to wind upward, but it was so pretty we did not give this a thought and continued on. The slope was gentle, so until we looked back at our RV, which appeared tiny, we did not realize we had climbed quite high. We were enjoying the experience, so we continued ever upward. After an hour, the terrain became much more rugged, but we kept going, not mindful that we did not have any of our protective gear with us. It just felt so free and cool in the sun on the high elevation. We have always been ones that need to see what is around the next bend wherever we are, on foot or in a vehicle. Exploring is in our blood, and we sometimes wonder if we were pioneers in a past life!

The air was growing chilly, but the views were magnificent and then the trail ended at some enormous boulders all over the mountaintop.

Bill asked, "Do you want to go on?"

I hesitated only for a moment because I always feel safe with my man! He climbed over the first huge rock and held his hand out to help me. I had never climbed over a huge rock boulder, but this was a fun challenge. Many, many more of these enormous boulders were between us and the top of the mountain, but we were now determined! We climbed carefully, and none of the rocks was loose. Ahead of me by a few hundred yards, Bill finally reached the top of the mountain. I was determined to make it there too. The last obstacles were the hardest because I was tired, but finally I made it to the top too, with his hand helping me over the last two gigantic rocks. We were at the top of a huge mountain and saw a flag where some other successful hikers had planted their victory symbol. We took each other's picture there and took many photos of the lovely views of the panorama below.

Then we made our way slowly and carefully down. At the bottom, I realized it had been so much easier because we had not worn heavy packs, nor had we encountered any drastic weather changes.

We were back down long before dark and drove on awhile. Then we saw a sign for a natural hot springs that Native Americans had used for many years. We relaxed in it, soaking our already sore muscles. We found a pamphlet that told us we had been to the 12,018-foot-high top of Medicine Bow Peak! Wow! We were proud of our stamina and accomplishment!

When we reached Mount Rainier, which is 14,411 feet in height, near Seattle, Washington, we camped overnight at one of the most beautiful places we have ever been. Our campsite was beside a roaring river rushing down the rocky base. I love it there, but later, when we brought a friend to camp with us, he noticed a sign at the campground which we had never paid attention to—Danger Rockslide, Avalanche Zone. We all decided to try to climb part of the way to base camp for those intrepid climbers who practice at Mount Rainier in preparation to attempt Mount Everest, which is 29,032 feet at the summit. One guide told us he had helped an eighty-year-old woman make it to Rainier base camp. We were in our late sixties and itching to try, but we knew we couldn't.

Then we decided to just try the Alpine Mountain trail on our own. It is a very steep climb behind the visitor center on a rocky path that wound around a side mountain, and we could keep Rainier in view. We were about 5,000 feet high when we ventured along a more challenging path across the middle of another very high mountain. This trail was only about twelve inches wide and consisted of loose large rocks creating a ledge in the middle of an enormous but ancient rockslide, now snow-covered at the peak. We were frighteningly aware of the warning on the avalanche sign we had ignored. We made it all the way across to a lower part of Rainier, but not to base camp, which is just over 10,000 feet in elevation. We guess we got up to about 7,000 feet and sat on a boulder to catch our breaths and watch a little marmot eat his flowers by a stream of melting snow.

I Can't Breathe

BILL DROVE OUR RV on to Hoh Rain Forest on the Washington Peninsula. We had loved this memorable campground before, and again we found an RV spot close to the Pacific Coast so the lapping of the huge waves could sing us to sleep at night. We parked at the base of Sitka spruce, western red cedar, Douglas fir, and Western Hemlock trees, some over three hundred feet high and seven feet in diameter. The roots, which were visible in front of our RV, were much taller than our motor coach. The mystical Hoh Rain Forest is one of our very favorite places in North America. It is truly magical, with huge ferns hanging from the ghostly branches. In the past, we had brought various sets of friends here to see the wondrous trees. We have returned here each time we have been blessed to be in the Pacific Northwest.

We took a hike around the campground, and then a heavy shower came, creating a very wet *rain forest*. The damp, cold air smelled fragrant with evergreen, and we were very happy to be there. There were no cell phone services here, and the highway out to this campground had instructions of what to do in case of a tsunami. This whole concept was foreign to us, but we were not afraid. Many people lived in the little town we passed about fifteen miles before arriving at the camp.

My sinuses were becoming quite stopped up, and my chest was tight, so I took a warm shower, which usually would prevent an asthma attack for me. But I only grew worse, wheezing heavily. I asked Bill to get my nebulizer machine, but we discovered I had forgotten to pack the tubing and mouthpiece that delivers the medicine, so it did no good. I was scared. I knew there was no rescue service because we had no phone service. It was not possible to back out and leave the park at night. I did the only thing I could think of: I took one of each of my array of hay fever and asthma medicines. Some were prescriptions, and some were over the counter. I used my inhaler and placed it beside the bed and put all the other meds into a zipper bag and gave it to Bill. I told him, "If I die in the night, this is the medicine I have taken tonight."

It was a terrible, suffocating feeling, but I did survive the night. At early morning, we drove straight to a pharmacy to get a nebulizer tube and mouthpiece. The pharmacist told me many tourists from dry areas got asthma attacks there because it was a rain forest, hence always very, very damp. I still love the place!

*****

From there, we went into Vancouver and then took a ferry to see Victoria, the capital and largest city of British Columbia, although it is off the mainland coast on Vancouver Island. We did not know it was possible to take RVs over on the ferry and enjoy wonderful campgrounds in several places on this island, but we were on foot this time. The city is beautiful. We had lunch at the gorgeous Empress Hotel, where we had once seen Queen Mary's Dolls' House in a traveling exhibit. It is the largest and most fabulous and intricately detailed dollhouse in the world, built by many architects and artists in the early twentieth century. We hoped it was still here, but it was not. Pamela and I and Bill's mom had been in awe of the miniature mansion years before.

On this day, we chose to go to the Butchart Gardens, a vast display of lush green plants and magnificent flowers of so many brilliant colors in an area of over two million square feet within a limestone quarry. In 1904, Robert and Jennie Butchart moved to this island to build a cement plant on the limestone deposit. When the quarry was depleted and abandoned, it left a cavern, literally in Jennie's backyard, and she envisioned turning it into a beautiful garden. She transferred topsoil by horse and cart to the quarry and began planting her favorite trees and flowers herself. She patiently toiled, adding more and more and gradually increasing her garden's beauty. Through 1929, her family helped the garden to grow and even created Japanese gardens by the sea, an Italian garden on their former tennis court, and an incredible rose garden, which delighted us with its beautiful scents.

On their grandson's twenty-first birthday, they gave the gardens to their grandson, Ian Ross, whose insights developed the gardens into the world attraction with concerts, special lighting, and amazing Christmas decorations. Later, family members of the next generation started a choreographed fireworks show and then added a children's pavilion and carousel. These gardens, which were in peak bloom when we were there, were most magnificent beauty we had seen on many of our trips.

Hanging Out
over the Pacific

I T WAS LATE autumn, and this was not our first time on the beautiful West Coast of the United States, perhaps the most scenic drive anywhere and maybe one of the most treacherous. We stopped to splurge on dinner at a restaurant in Carmel, California, and stayed longer than we had anticipated. We left close to 8:00 p.m., and we were looking forward to the orange and gold sunset we would see over the Pacific Ocean as we drove south, and we felt sure we could make it to one of the two RV parks listed in the *Woodall's North American Campground Directory*, the bible of campgrounds. However, we were on the road when I started calling, and the managers of both anticipated campgrounds said they were filled for the night and had no place for us.

We had not planned well, and darkness was rapidly upon us. There was nowhere to turn around on the winding two-lane highway. The cliffs were on the east side of the road, and the Pacific Ocean was a sheer drop beside my passenger door. There was nothing we could do but continue southward. Even though Bill had a stellar driving record for hundreds of thousands of miles, the unlighted narrow S curves were terrifying challenges, and we were missing the breathtaking scenery we remembered from our other drives on this highway. After a couple of hours of driving slowly, we came to a pullout rest stop on our west side, and Bill pulled in, thinking we could stay here for the night. We got out of the RV to survey our situation and peer over the edge at the huge waves far below. We both shook our heads. It was earthquake country, and one rumble could drop us down the cliff and into the ocean many yards below. Bill drove on carefully.

Close to midnight, we saw a brightly lit bar on the east side of the road up the mountain at the top of a steep driveway. I said, "Turn in, and I'll go persuade them to let us stay in their parking lot overnight. My white hair and a few tears, which will not be fake at this point, can be very persuasive!"

I was a little nervous because I had grown up in a "tea-totaling" home, and I had never in my life been in a bar. I think my mom had made me believe the devil himself lived inside any bar. However, I was happily surprised not to find the boogeyman or dark evil lurking inside. The sympathetic bartender could readily understand our predicament, as we had not been the first to ask to park overnight. He agreed and seemed happy to help! We slept peacefully, and the next morning, we were able to see the rest of the exquisite coastal drive and stop for photos at designated scenic stops in route.

We toured the enormous William Randolph Hearst Castle in San Simeon, on a hill overlooking the Pacific. This castle, comprising over 90,000 square feet, was the crowning glory of the publishing tycoon who built it between 1919 and 1947. In the Roaring Twenties, he hosted numerous parties and houseguests who enjoyed bowling, golf, and the largest indoor swimming pool in the world and to us, the most amazing part of the mansion! He was a collector and had prize ornaments, furnishings, paintings, and rugs from all over the globe, making his mansion a true art museum. And one of his infamous private collections was of live exotic animals, which he imported from many countries for his own zoo. At that time, these animals had never been seen in the United States. We noted where the zoo had been. Our travels in our RV have given us access to so many memorable places in the United States.

After the Earthquake

OUR CHILDREN IN Los Angeles had recently experienced the terror of the huge earthquake which destroyed many homes and buildings, highways, and bridges in Los Angeles in 1994. We wanted to be of comfort to them, thankful they were not personally affected in a severe way from earthquake damage. We stayed for a couple of weeks at an RV park near their home, astonished at what an earthquake could do! Like the COVID-19 pandemic, it forced thousands of people to work by Internet from their living quarters to keep highway traffic at a minimum.

For a respite, we took Blake, his wife, Beth, and our little granddaughter in our large RV to enjoy the peace of the incredibly tall trees in the magnificent forests at Sequoia and Kings Canyon National Park, which had originally been designated to preserve 631 square miles of forested mountain terrain and in 1976 got the additional designation of UNESCO Biosphere Reserve. We hiked and cooked on the grill and just relaxed. It was peacefully perfect, and we were thrilled that they enjoyed the camping experience with us.

Driving through King's Canyon in the giant forest of old-growth trees, we marveled at the General Sherman tree, the largest living single stem tree on earth. It is estimated to be about 2,700 years old and is over 286 feet high. Second to this is the General Grant tree. How soothing it was to place blankets on the needles of the clean forest floor and lie there to look up at these old monarchs and see them from Baby Jordan's viewpoint!

We had recently visited one of our favorite places on the Pacific Coast, Klamath, Oregon, near Crater Lake. Walking on the white sandy beach with driftwood of huge dead trees is a magical experience. Nearby is what I call the Enchanted Forest. Its huge trees protect from above, beautiful ferns line the pathway, birds sing, and the calming evergreen scent make it one of the most inspiring and peaceful places anywhere.

Near there we had visited the Avenue of Giants, where there are three giant redwood trees you can drive through in a car: the Shrine Drive-Thru Tree, Chandelier Tree, and Klamath Tour-Thru Tree. These trees are still living, and the circumference of their huge trunks inspired some people in this privately owned forest to carefully carve out the passageway through the trunks. They took great care not to harm the living part of the trunk, and the trees have, for years, survived the savagery done them. Old-growth sequoias in their centuries of life have also miraculously survived huge forest fires, floods, and terrible storms. They are living miracles.

We did not make it as far as Yosemite on that trip, because our children needed to get back to work. Bill and I have been to this beautiful national park in the central eastern part of California. The altitude ranges from about 2,000 to 13,000 feet, and it covers about 750,000 acres with diverse plant and animal life. It was among the earliest of our national parks. In 1864, President Abraham Lincoln signed the Yosemite grant to protect Yosemite Valley from development. It was established as a national park in 1890 and is a UNESCO World Heritage Site. It is truly beautiful, and we especially love the rushing waterfalls and enjoy the more level hikes. We had listened to many of John Muir's recordings describing his beloved mountains there. We wanted to experience the winter wonderland, which he describes so beautifully. Once we did arrive there in a snowstorm. However, it was so foggy we could not drive through, and even when we were walking visibility was very poor, so we were disappointed. Yosemite is one of the most visited of all our national parks, attracting five million visitors in 2016. RV spaces must be reserved months ahead.

Look before
You Leap

W E HAD SEVERAL experiences through the years in our nine
different sizes and models of RVs that taught us we must
get to know the vehicle size and specifics before we take it
on a trip. In the early years, we had grown accustomed to our smaller
RVs, and we felt we had luxury when we changed to larger ones.
When we bought our first larger one, we packed in a hurry, eager to
get on the road to see our family in New England and the great sights
along the way. Should we study the RV manual that came with our
new purchase first?

"No, we can look at it along the way. Let's just go," Bill said.
(We both hate to read instructions.)

We made it successfully with no problems all the way to New
England, and often we had chosen small byways instead of major
highways, which have dreadful traffic. I was eager to stop at little
unique shops in quaint small towns, but after several days of arriving
at about 4:45 p.m., with stores closing at five, I accused Bill of planning it that way since he is not a shopper! We laughed about it as it
happened more and more often.

One day a little shop beckoned me, and it was only two in the
afternoon. Bill looked for a parking spot, but alas, there was nowhere
to stop. Our smaller RVs had been able to fit into street parking, but
the few more feet of this new one required a minimum of two parking places end to end, and nose-in ones were impossible. We were

not yet towing a car. We realized we could only park in large parking areas of malls or big box stores like Home Depot. These stores provided convenient indoor walking in wet weather. We learned that Walmart encourages RVers to use their parking lots in super centers, which are guarded at night. The store managers knew RVers always need groceries and things. Often our expenditures there would be close to $100. We wish Walmart still sponsored a map book with listings for their stores that allow overnight parking.

One day we needed to stop for gas, and the only station we could find on this long stretch between towns looked small. Although we knew our RV was listed as twenty-eight feet long, the outside length was a few inches longer. The height was listed in the RV instructions, and we could see the air-conditioning unit on the roof, but it was unclear whether the listed height included the AC unit. Bill was a good judge of heights, so he figured we could safely get gas at that station, where the roof over the pumps looked to be of questionable height. We got the gas easily but had failed to see that the exit was down a sharp incline! As our front end tilted downward, the ceiling of the station exit sheared off the top of the air conditioner on our roof, and we took a bit of the station's roof with us. After that, we always memorized the total height of our vehicles.

Heights of bridges and tunnels are marked, and on a very curvy road in New England, we stopped quickly just before we got to the entrance of an old stone bridge that was too low. We were thankful there was no traffic, and Bill could back away and turn around just in time. Structures built since mid-twentieth century are tall enough for semitrucks to go through, and RV heights and outer widths meet those standard measurements.

We memorized our weight also and added a few hundred pounds for ourselves, canned goods, gasoline, and water. We watched the ton limits of bridges. On old roadways, No Trucks Allowed signs are not just for keeping us out of being snooty, sophisticated neighborhoods. There is a reason those signs are necessary, and it is best not to investigate why! And if you miss a No Outlet sign, it is particularly treacherous, especially if you are towing a car. But sometimes these are not marked, as in crowded parking lots.

I was driving on a snowy day and pulled into a church parking lot to change drivers. I drove around the church to be pointed to the exit before stopping. But it was not a U-shaped driveway and I ended up trapping us at a dead end. At that time, we had traded up to a thirty-four-foot RV and were towing a car, making backing up impossible. Poor Bill had to unhook our tow vehicle, maneuver the RV out of the situation, and then hook up again. Not easy in a snowstorm or in any situation!

We were not towing a car when we entered an older state park, where the picturesque sturdy stone walls and lodge were built during the Great Depression by the Civilian Conservation Corps. Vehicles were small then, and the circular drive to the visitor center had low stone walls on each side encompassing the grassy lawn. We learned circumference of a circle counts! Our vehicle did not get stuck, but we got huge scratches on each side as we scraped around the circular driveway we should never have entered.

Another time we were with our son Tom and his, wife, Anna, to drive them from Los Angeles to visit Blake's family and ski in Park City, Utah. To our dismay that morning, our diesel engine in the RV did not sound right. Bill was fortunate to get it into a repair center, and they worked on it all day, delaying our leaving LA until high traffic time in the evening. We had planned to spend the night in Las Vegas. Tom and Anna had reservations at the Circus Circus Casino Hotel, and we planned to overnight in the RV campground behind that casino. Although we had invited Tom and Anna to stay with us also, because our RV was quite large, with an extra queen bed in a separate area we could close off, they preferred the hotel.

It was about midnight when we all checked in, and Bill and I went to bed in our RV. But about 2:00 a.m., Tom called and sheepishly asked if they could come stay in the RV. We said, "Of course!" and hurriedly made their bed and lit a candle for them and poured some wine, so it would be appealing and welcoming. We had always hoped our family would travel with us sometimes as adults. We were ready when they knocked on our door and entered. They were so upset. Their prepaid room was unmade, filthy, and strewn with beer cans and pizza boxes when they checked in. When they were reassigned another room, they pushed the elevator button and when the door opened, the elevator reeked of the vomit on its floor. The third room they were assigned smelled strongly of cigar smoke and even had dirty diapers in the bathroom. We were all disgusted and revolted! Delighted with the peaceful welcome in the RV, they slept well.

The next day, we happily arrived in Park City, where we had an RV site reserved, so we unhooked the car and set out to drive in the deep snow at dusk to take Tom and Anna to Blake's house. However, on the way, a truck stalled in front of us, and Bill swerved to stop in time, but could not avoid clipping the driver's side front of our car. The damage looked minimal, and the truck was not harmed, so we drove carefully on. All seemed fine, and the dent in our car could be handled after we got home. We had a fun time, and Anna learned to ski. We loved the skiing and sledding with the grandchildren and even flying down the icy hillside on inner tubes.

But that was not all. When Bill and I left the rest of our family and headed toward Texas in our RV, we stopped overnight in Salt Lake City. The next day as we left the city, a very high wind was blowing furiously. We were driving down an incline when a vicious gust caught the electric awning over our stairs on the passenger side. We flapped along in alarm with semitrucks passing us and nearly clipping our open awning. Bill pulled over to the first safe place he could find and had to remove the entire awning.

Our trip west had lasted about a month of happy experiences when we finally reached our home. The RV repair center was able to replace the awning, and no other damage had been done. The car garage mechanic told us the little dent in our car front had knocked our tires out of alignment and caused our tires to wear badly, so we had to have two new tires and realignment. Sometimes, we wonder if traveling by air and hotel might be easier and ultimately cheaper, but we enjoy the RV road trips too much to think of giving them up, and it is always comforting to have our own bed and bathroom.

Since roads have standard widths for lanes and all vehicles comply within safe limits, RV width is not usually a concern. However, it can be if you are in a small crowded town at lunchtime. We were in one in Kentucky, and the two-lane Main Street was not only crowded but also had parked vehicles on both sides. On our passenger side, we encountered a parked oversized delivery truck and the side mirror stuck out widely, as did ours. Bill went slowly and thought we were safe, but we clipped the other mirror and broke ours off, and there was nowhere to stop.

We also have discovered seasons matter. We arrived in mid-June for our week at Glacier National Park. It was a beautiful, sunny, and crisp/cold time of year there with high winds. On the first day, we had planned to drive our car on the picturesque Going-to-the-Sun Highway, a narrow winding two-lane hugging the steep side of an enormous mountain above a deep valley. We found that the road was always closed until June 20 or 21, the first official day of summer. There were good reasons for this: snow was still deep, and winds were ferocious. We extended our stay until the road opened, and we booked a narrated tour in a small bus. The views were amazing, and we had beautiful photo-op stops on the breathtaking drive. We realized why RVs were not advised and large ones not permitted on this road.

Another time we were driving through the Rocky Mountains in Colorado in mid-May. The winding mountain road, also a narrow way with high mountains on one side and deep drops on the other, had just reopened that day after being closed all winter. However, the Avalanche Danger signs made us feel quite uneasy. As I looked up at the snow-covered mountain high above on my side of the RV, I noticed snowmelt dripping beneath the deep ice pack. We hurried safely through, and we were glad it was only a short stretch because it certainly appeared that an avalanche was about to happen.

Another important thing to learn when you get an RV is the capacity of your freshwater tank and how to measure the intake. A couple we know were happily setting up for the first night in their new large motor coach, a retirement gift from their friends and family. They hooked up the freshwater hose and went inside to prepare dinner. They had excitedly invited another couple to travel with them on this inaugural adventure. The four retirees had a wonderful evening but decided to head for bed early. The other couple went to the back bedroom and called out, "What is making this bed hump up in the middle? We can't sleep on this! Are we on a large rock or something?"

The driver ran outside and discovered he had left the water hose on full blast and had far overfilled the big plastic water tank, which was located beneath the bed. He had not known to open the over-flow valve or disconnect from the campground faucet. Fortunately, he could let out the extra water before the tank would have burst and flooded the RV. When he relayed the story to us, since we had had many years of RVing in various rigs, we laughed and said, "When you take a house on the road, something will *always* happen!"

We Survived!

O F COURSE, THERE are some incidents that cannot be predicted. It was summer in the Midwest. We had left Hopkinsville, Kentucky, where Bill's great-grandparents had lived. We were happy to find photos and ancestry history in the museum there. Heading on westward, we came to the convergence of two mighty rivers: the Mississippi and the Ohio. The huge modern arched steel bridges are two lanes wide, with crisscrossed steel girders on the sides. The sky was growing very dark, with ferocious clouds gathering, but we were on a little two-lane road with deep ditches on each side and a long line of five o'clock traffic waiting to cross the bridge. We could not turn around.

It was finally our time to enter the Ohio River bridge when the wind started howling at high velocity, and we realized conditions were right for a tornado. We were on the second bridge, crossing the Mississippi River, when we saw we were meeting a car carrier loaded with vehicles, and it passed us in the middle of the bridge just when a powerful gust began hitting on the carrier's far side. We had visions of those cars being blown onto us. That didn't happen, but as soon as the carrier passed, the powerful wind force immediately hit us. We heard a loud clicking noise we could not identify. We were forced to keep up with the speed of all the traffic trying to escape the storm at forty miles an hour and could not stop, but the clicking grew louder. We were unaware that the wind had caught our twenty-four-foot rolled-up awning on the passenger side and had blown it partway open. Then we realized the steel arms of our awning had partially extended and were hitting each of the upright girders of the bridge's sides until the awning and both its arms were ripped off and fell into the churning Mississippi River.

Bill managed to keep our rig upright, and as soon as we were off the bridge, he found a level place to park. Between the tremendous gusts of wind and torrential downpours, he climbed the ladder on the back of our RV to rip off the remains of the tattered awning and be sure there was no greater damage. The storm was getting worse, so we rolled slowly another couple of miles to a large truck stop. We lived in *Tornado Alley* and knew to park facing into the storm. We hurried inside to take shelter from the impending tornado. Along with many other travelers huddled inside, we watched as the furious funnel swirled past just outside the parking lot and missed us all by perhaps a scant half mile! Everyone in the station cheered. Quite shaken, we asked if we could stay overnight in that parking lot, and the manager agreed. We were very grateful to be safe, and our RV was not damaged further. The next day was lovely and sunny.

On another trip through the Midwest, we were in a nice campground and already in bed. An urgent knock at the door made Bill respond.

The manager shouted in alarm, "A tornado is headed this way. Every person and animal *must* get into the space between the two concrete bathhouses *now!*"

We quickly got raincoats and our little dog and ran into the indicated safe space only about two feet wide and completely filled with anxious campers packed in. Misery does love company, but not quite this close together and preferably without smokers! The storm passed over us, and we all felt bonded in our great relief.

A Deer and Mother Dear

FTER MY MOTHER was widowed, she loved going with us on RV adventures. She liked to perch right behind Bill's driver seat and talk constantly, leaning over his shoulder. I admonished her to sit back and wear her seat belt, but she continued to read aloud every sign we passed and constantly try to entertain us with her chatter. Finally, Bill asked her a theological question he knew would irritate her, and she finally sat back quietly.

But she was good company and fun, and she loved Bill's teasing. He could always make her laugh. We were driving along the beautiful Blue Ridge Parkway through the mountains with lovely fall leaves, and the scenery was spectacular! The speed limit was thirty miles an hour, and thank goodness, Bill always stayed below any speed limit. Suddenly a doe ran out in front of us, and there was no time to hit the brakes. We hit her as she sprinted to the other side. But she was able to limp on through the woods, so we hoped we did not hurt her seriously.

The next time we were in Walmart, I bought the little high-pitched squealers that mount into the front grill of a vehicle. Wild animals, especially deer, can hear the sound and be frightened away, but people and dogs cannot hear it. We bought one set for each vehicle, hoping we would never hit an animal again. When we later were driving in Colorado and saw a big moose about a half mile ahead, I quickly got out my camera, but the moose heard our squealers and ran long before we reached him.

*****

For her eighty-fifth birthday, we asked if Mother would like to camp with us in the RV in North Carolina at the Cherokee Indian Reservation, where we have fond memories of many happy family vacation when I was growing up. She was thrilled. We stayed at a nice RV campground. On our first night, there was a little event: a pop-up camper vehicle was beside us with a family of four. We heard crying late at night and looked out the window to find a little girl about six years old in tears, wandering near our RV. When we asked where her family was, she pointed to the pop-up and said mournfully, "I rolled out of the bed up there and landed out here. I can't get my mom to wake up!"

We took her over to her parents, whom we roused, and later laughed together about the unexpected occurrence.

We were eager to show my mother the ways the town of Cherokee had modernized since she was last there. We had all noticed no more little adorable bear cubs were chained to Stop signs for people in cars to feed. Mother was a strict Southern Baptist lady and was strongly against drinking and gambling. In the prior few years, an elaborate casino had opened in town, and Bill was out to tease her. We were looking in the little Indian souvenir shops along the street, and these still had the popular items that were being sold when I was a child. Mom and I smiled and said, "Hello," to the friendly Indian chief in a full feathered headdress who lured tourists and kids into these shops. He or his ancestor had been one of our favorites in my childhood, and my siblings and I always saved our allowances to go into his exciting store and buy something special. I bought moccasins and later a beading kit so I could try to learn the Cherokee's beautiful skills. My brother chose a feathered headdress, so he could be like our big chief friend at the door. My sister had to have the precious little Indian dolls in native attire.

Bill winked at me and said, "I'm going into that building across the street, and you and your mom can come when you want to."

We did not think Mother would recognize this as a casino, but she was very astute. A little later, when she and I reached the door, she balked and planted her feet. She was not about to enter that *den of iniquity*. Her fear conveyed that she thought the *devil* was on the other side of the door awaiting us. Bill laughed and opened the door and took her hand and said, "I want to show you something. Here is a quarter. Put it into this little slot and see what happens when you pull this handle."

Of course, she did not want to offend Bill. She did as he said and pushed her quarter into the slot. When she pulled the lever, perhaps she was expecting a gumball to roll out, since candy and gumball machines were everywhere in the USA at that time. When she pulled the handle, out came *two* quarters!

"This is fun!" she exclaimed.

Bill responded with a big smile, "Yes, and now you are an official gambler. You have already doubled your money."

She almost ran out the door!

I had loved my childhood autumn weekends in Cherokee, but wherever my family went, we *always* attended Sunday morning church. Back then, the little Indian church was very small, with a congregation of under a hundred people. We attended Sunday school when I was eight and my little sister was five. She had long pigtails. I was supposed to take care of her in the children's Sunday school class. When we went in, I was terrified to learn that Chief Walking Stick was our teacher. I just knew he would covet little sister's long brown pigtails and scalp her! I suffered my miserable imaginings all through the long class. Then with her scalp intact, we met our parents and baby brother to go into the church service.

In the tiny sanctuary, the minister, who was also a chief, announced he was sorry, but the pianist was sick so singing would have no accompaniment.

Mother punched me with her elbow and leaned over and said, "Bonnie, go use your talent for the Lord. You can play the piano for them."

I had taken only one year of piano lessons and loved to pick out familiar pieces by ear. But I was in *no way* going to play for a group of strangers! I refused, and suddenly felt I might be struck by lightning because I was saying *no* not only to mother but also to *God!* The guilt of that had haunted me for fifty years, and before we came to Cherokee, I had told Bill if that little church needed a pianist again, I would *have* to play for them and clear my conscience. Thankfully, when we arrived in Cherokee, I saw that little Baptist church was now a large building with many members and professional staff, including an organist. Thank goodness! And I was saved because Mother preferred to experience the Sunday worship service given by the park ranger at the campground that day.

Bill Enjoyed Teasing Mom

NOTHER TIME A few years later, Bill wanted to take Mother camping again because she really was fun to be with. We went to a Table Rock State Park close to Greenville, South Carolina, where she lived. We set up the RV in the beautiful wooded campground, and Bill asked Mom if she liked to fish.

She said, "I have never been fishing. I would love to try it!"

Bill brought out the poles and bought some worms. We took a chance on needing a license because we knew this would not last long, and we could get the permit in the morning if Mom became hooked! He set up our chairs near the lake and threaded the worm onto her hook and showed her how to put the line into the water. We quietly waited but not for long. Suddenly Mother caught a fish, about a three-pound bass. She was as excited as a child, so Bill dressed and cooked her catch for dinner.

By the time we finished, it was nearly dark, and Mother began exclaiming that she was getting too old, and she was ready for God to take her to heaven. She had had a physical exam the day before we started on this excursion, and the doctor had exclaimed, "Mrs. Burgess, what have you done!"

Mother was frightened that she might have made a huge error because his voice was so emphatic. She timidly asked, "What do you mean?"

He replied, "I want to know your secret. At nearly ninety, you are healthy enough to donate your organs! I have never had a patient like you!"

Mother thanked him but did not know how to respond.

She related the tale to us and was almost tearful. "I don't want to live so long. My eyes are failing. Lord, just take me."

It was sad to hear her say that, so I cheerfully reminded her, "Mom, the doctor was asking your secret of long, good health. You have never smoked or had alcohol to drink. You exercised and rested each day. You have just lived a good Christian life and have trusted God."

Bill said, "I have to run an errand. I'll be back in a few minutes."

He drove away in his car, leaving us at the picnic table with me consoling Mother. In a little while, he returned with a big grin and a sack. He said, "Nelle if you don't want to live so long, you can stop right now. Here is a pack of cigarettes and a fifth of whiskey. Let's get started!"

She doubled over in laughter but did not follow his suggestions!

*****

Bill loved to tease Mother. She was a good sport and enjoyed it so much. When we were driving her from South Carolina to our home in Texas for a visit, we stopped at a truck stop for dinner because we had learned they had good home-cooked meals in the evenings. Mother was skeptical, I could tell, but she didn't say anything negative. I remembered when I was a child during the polio epidemic era, she was very cautious that we never ate in a place that did not have the grade A certified government certificate displayed in the window. And she had taught me that in those days, we should always check the restroom before deciding to eat there. She believed the standard of cleanliness there indicated the condition of the kitchen. (But that was not true since customers are not careful in restrooms.)

She was pleasantly happy with the meal, which was truly prepared there by skilled cooks with homestyle recipes (not so today, with frozen foods delivered to restaurants across the nation). When we finished eating, Bill decided he was too tired to drive on. Located in mid-USA, this was one of the largest truck stops. RVs were welcome to stay overnight. We knew it would be quite a different experience for Mom. Truck generators roared, and a loudspeaker in the parking lot announced, "Customer number 12, your shower is ready."

Bill, with a gleam in his eye, said, "Bonnie, you are up next."

Mother startled and looked horrified!

Bill then told her, "Nelle, you will enjoy it. The showers here are really clean and larger than in the RV."

Mother turned her head so as not to show her feelings. Bill and I began laughing, and we explained to her truckers who are on the road all day have nice facilities here since they sleep in their rigs.

I said, "Mom, he is pulling your leg! Of course, we don't shower in there! But there are good facilities for those who need them. In fact, truck stops have a lot of amenities which even airline terminals may not have except for international flights. We knew you would enjoy this adventure, and you can tell all your friends about your vagabond daughter and hobo son-in-law!"

We all enjoyed a good chuckle.

*****

Mom wanted to ride in the RV with us to attend her grand-daughter's college graduation in Alabama. All the South Carolina relatives were there to celebrate, and Mother offered to treat every-one to dinner at a restaurant after the ceremony. Cher, the graduate, brought her boyfriend along too. There were twelve of us around the long table. Cher knew her grandmother was a serious tea-totaler, but this was a special night, so she ordered a cocktail, and so did most of the others, except Mother and me. I was afraid to drink in front of Mother since I had been so warned of the dangers of alcohol when I was growing up. My sister and brother did not drink often, but they also had respectful fear of her wrath. Cher thought she was being discreet when she told the waitress with a wink to bring strong lemonade, but *Honey* and Bonnie would have water. Mother did not say anything, but we all figured she knew but did not want to ruin a happy occasion.

At the end of the lovely meal, she took the ticket from the waitress, since she had wanted to treat everyone, but when Mom looked at the over $300 bill, she almost fainted. And then she noticed there was a separate bar bill. She gulped and said, "I'll pay for the dinner, but not for *alcohol*."

This became a family story that always made us laugh.

Exploring Utah with Our Grandson

O
UR OLDEST GRANDCHILD loved camping, hiking, and exploring nature, and many times, he was happy to accompany
us in our RV. Just after his junior year in college, we were
delighted that he jumped at a chance to meet us for ten days for a trip
to some of our favorite places: the five national parks in Utah. With
many different types of scenery and adventures, we would make that
our destination. In joyful anticipation, we met his plane in Las Vegas,
knowing Alex is smart and is great company. We all chose to get on
the road and save Sin City until our return, the last night before he
would catch his flight home to his summer job in New Jersey.

Just outside Cedar City, Utah, near Highway I-15 north is a
prehistoric trail. Tribes coming from Central America set up camp
here for a while before moving on to trade or settle in the great West
beyond this point. As more and more people walked along this way
in ancient times, it became necessary to leave special information to
help newcomers find their way. Pictographs in the red stone cliffs,
which gave information about local seasons and weather predictions,
were inscribed for nomadic newcomers. Also, twelve specifically
placed small mounds in the red ground were built centuries ago and
are still in evidence today.

Twentieth-century archeologists and anthropologists spent
decades trying to decipher the meanings of these obviously important pictographs. They realized this must have been a highly spiritual

place for the prehistoric travelers because on summer and winter solstices, the sun set in the narrow opening between two of the natural rock formations. All over the world, when similar sunlight radiates at a natural "window" during solstices, the occurrence is considered mystical, and the places are deemed holy. Finally, scientists discerned that if one stands at other times during the year on one of these little mounds and views the opening at sunrise, the months of the year can be determined by the path of the natural light rays. The mounds seemed to serve not only as a clock but also as a calendar.

A strange calendar marked in the pictograph seemed to make the middle week of May and the middle week of August significant. After many scientists studied the meaning of this, it was decided that this was to tell newcomers that babies should be conceived in August to give birth in May. The reason this would be so important for the original nomadic people was that a baby born in May would be old enough to withstand harsh winters when the snows set in. Hence, the origin of present-day calendar date for Mother's Day was set by President Woodrow Wilson as the second Sunday in May. Alex was fascinated.

We drove over the Devil's Backbone, where the highway clings to an impossibly narrow ridge of the high mountain overlooking Hells Canyon en route to Capitol Reef. This is the newest national park, where the rock formations are an open book, revealing the geological history of the earth. Geologists come from all over the world to study these formations because they find more evidence easily interpreted than any other geological formation on earth. The different colors in the giant mountainsides tell scientists not only the mineral contents but also the age of the layers of formation. One place is called Waterpocket Fold, which looks like a folded rock." Another seems to be red-and-white ripples of waves suddenly turned into rock, frozen in time.

At Zion National Park, the gigantic boulders and bare rock mountainsides guide your eyes to look up at God's heaven, hence the biblical name chosen for this beautiful, rugged place. Alex loved jumping from rock to rock in the swiftly flowing shallow stream in the valley leading into a canyon that could suddenly fill with rushing water and drown people during a flash flood, so none of us ventured as far as the canyon. In our car, we drove to another parking area and hiked to the top of Cathedral Rock, where we could view far and wide. We could peer straight down into a deep fault that had split the two sides of this formation. From below, it does look like a cathedral. One huge mountain in this area appears to be carved in squares, giving it the texture that reminded me of elephant skin. Alex loved exploring and climbing at every stop. Often we followed him up or down a steep incline, and he was always so thoughtful and solicitous, offering his hand to pull me up or steadying his granddad by holding his arm. We all had sturdy hiking boots, which made some climbs possible that would not have been wise with less sturdy shoes. We even saw some youngsters in flip-flops and could not believe anyone wore such unsafe shoes for this climb.

We discovered Alex was not so fond of long drives as we made our way many hours to Dead Horse Point State Park, a more difficult place to get a campsite because it is smaller, so we were glad we had reserved one. We enjoyed a day of hiking and finding wading pools in the weird impressions in the flat rocks after rain. The beautiful Colorado River in the canyon, which wound around a small island, made the horseshoe shape in the rock formation, making this one of the most photographed scenes in the world. Our grandson is quite knowledgeable about creepy things, and he found a lot of interesting reptile and amphibian wildlife he was fascinated to observe.

At the campfire one night before dusk, Alex, a very talented artist, showed us his sketchbook with the drawings he was making all along the way. We were in a rather private campsite protected by large shrubs. However, we were spotted. We looked up to see a strange-looking green car passing slowly with large cameras on top, and then we saw the words Google Earth on the side, and perhaps our photo is now virtual worldwide!

We found a very tempting red rock mountain formation to hike with a steep incline up a long way. This hike looked clear, with no bumps, bare rocks, or steps. I was not sure I could make it up the steep hill, so I asked Alex to test it for us and signal us. At the top, he motioned for us to follow, and we did. It was steep, but his hand was ready to steady us if needed or to pull us on up. We were so very glad we did go up for the view of another mountain that did not look real. It was across the deep canyon, and the other mountain glowed in the sunlight with an iridescent metallic green-and-blue brilliance. It was stunning! With Alex's help, we made it safely back down again.

We moved on to Canyonlands, Bill's and my favorite of the amazing Utah national parks. At Canyonlands, Alex got out of the car to explore before we gathered our camera, jackets, etc. We were excited to watch for his awe when he could see the views below. We lost sight of him for a few minutes and were concerned. Then we saw him, but really felt inner panic!. He had walked the very narrow ledge directly overlooking the sheer drop of two thousand feet and was sitting with his feet dangling over the edge, utterly fascinated! Even though he was twenty years old, we were entrusted with his safety, so Bill called him to please move back from the edge. He did so and came back to gaze at the wonder with us. We three had several glorious days of hiking and discovering the beautiful views from the flat top of the *Island in the Sky* area of Canyonlands, where the mountains surround the canyon cut by the Colorado River breathtakingly far below. Some brave souls are always backpacking for that deep and rugged canyon's primitive camping. But permits from the national park headquarters are required for the safety of all campers who might get lost in that wilderness. Alex would have loved to do that, but we were not up to it ourselves and did not seek a permit.

However, Bill bravely dared a fun excursion. He drove our small GMC all-terrain car down the unbelievably steep solid S curves of White Rim Trail, about a hundred miles to the bottom of the canyon. That took hours of very slow driving, with the steep cliffs jutting up beside us on one side and straight down the cliff on the other side of our little car. We had no idea what would happen if we met a car, and we could not imagine the brave people who created this road. We made it safely down, and at the bottom was a sign warning that sudden flash floods could wash cars and people away. That was alarming as we sat and ate our picnic on a rock, hoping that didn't happen, but rain was predicted. Bill knew that the road out of this place was flat, and we were not far from the town of Moab. On our way out, we passed beautiful, brilliant blue lakes and later learned the bluing was added to these salt flats, where the water collected after rain, and the salt was later mined and refined.

*****

Alex had chosen his college major to prepare him as a certified jeweler. He had learned all about rocks and gemstones and foresaw the graduation project he could use them for in the next semester. In the little hippie town of Moab, Utah, we knew there was a great rock shop and took him there. He talked to the owner and asked if he himself had found the rocks which he sold there. The man responded in the affirmative and offered to tell Alex where it was okay to look for some himself. We three set out the next day to find the remote road the man had indicated and saw several Do Not Enter signs on side roads, where obvious mines were active. The rock merchant had told Alex the mine he was sending us to was inactive, and we would find malachite and azurite, which were legal to keep if we found any rocks we wanted. However, when we got to the place to which he had directed us, the sign said Keep Out. The cave entrance was not blocked, and Alex peered just inside but could not see anything in the darkness within. Then I saw some green rocks in the hillside out beyond the cave entrance.

He ran back to the car, where Bill had some tools he could use, and Alex started chopping rocks in the ground. He and I collected many green specimens. They were not shiny, so I would not have recognized them as valuable, just unusual. But Alex assured me these could be polished into beautiful pieces for jewelry or other art projects. We gathered several bags of them while Bill watched nervously for authorities to come and kick us out or maybe arrest us. We have always teased Bill as our *Dudley Do-Right*. He is a rule keeper, while I think breaking rules can be fun—within reason! We made it safely away with our heavy treasure trove and then realized Alex could not fly with this twenty-pound booty! So we planned to bring it to him in the fall when we drove to New Jersey for his birthday. We did so, and months later at his graduation art show, we recognized the green malachite rocks being used in his innovative diorama.

For the final day and night of Alex's stay with us, we set up our RV at our favorite campground in Las Vegas: Oasis RV Park. It is a beautifully landscaped park with all the amenities, including a doggie bath facility, which our little white dog really appreciated. We all had fun for a little while with a limit of $10 each in quarters to spend on the slot machines in the campground store. (We did not come away rich, which is a good thing, so we did not become addicted to gambling!) Slot machines are available at so many stores in Vegas, and even in McCarran International Airport.

We took Alex to a seafood buffet restaurant for dinner, which could have seemed crazy here in a desert midcontinent, but we knew it was a highly acclaimed restaurant, and Alex loves seafood. It was messy fun as he taught us how to crack crab legs, a new experience for us! Then we wanted to show him the magnificently imaginative buildings on the Strip. Since he is an artist, we knew he would appreciate the amazing architectural designs. We walked through many of the major casinos, but he was not interested in stopping to gamble. By the time we returned to collapse into bed at the RV, our pedometer said we had walked seven miles! The next day we hated to say goodbye, but we look forward to many more Real Ventures with Alex, our only grandchild who likes camping.

Native American Heritage

AFTER **A**LEX FLEW home, Bill and I were returning to Texas and decided to go to see the archeological relics in Chaco Culture National Historical Park in New Mexico, which is also a UNESCO World Heritage Site and preserves the largest collection of pueblos and important pre-Columbian historic areas of the United States. We carefully drove about ten miles in our RV deep into the canyon on very rough, unmaintained dirt roads. From where we parked, we hiked across a desert field of scrub grass and cacti to the huge complex built by hand centuries ago with sandstone blocks and timbers carried from far away. This pueblo center was constructed and inhabited beginning about AD 850 in a semicircular configuration that defined and depicted the various annual solar and lunar cycles. It was a spiritual center for both local and traveling tribes. We enjoyed going in and out of the many openings in the little rooms. As far as archeologists can determine, this pueblo was abandoned in about AD 1250 during a very severe fifty-year drought. After about an hour of exploring here, with only a few other visitors present, we were hot and tired, so we started walking back the long way to our car. My foot suddenly felt very uncomfortable. Puzzled, I walked a few more steps and then stopped to inspect it to discover the sole of my comfortable old boot had simply fallen off awhile back! Not a pleasant walk back through prickly desert vegetation!

Driving back out of the canyon, we went on toward Farmington and stopped near the town of Aztec at another Native American heritage place still within the Chaco National Heritage area: Aztec Ruins National Monument. Here we found a very different, less well-preserved collection of little buildings in a community from centuries earlier. We could walk through this, sometimes looking down at it because some of the ruins were not high. We walked inside the Pueblo Great House with walls for four hundred rooms still partially intact, built by hand more than nine hundred years ago. It was incredible to find fingerprints of the original builders still visible in the adobe. We walked another half mile to go inside the reconstructed Great Kiva to see the place of gatherings and worship for the ancient Puebloans. Our RV travels through the American Southwest have enabled us to see many Native American pictographs, ancient buildings, present-day museums, and shops. We have grown more and more fascinated with learning about and now meeting and honoring many of these people with various tribal ancestries.

We wanted to return to Santa Fe, where years before, we had had an incredible opportunity that probably piqued our interest in Native American arts and culture. We were casually visiting San Ildefonso Pueblo in the Rio Grande Valley of New Mexico with friends in our little RV. We stopped at a shop to admire and purchase some pottery on display. We inquired about the unusual black pottery, and the manager proudly told us that Maria Martinez, who was famous for her black pottery, lived in that pueblo. A little girl, who told us Maria was her grandmother, wanted to take us to meet her. We were thrilled to be invited into her very neat small adobe home, where she, quite elderly, sat beneath her patterned woven blanket. She welcomed us, and we bought her biography, which she autographed for us.

We talked to her about her technique, as we had with the maker of black pottery in Oaxaca, Mexico. Maria explained that she had always liked making pottery from the local red clay since she was a child creating pieces for her doll. As she grew up and her pottery-making skills increased, Dr. Edgar Hewett of the Laboratory of Anthropology in Santa Fe brought her shards of black pottery he had discovered and asked her if she could figure out the technique.

She tried over and over until she figured out how to turn the red clay pieces black by firing them in a cool fire covered with dried cow manure, which trapped the smoke. The slow baking turned the pottery black. Maria's husband, Julian, painted the Indian designs on her black pottery until his death, when her sons took over the design work. Maria's unique black pottery is a celebrated art form, and she was invited to the White House four times. She received honorary doctorates from the University of Colorado and New Mexico State University. She is considered one of the most influential Native Americans of the twentieth century. We could not believe our good fortune to get to talk to her in her home!

In more recent years of stopping at Santa Fe, we stayed at a KOA Campground in July and quite by accident, learned there was to be an Indian powwow nearby the next day. We eagerly went and were intrigued watching the colorful tribal dances, taught to each generation through the centuries. We thought the men's beautiful handmade soft deerskin costumes with traditional tassels and feathers, and the women's deerskin dresses with hand-painted designs, elaborate beadwork, and clacking pieces of metal, must have been handed down from earlier times or carefully copied to keep traditions alive. We assumed each design had a special meaning. We realized we were tapping our feet to the drum beat as the chanting and singing grew stronger and stronger. It was like a cultural county fair, and we discovered our favorite food there was fry bread. The celebrations continued well into the night. However, I began sneezing, and finally we had to leave. I had forgotten that at this time of year, I am allergic to the bright yellow blooms all over New Mexico, and on future westward summer trips, we took another route.

RV Evenings Happily Reminiscing

AS WE RESTED in our RV at the campground, we recalled our first trip to this state when we had been married about eighteen months and determined to have our own Christmas instead of dutifully returning to our families' homes for beloved traditions of the holidays. Friends of Bill's parents, who had a home in Ruidoso, New Mexico, invited us to stay with them after Christmas and learn how to snow ski. We were very excited and drove our little Plymouth there, as we had never even contemplated an RV in those days, just before our college graduation in the spring. We had no money for ski clothes, so we decided our jeans and winter coats would have to do. We took beginner lessons and had many tumbles in the snow trying to snowplow down the baby hills, but it was fun for the two days of tickets we had purchased. We were able to use the clothes dryer at the house each night to dry our very damp ski things. On the third day, we wanted to go exploring and drive to Taos to see the Indian crafts. We headed out, not asking instructions, and found a small road through the woods that looked like a shortcut with no traffic, so we took that. I love forests, and this one was so beautiful in the snow.

Bill had difficulty driving and had to stop many times, hoping we were not stuck. We didn't even know about snow tires since we had not lived where snow and ice were a normal part of winter. When we made it to Taos, we were drawn to the fascinating Indian crafts and souvenirs available in the shops and had fun deciding what our little budget could stand. When the shopkeeper asked where we had driven from, we said Santa Fe. I told how much fun it was to drive through the snowy woods. He looked incredulous! "Oh, no one uses that little road in winter! I'm surprised you did not get stuck. You must return on the highway!"

Another memory we still recall fondly nowadays was when we were first married, at ages nineteen and twenty-one, I tearfully said goodbye to my South Carolina family, and we drove away in a little Ford car pulling a small U-Haul trailer. I was so happy to begin life with my love, but I was totally blank when I tried to imagine the apartment Bill had chosen for us near Southern Methodist University, where we were to complete our college educations. I could only imagine a void, and I began feeling homesick. For the first eighty miles, I was able to choke back the lump in my throat and blink back my tears, but suddenly, the floodgates of my heart opened, and I began sobbing out loud. I was so happy to be married now but so sad to be leaving everyone I knew.

Bill was very concerned and tried to console me, but that made his driving so difficult, with about eight hundred miles to go! I tried valiantly to stop crying and succeeded for a while, and then the sadness overcame me again. This happened over and over until we neared the Mississippi River at Greenville, Mississippi, and I had left my family in Greenville, South Carolina. In my heart, crossing the Mississippi River seemed to be the line of demarcation, and I had no idea when I might ever cross back. I was sobbing uncontrollably. Suddenly, my new husband, the love of my life, pulled over to the shoulder of the highway, at a loss of what to do.

Then in total bewilderment, he said, "If you can't stop crying, I'm going to turn around and take you back!"

That shocked me into reality, and I did get control of my homesick feeling, and for the first few months in our modest little Dallas apartment, I tried hard to keep my tears to myself, crying only at times when he was at work, or I was in the shower. But through the years, Bill made sure to drive me and our children back to South Carolina at least twice a year, and I flew on other times when he could not leave work. We figure that in our nearly sixty years together, he has driven us back to South Carolina on enough trips to equal about a million miles! He really kept his promise to keep me close to my distant family, and five years ago in retirement, he suggested we move to South Carolina since our children and grandchildren live in places too far from each other to be our retirement location. Our RVs have made many of these trips so much easier. I am so glad he likes to drive because, with family always far away, part-time nomadic life seems to be our answer.

Habitat for Humanity RV Build

A T ONE POINT, when empty nest was ours and we had already enjoyed RV trips so much, we contemplated making that our full-time home. We had a large RV that was quite comfortable, so we decided to give life on the road a try, to live full-time on the go in our RV. We bade goodbye to friends and stayed on the road for nearly three months. We had so many great adventures and loved the outdoor life in the mountains, hiking trails, having cookouts, sightseeing, and traversing many states and different climes. We happily passed the test of togetherness, which has made our life happy even while sheltering in place during COVID-19, which was less of a challenge for us than for many couples.

When we returned home to Texas, our friends were very curious about our experiences, and would we *really* sell our home and live in our RV? We were not sure. We would hate to leave friends of many years, but our little town did not have hiking trails, shopping, or much entertainment. However, those were not serious factors in our decision because we loved Paris, Texas, and our many friends there who had become like family to us. The main problem that plagued our decision was, "What would we do with our *stuff.*"

While we were puzzling over the question of life on the road, we drove to Bend, Oregon, to volunteer on a two-week RV Build for Habitat for Humanity. There were about twenty RV couples gathered to help the local Habitat group complete a nice house they had begun. We learned that these RV Builds were popular. Local organizations provided a place for the RVs to make camp, and locals hosted the evening meals around the group's campground. We found it lots of fun to meet other RVers from all over the USA and enjoyed sharing stories.

The building of the house was a great experience. Our jobs were designated by the local club, but I quickly failed my job! I had been assigned to tape and bed the Sheetrock. However, I did not understand the proper process, and my tape quickly fell off! I was discouraged and embarrassed, but the kind people gave me a paintbrush instead. Painting I could do since they also had a good drop cloth in place. (My only wall painting at home had resulted in having to have new carpet!) Bill was appointed to be on the roofing committee since he had a little experience with roofing houses for the workers at our farm. The leader of his roofing team was a very sharp and capable woman, who was a perfectionist and knew what she was doing. She directed the roof project to completion and to everyone's satisfaction. Bill learned a lot from her.

We became friends with her and her husband in the evenings as we relaxed and ate dinner. Gary was a retired college professor. They were full-time RVers, and they told us all about their life on the road, which they had enjoyed for several years. We really liked the camaraderie of the group encampment. We learned from others that there are many Habitat for Humanity RV Builds in more places and other RV volunteer groups gathering to help with other organizations.

Avis and Gary also joined Methodist RV Volunteers to build churches, repair houses, or other jobs in many places in the United States. When we asked what they did with their *stuff* when they first sold their home and went on the road, they told us that their daughter lived on a farm with plenty of space for them to park when they returned to see family. Also, they owned a storage unit on that farm where they kept anything they could not part with.

That last evening before we all went separate ways, Avis passed around a sheet of paper and asked us each to list our names, phone numbers, email and physical addresses, and our birthdays and anniversaries. We thought this was odd but assumed she might be doing it for the Habitat local group as a sort of secretary of the build. A few months later, we received a happy anniversary email from them, talking about the place where they were then volunteering. We thought this was very nice and enjoyed many birthday and holiday messages from them through the years. Once when they were on a volunteer project fairly near our Texas home, they came for a visit and told us they often visited new friends from the road when they are nearby. It was a great way to keep up with new friends, and they were diligent.

By that time, we had decided that full-time RV life was not for us, but we had learned a great lesson: none of us needs as much *stuff* as we own. An RV can truly hold whatever is *needed*. But family memoirs and photos were our drawing of the line in the sand. Cell-phone photos had not been invented then, or that might have changed our minds, but we chose to keep our RV life special for our many trips through the years. But each time we see a storage unit complex, we shake our heads and mutter, "If people can live without their stuff, which is tucked away in storage, they do not need it after a year!"

Crater Lake

SEVERAL PEOPLE WITH us in the Oregon group had described Crater Lake, just ninety miles away, as a *must-see* during our weekend break in the middle of the Habitat for Humanity Build. On Saturday morning, Bill and I drove to the north entrance of Crater Lake National Park, the sixth one to be preserved in our National Park System. It was winter, and the highways were clear, but when we arrived, the entrance road was deep in snow, and the north entrance was closed. Disappointed, we asked some locals if there were any way to see the lake at this time of year. They directed us to the south entrance, about ten miles away, where we found the roads clear and easy to drive, but the banks of cleared snow on the sides were higher than our RV. We didn't go to the visitor center since we were only there for the day. We saw only one other couple driving slowly around the lake on Rim Road through the park. We came to a place where there was a stone wall with not too much snow on it, overlooking the snowy landscape and frozen lake far below us, so we stopped to eat our picnic lunch. It was a beautiful sight and made us determined to return, which we did the next summer.

In July, after being with our Los Angeles family, we headed for Crater Lake to stay and hike in this national park for a few days. We had learned that at 1,943 feet deep, this is the deepest lake in America and one of the deepest in the world. Famous for its incredible clear deep blue color, it is not fed by a stream or spring or any other water source. Only snow or rain fill this deep volcanic crater at the top of Mount Mazama. This Cascade Mountain Range receives an average of 43 feet of snow annually. A volcanic eruption collapsed this 12,000-foot-high mountain 7,700 years ago, and according to the legend told by the Makalak natives who lived in the surrounding area, the collapse was caused by a battle between the Spirit of the Mountain and the Spirit of the Sky. Because no minerals or sediment are brought into Crater Lake by ground water sources, it is one of the cleanest, clearest lakes in the world.

We were totally engrossed with the magnificent photo ops during our 33-mile drive around the Rim Road and stopped at all the picture points so that this filled a gloriously gorgeous day. We kept hoping to see a bobcat, although we knew these are nocturnal animals. We often saw deer and elk browsing in the thick forests. Our favorite little creatures we spied many times were the adorable little picas, which look like fat little brown squirrels squashed into miniature.

We were eager to take the boat tour on the lake to Wizard Island, a volcanic cylinder which protrudes up 750 feet from the water. However, the hike over a mile down the steep 700-foot slope to board the boat was challenging, but we kept telling each other it would be worth it! The boat ride was not only fun but also informative as the guide told us many fascinating facts about this mysterious lake. Scientists have studied the flora and fauna very deep within these waters and learned that in some places far below, the icy cold water is periodically pierced by extremely hot funnel fumes from the volcanic depths. At these places live strange species not known anywhere else in the world. Also, people who are brave enough to swim or wade at the lake's edges may be privileged to encounter little Mazama newts, which exist only here and nowhere else on earth. These hide under rocks or logs to escape from the invasive non-native crayfish. We declined to swim because to us the water was freezing! The boat stopped at Wizard Island, where everyone got off to climb up the center of this rugged cinder cone. We didn't make it all the way up, but it was fun just trying on this actual volcanic rock. When we returned to shore, we had the tough hike back up the steep hill to our campground, and our muscles were shaking when we collapsed into rocking chairs beneath our RV canopy. The crisp, cold air was stimulating, and we soon recovered.

At twilight, we hiked to Sun Notch to see the castle in the lake, known as Phantom Ship. We had learned at the visitor center that it is the oldest exposed rock in the caldera and is the height of a sixteen-story building. Geologists have determined that this natural island made of lava rock is four hundred thousand years old. It looked to us more like a magnificent castle with many turrets, like the sandcastles we had aspired to build with our grandkids on a sandy beach by the Atlantic Ocean earlier that summer.

Crater Lake National Park's beautiful forests have miraculously evolved to withstand the raging forest fires of the West. Scientists have learned that the fires caused by lightning are nature's way of making certain seeds germinate and of creating fertile soil for these gorgeous forests. We talked to a couple we met in the campground who had been present here when one of these horrific fires broke out. National park officials in past years tried to fight them to protect campground buildings, but scientific studies have now proved that it is better to protect people by making them get out and letting the forest burn naturally but guarded. We were thankful not to be present when that happened. The campers told us it was very scary to see the brilliant flames raging around them. Sadly, many forest fires are caused by people being careless or maniacally criminal during what has become known as fire season in California, and these fires can swiftly get out of control and cause great devastation, as seen in news reports.

Safety Always First

WE HAVE FELT safe in campgrounds, especially those so well run by our national and state park rangers. However, as campers, we all are in nature and are at her mercy. We had stayed in a provincial park in Western Canada in a very stormy time, and fortunately we had left after only one night because we had a different destination we had to make by afternoon. We forged some enormous puddles and flash flooding to get out but thought nothing more about it. The next day, we learned on the news that the campers we left behind were stranded because the roads completely flooded. Canadian authorities were dropping food from helicopters to those who had become stranded for days, and some had to be airlifted out.

Once at a state park in North Carolina, we were safely tucked into our RV bed during a loud storm while we slept unafraid. The next morning was clear, and we left our RV to walk our dog. Just across the camp road from us was a campsite where a mother and her first-grade son had camped alone in a tent. What a terrifying experience for them because a huge tree was toppled by the storm and landed only about three feet from their tent.

A friend of ours a few years earlier had led a Boy Scout Troop in South Texas on a campout for earning badges. They had a wonderful time until one of the well-known Texas tornados blew in. The leader quickly herded the boys together, but one had strayed from the group and was missing. The storm savagely blew through while the leader searched for the boy, but sadly a tree had fallen on him.

We have been to many lectures and campfire talks given by park rangers in various campgrounds around North America. These are very interesting and informative, telling campers about the local points of interest and special hikes, and also they advise what precautions to take for local hazards. These lectures and signs at park entrances are important for wise, safe campers to read and heed. At one campground beside a large lake with boat ramps, there were signs that the bottom of boats had to be scraped and sanitized before and after being launched in this lake because invasive species were carried from lake to lake on the bottom of boats and could kill native species of flora and fauna in lakes where these species were not natural inhabitants. At another campground, we learned not to bring in firewood from another place because of invasive insects that could be transported in the wood. Most campers have never thought of environmental impacts, but thankfully, our national and state parks are making us ever mindful of caring for our beautiful earth. Every camper must strive to be informed and responsible. Recycling trash is now required in most parks, as it should be in everyday life.

Traffic Lights Really Extend Travel Time

IN THE EARLY years of our trips by car, and later by RV, driving from Texas to see family in South Carolina required going through Birmingham, Alabama, which was a nightmare. The stretch from Bessemer to Birmingham had thirty-nine stop lights, and they were timed so that we had to stop at every one!

Because our children live on both sides of the United States, we enjoyed many *real ventures* across our continent. Most trips included Tennessee, a state we love because we are drawn to mountains! This Blue Ridge section of the Appalachian Mountains is deep green with evergreen forests interspersed with dramatic autumn color of many species of hardwood trees. Interstate Highway 40, which traverses the long state, is always crowded, and scores of eighteen-wheel semitrucks use this as the best route across America too. The views from the highway down the steep mountains are lovely but can tempt the driver to be distracted, and in winter, the snow, ice, or falling rocks can be a danger. The highway is well maintained, but if you hit a traffic jam, ugh! We have been stopped for hours, along with hundreds of other vehicles in both directions on a couple of occasions. There is no way to escape, with high mountains on the northern side and the steep mountain slopes on the southern side, and many miles stretch between side roads leading to a town or rest stop. So be equipped with food, water, and an empty bladder, and in winter, blankets.

However, we have learned to take another route in winter, selecting, instead, Interstate Highways 30, 20, or 10. Wide interstate highways were started just after World War II by President Dwight Eisenhower to provide safe landing strips for airplanes during emergencies. By 2008, much of the infrastructure of highways and bridges in the United States needed upgrades and serious repairs. Under President Barack Obama, Congress passed the bill to provide money for the states which would accept it to provide work for many who were unemployed during that drastic recession and to accomplish the much-needed construction for repairs.

We now deeply appreciate the Interstate Highway System, and even though we often are stopped in our travels for road construction or maintenance, we try not to complain. But one stop while we were traveling through Mississippi almost became disaster: We came to a total standstill of traffic both ways, and we were in the outside lane of three lanes traveling east. Far ahead we could see flashing lights of emergency vehicles, but we could not see the accident. After about forty-five minutes at the standstill, I got out of our RV and walked back to ask the driver of a semitruck if he knew what the accident ahead entailed, or if his communications with other big rig drivers had any information about how much longer we must wait. He was very nice and gave some hopeful news that the traffic jam may soon be freed, so I thanked him and stepped back into the wide shoulder of the highway without looking. To my terror, a car that was impatiently bypassing the long line of stopped traffic zoomed past me and missed me by perhaps two inches!

Total Darkness

L EAVING OUR FAMILY in Los Angeles, Bill decided we would meander and visit places new to us along the way to see our family in New Jersey. He read that Lassen Volcanic National Park in the Sierra Nevada mountain range of Northeastern California is the least visited of all our national parks. We wondered why and decided to learn for ourselves. We easily found a good RV site near Manzanita Lake and set up for several nights. This park was dedicated in 1916 to preserve and protect the largest *plugged volcano dome* in the world. This type has steep sides and a rounded mound, which was formed when *viscous lava* welled up into a crater but was too stiff to flow away.

At the visitor center, we learned there are three different kinds of volcanoes that geologists recognize, and examples of them and other volcanic activity are all in Lassen: *shield volcanoes*, which are from a lava flow and look like a shield lying flat on the ground; *composite volcanoes*, which are conical in shape and were built up by many layers of hardened lava; and *cinder cones*, which are steep cone-shaped hills of loose fragments of ash and cinders downwind and around a volcanic vent. There are *fumaroles* and *boiling mud pots* in the southern part of the park, evidence that the volcanic activity is still continuing below.

Volcanic soil is very fertile, so the scenery was lovely. On our walk through King's Creek Meadow, the ranger explained so much about volcanoes and how the administration monitored for everyone's safety in case one of those was about to erupt nearby. We saw lots of steam rising from the mountainside at Devil's Kitchen, signs of still-active volcanoes. We learned that sleeping volcanic mountains gradually build up their tops to a point, and many of these have the potential of erupting (maybe in a thousand or so years? We hope!). He pointed out the huge snow-covered Mount Harkness in the distance, whose flat top indicates it had erupted in the past. That night we placed our folding chairs beside the beautiful lake for the ranger lecture about the night sky and constellations. We have never before or since seen such an exquisite night sky, far from city light pollution, and in the clear, crisp, dry air, millions of stars sparkled above us like diamonds on black velvet. Magnificent!

The next day, we asked a ranger to recommend a hike. He said to meet the group at the base of the cinder cone to hike to the top at dusk and watch the rising of the full moon. We were excited to do this and looked forward to it all day. He had given us good map information to get to the meeting point, about thirty miles away. When we arrived at the appointed 6:00 p.m. time, no one was there. We double-checked the map he had marked, and we were in the right place. However, the large forest at the base of the cinder cone was smoldering, and smoke lazily rose throughout the burned forest. We, at first, feared a forest fire, and then we realized it had been a carefully monitored burn of undergrowth, which we already knew helps forests. We waited a half hour in the growing dusk and decided to climb the enormous cinder mound by ourselves, assuming the group might have gone ahead or would come up later. We took a blanket and water as directed, but the ranger had told us not to bother with a flashlight as the bright moon would light our way in a wonderful, mystical way.

We could not see to the top of this huge 700-foot-high cinder mountain, and the main mountain top was 6,000–6,900 feet above sea level and made of loose black lava rocks, called scoria, each about the size of a golf ball. It was an unbelievable challenge to climb a cinder cone, which we had never imagined. Thank goodness we had sturdy hiking boots, or the four-mile round-trip hike would have been impossible. Each step we took was about two feet upward, only to slide back at least one foot, repeated with each step the entire height, and time was growing later and later. The sun had set behind the black mountain. When we finally reached the top, we were exhausted, and it was awesome to peer down deep into the two concentric craters, the widest of which, we had read, was just over 1,000 feet in diameter, and the smaller one inside it was about half that size.

It was a warm glowing twilight, so we walked about halfway around the crater and then back and settled our blanket on the top. No one else was anywhere around. The darkening silence was intriguing, and we were not afraid, just eager to see the magical rising of the full moon. We kept looking out over the smoldering forest until we could no longer see it at all. We waited in pitch darkness, thinking perhaps clouds had covered the moon, although some stars were appearing. After an hour in total blackness, we decided we must start the return trek. We gathered blankets and water bottles and started slowly down. With no flashlights (as we had been instructed), we could not even see our boots, but the solid black rocks kept sliding downward beneath every step. Again, it was one step forward but then a half-step slide straight downward on the very steep side of the cinder cone—all in total blindness! We had once experienced a whiteout while skiing, but never had imagined a total blackout! I could barely see Bill's form ahead of me. It took about an hour to descend carefully, and *then* the full moon appeared behind the mountain. While seated, we had been facing 180 degrees in the wrong direction!

We were relieved to get into our car and start back the long gravel miles to our campsite, but Bill discerned a problem. He drove slowly past the smoking part of the forest ashes, and as soon as we were on the rough road, he stopped to figure out the problem with the flashlight we had left in the car. We had a tire going swiftly flat and nearly forty miles to drive. There was no cell phone service, so we had to bump our way back, which took over an hour and a half. But we made it, and the next day Bill changed our car tire, glad that we now always tow a car behind our RV and the flat was not an RV tire.

We now felt very well-educated about volcanoes because the year before we had been in Idaho, where we were able to walk through a lava tube, which is a tunnel formed by hot lava flowing beneath the hardened surface of the lava flow during a volcanic eruption. The lava tube empties and leaves a cave, and we had found these fun to explore. We had been fortunate to discover the Shoshone Ice Caves in Southern Idaho, which are in a huge lava tube frozen with ice year-round. Geologists know this area as one of the earth's natural wonders, and visitors descend 100 feet beneath lava on guided tours every thirty minutes through a world of volcanic wonders and ice, about 1,700 feet long, 50 feet wide, and 45 feet high.

We Enjoy Car Races

A

NOTHER SUMMER, WE ventured to Portland, Oregon, to attend the IndyCar Series race with a friend who had arranged passes for us to meet a driver who was his friend. It was a fun day, and I learned about Indy cars and spoke to some of the drivers, and Bill, a longtime racing fan, was having the time of his life.

A few years before this, when our children were still young, I was assigned to write a magazine article about the first Formula 1 race ever to be in Dallas, Texas. I had never been to a car race, and we were all excited since this race featured famous international drivers. It was at Fair Park, where a special asphalt racetrack was designated for this big event in midsummer. When I went to the press pass desk, I was quite puzzled because I was given our passes with no questions, but two journalists from very high-profile magazines in line next to me were turned away. When I related to Bill what had happened, he immediately knew.

He said, "Your syndicated newspaper column is called *Formulas for Fun*! They must have assumed you are a Formula 1 race car journalist!"

We both laughed at the wonderful mistake because my weekly newspaper feature was about fun things for parents to do with children!

But this event turned out to be exactly that: our family loved it! One of the top TV shows at that time was *Dallas*, and our family watched it frequently. We were just leaving the Fair Park Formula 1 race stands near the track when a helicopter landed, and out stepped the cast of *Dallas*, and *they* took *our* pictures! Our children were ecstatic! But alas, my article was never published because in the Texas summer heat, the track started to crumble, finally ending the race and the dream of having any more car races there. But that *vroom! vroom!* of the motors got into my blood and I became a car race enthusiast also. It was twenty-five years later when we were able to take our grandson to a NASCAR race at the Texas Motor Speedway.

*****

When our grandson Nicolas was three years old, Bill grew tired of playing on the floor with him and said, "Get on my lap and let's watch these cars on TV going around the track. You choose whether the M&M car or the car with fire painted on the side will win."

From that day on, Nicolas was hooked on NASCAR! He chose the driver Jeff Gordon as his favorite and watched many Sunday-afternoon races with his dad. By the time he could read, he sub-scribed to racing magazines and memorized the statistics on many races and drivers, but he always remained faithful to Gordon. When Nick was twelve, I was able to interest several magazines in an article about this young NASCAR fan who idolized Jeff Gordon, the num-ber 1 favorite of thousands of fans. His mother flew to Dallas with Nicolas, and I got permission for press passes to be waiting for us, as well as an interview appointment with Gordon.

On race day, it took two hours in the heavy traffic to arrive at the track and get to the line for our passes. When we arrived at the press desk, the lady in charge looked us over and immediately asked how old Nicolas was.

I replied, "Twelve."

She said, "He cannot have a garage or hot pass. No one under eighteen is allowed in these areas at NASCAR races."

I responded, "But I have an appointment for Jeff Gordon to talk to him, and five magazines want this article about his dedicated young fan!"

She said, "I'm, sorry ma'am, but only the president of NASCAR could okay a pass for him. And besides that, full shoes and long pants are required attire, and he has on shorts and flip-flops."

I asked, "Where is the president of NASCAR? I am going to talk to him!"

"He is in a tent at the back of the lot. Here is your pass."

I instructed Pamela and Bill to find the right clothing for Nicolas because I was *not* going to allow his disappointment, nor fail to arrive with him for our interview with Jeff Gordon! I left them, and Pamela squeezed Nicolas into her own tennis shoes, while Bill got his own black rain pants from the car trunk and belted them around Nicolas's waist and rolled up the legs to fit, so he met the dress code requirements for spectators.

At the tent where I found the NASCAR president, I explained the situation to him, and he was only too happy to write a note granting Nicolas's permission to enter and to have garage and hot pit passes, so he could get close to the track while the race was in progress. I was glad that when I was a graduate student in journalism class, I had been taught to be persistent but always polite. I quickly returned to our family with the good news and gave the note to the astonished lady at the desk, who promptly gave Nick his official credentials.

It was fun to take Nicolas to the garage, where he talked knowledgeably to the workers, some of whom he knew by face and name from the many magazine articles he had read. He knew all about the makes and types of cars and even recognized some of the owners and made conversations with them. This immensely helped me in my article research and yielded great photos.

Our appointment with Gordon was at 2:00 p.m. to meet him at his trailer after his qualifying race for pole position. We arrived there at 1:00 p.m., and a crowd of autograph seekers were already gathering. I instructed Pamela and Bill, each with a camera, that they *must* get good photos of Nicolas with Jeff because the interview would not last long. Nicolas and I were close to the entrance of Gordon's trailer when Nick looked up and said, "Oh no! We are not going to get the interview because there comes Jeff, and he does not look happy. I guess he did not qualify well."

I said, "Nicolas, I interviewed Jeff yesterday, so we may not get the interview today, but we *must* get a picture of you with him, and you *must* get his autograph on that beautiful Gordon jacket you worked so hard to pay for. Here's what we'll do: You take this permanent-ink felt-tipped pen and stand in front of me, and when Jeff arrives, you hand it to him with the jacket. I am in front of his trailer door, and he cannot get in until he gives you that autograph, and we get the photo. He knows to expect us here."

Nicolas agreed. Pamela and Bill tried to fade into the crowd, but I sternly dared them not to fail in the photo assignment.

We were successful! The photos of Jeff giving Nick the autograph were terrific, and I got my article, even though the interview did not happen. Nicolas was elated, and his autographed jacket hung proudly on his wall for years!

Bill and I loved seeing the many grand RVs that the race-car drivers own and often live in for privacy at races. The tracks offer excellent accommodations for these RVs, and we could not go behind the fence to see them up close. But it seemed to raise the level of RV reputation higher than road rats, as some people we know had thought of our chosen vacation style.

It was a misty, rainy morning, and I wore a long black raincoat with a black hood since I'm cold natured. Nicolas was at first embarrassed by my attire because in the past, he had teased me by saying I look like the Grim Reaper in it. However, as we showed passes at various racetrack gates, we became memorable. Soon we were no longer questioned, and he was the only child able to go into the garage area! He sensed that he was being closely watched by many officials, and he conducted himself very maturely.

Years later, Nicolas achieved his dream and was hired by NASCAR; ironically, his job was to certify the special passes. When he gained confidence and experience, he related to his boss the experience he had as a twelve-year-old. After working for NASCAR a few years, Nicolas was talking to the president of NASCAR at one of the races and asked, "Why and when did you lower the eighteen-year-old requirement and allow younger fans to come to the races?"

The president told him that years before, they had carefully observed a young man who came with his grandmother, who was a journalist. The boy had conducted himself so well, it led the officials to reconsider the age limit.

Nicolas asked, "Did that grandmother have on a long black hooded coat?"

The president said, "Yes."

Nicolas replied with a grin, "I was that little boy!"

Train Lovers' Delight

O N SOME OF our many trips across Tennessee, we have discovered excellent places worth the problem of finding a place to park an RV. One of these is in Jackson, where conveniently the parking lot will accommodate RVs and big rig trucks in a dusty side parking area of the Casey Jones Home and Railroad Museum. It is located next to the birthplace of Jones, the engineer immortalized in "The Ballad of Casey Jones," which many children learn to sing on the playground. Jones was an engineer in the late 1800s for the Illinois Central Railroad and ran the passenger service from Memphis, Tennessee, to Canton, Mississippi. He was known for being exceptionally punctual, keeping the railroad schedule perfect.

However, on April 29, 1900, he had to do a double shift because a scheduled engineer failed to come for the day's run. He was tired when it was time for his own shift, leaving Memphis about midnight. Due to the absent man for whom Casey was filling in, the night train for Canton was over an hour late in departing. Jones knew he could make up for lost time and arrive nearly on schedule because the engine number 382, known as the Cannonball, was so fast as to be immortalized in the song. But when he rounded a bend in the track approaching Vaughn, he was unaware that another train had broken down directly in front of him. Jones's unbelievably skilled maneuver to stop his train just in time saved all the passengers. But the effort cost him his life at only thirty-seven years of age and father of three children. The film at the museum told the story and enlightened us about the railways in the USA.

The museum is any train lover's dream. Examples and stories of so many different types of railroad cars and history through the years were fascinating, and the director added much to the tour of anyone who asked. We had our photo made beside the thirty-five-ton locomotive, which is similar to Jones's train. Souvenirs of every kind of train or items used on a railroad are treasures for many adults or children to purchase. We enjoyed visiting the Jones's home, with its lovely Victorian decor.

At Brooks Shaw's Old Country Store in Casey Jones Village, we enjoyed one of the best meals ever on our travels. The Southern homestyle country buffet included Southern fried chicken, collard greens, mac and cheese, catfish, and much more, so we try to time every trip through Tennessee to be there at mealtime. Not only is the buffet delicious, but also the old-timey soda fountain with root beer floats, banana splits, and sundaes. This country store is a step back in time, with bulk candies in wooden kegs and other fun things for sale in this replica of historic general merchandise stores, which were mainstays of every town a century ago. Of course, when we left, we were so full we decided to spend the night in the parking lot in our snug RV.

Looking for
Country Stars

MOVING ON TO the Arkansas side of the Mississippi River, we found the special Tom Sawyer RV Park, where we have since spent many lazy, restful days and nights watching barges and tugboats slowly travel up and down this water highway. For restrooms and the laundromat, the RV park has rustic-looking wood buildings on stilts, reminiscent of the kind Tom Sawyer and Huck Finn would have called home (although modern facilities are within). There is even a tree-house cabin and many artistic innovative yard decorations, benches, and other clever items that might have been lifted directly from Mark Twain's descriptions. Safely on her leash, our little dog loves to roam on the flat grassy open land beside the river and sniff the tiny water-borne flora and fauna that sometimes drift ashore. A fishing pond parallels the river, for anyone who wishes to cast a line.

On another RV trip through Tennessee, we took our niece Bryann, who had just graduated from the University of South Carolina as a music major in the LIFE program. She loves country music, which is also one of our favorite genres, so she helped select where we should stop. On our first night near the Mississippi River, we thankfully missed a tornado, which we saw pass over the area without touching down. In Memphis for a few days, we wanted to enjoy the famous Beale Street, home of blues, rock and roll, and soul music, brought to town by slaves, who moved from plantations to settle there after the emancipation.

At midday, we strolled in and out of the restaurants and bars where open doors let the haunting strains of vocal and instrumental music float out to beckon us. At lunchtime, we entered B. B. King's Blues Club to hear a choir concert of young black singers. The music was not only beautiful, but also the choir of young adults was very well-trained. We asked about the choir when we met their director, Jeff Kollath, who was seated near us at the bar. We learned he teaches at the Stax Music Academy where mainly at-risk youth, who might not ever have been able to develop their talents and love of music, receive a well-mentored music education. The Soulsville Charter School in the same campus prepares these students with a solid, well-rounded education to help them be ready for college opportunities.

Mr. Kollath was so kind to our niece, and he was quite perceptive of her talent and love of music. It was evident from Bryann's questions that as a musician herself, she felt keen interest and empathy for others who might not have had access to what they loved. He invited her to apply to be an instructor for their summer music program. We saw how attuned he was to the youth and those who could become great musicians if they had a good, free music education. He was a compassionate school administrator and a great man who cared about children of few opportunities and helped them develop their natural talents. We have often wondered how many musicians he has helped develop. The Stax Museum nearby is one of only a small number of museums in the world dedicated to soul music and contains the legacy of Stax Records. We all had fun there learning about the historic recording studio, which began in an old theater in South Memphis in the 1950s. So many greats were discovered and recorded at Stax under several different record labels.

Then we found Sun Studio, where Elvis Presley was first discovered and recorded just after he graduated high school in 1953. He had gone to Sun to record two of his songs as a gift for his mother: "My Happiness" and "That's When Your Heartaches Begin." There at Sun, rock and roll, country music, and rockabilly music were recorded throughout the 1950s. Our tour there was fascinating. We saw all the old instruments in the tiny recording room, where Presley, Johnny Cash, Carl Perkins, and Jerry Lee Lewis, dubbed by the local newspaper "Million Dollar Quartet," had an impromptu jam session. Bryann was thrilled to be able to sing a few bars on the same microphone used by Elvis Presley to record his early songs there. This museum has thousands of important, priceless pieces of memorabilia from mid-twentieth-century musicians.

Our next stop was the KOA in Music Valley of Nashville, home of *Country Music Hall of Fame* and the *Grand Ole' Opry*. Across the South, people are known for their warm hospitality, and we all found that to be generous in Nashville. Bryann had her photo taken with a guitar and microphone at the photo booth of the visitor center. We all were fascinated with the many large glass cases of costumes of performers deemed worthy of this Hall of Fame. Bryann's favorite singers at the time were Carrie Underwood, Luke Bryan, and Brad Paisley. She was hoping for an autograph if we should pass one of them on the street. In a large hotel on Music Row, we saw a group of four people enjoying dinner. Bryann was sure one of the men was Brad, so with my permission, she approached him with a pen and paper, but up close she realized, from the questioning look on his face, that he was not Brad but perhaps his doppelganger. We were both embarrassed and quickly exited the hotel.

We had press writer permits to go to Bluebird Cafe, which was so small we had to stand in line for two hours in the hot afternoon sun hoping there would still be room for us when the doors opened. Bryann was thrilled when we were admitted, as it was a special place where many new musicians had been discovered and later enjoyed great promotion and fame. Herself a singer and pianist, she had dreams of someday being discovered here. Her knowledge of country music was encyclopedic. She did not perform but with joy absorbed each piece of the music presented, and she talked to several of the newbie performers afterward.

That night we had tickets for the Grand Ole Opry at the iconic Ryman Auditorium. We loved every minute of the down-home country performance, and often we stood and sang with the professionals, as the audience was encouraged to do. Afterward, we joined the backstage tour, and it was fun to see the dressing rooms and mail-boxes of so many stars. One of the female performers took Bryann under her wing and gave her some special insights backstage that normally visitors did not get to enjoy. It was a great last stay in this trip across Tennessee, and we returned our young lady to her family and home in Saluda, North Carolina, with stars in her eyes and dreams in her heart.

Again and Again to Tennessee

O N THE WAY home, we detoured through Pigeon Forge, Tennessee, which holds a special memory for me. The visitor center invited me to my first press trip. I had been a published author and journalist for years, but after my first two books were published in the 1980s and the publishing industry hit a low with the introduction of the World Wide Web in the 1990s, I only got rejections for my new manuscript submissions, which released my tears. In 1999, for my birthday, Bill gave me a new computer, which had a little magic button that said, "Publish your own work."

We had just returned from a trip, so I wrote about it and hit the Publish button, and there it was on the World Wide Web. I didn't understand cyberspace and had no idea where my published work was being seen, but this new computer with its magic button was like giving a drunk a liquor store! I was so excited I showed my neighbor, who said, "That's great! If you ask other people to write about their trips, you will have a magazine." And so, I did.

I studied everything I could find to learn more about HTML, email, links, key words, and so much more. At that time, there were no similar e-zines on the Web. Mine, www.RealTravelAdventures. com, was unique in that I did not sell anything nor advertise any products. Soon I invited other writers to send me their articles for publication. Pigeon Forge and other visitor centers discovered our e-zine and invited us to come write about their places. As subscribers and links grew, my travel e-zine had thousands of followers and moved to the top place on search engines for travel. And this resulted in our enhanced world travel life, not only by RV (still our favorite) but also by car, train, plane, ship, bus, and on foot.

*****

Pigeon Forge, Tennessee, is a quaint little town in the Blue Ridge Mountains and the home of Dollywood, Dolly Parton's wonderful country theme park. All the rides, stories, crafts, shows, and hotels have the down-home welcome feel that Dolly's music conveys. The rides are super fun, especially the exciting Barnstormer swing, on which we were lifted high up at forty-five miles per hour on a 230-degree rotation of heart-thumping fun to top a barn, which we felt like our toes would scrape. I was not brave enough to ride the Lightning Rod, which is a roller coaster that goes forty-five miles per hour and up twenty stories high.

There were so many fun rides from which to choose, but I love to make things, so I spent hours at the Craftsman's Valley watching talented East Tennessee artists create useful items, which Appalachian locals have been making for centuries to use in their homes. Of course, modern tools and materials have made the tasks easier while keeping the traditional skills and history alive. I tried my hands at candle making, watched the blacksmith, carved some wood, bought handmade soaps, and copied recipes in the excellent country restaurants with down-home cooking. The shows were numerous, and the one I found most fascinating was the bubble blowing, in which we watched the bubble master create imaginative figures and cluster designs by blowing the soapy mixture in a variety of skilled ways.

Soon I planned our RV trip back to Pigeon Forge and Gatlinburg to show Bill all the great places I had learned and written about. We were drawn to the beautiful thickly forested Great Smoky Mountains National Park. Our guide from A Walk in the Woods was very knowledgeable of her local flora and fauna and delighted in sharing the information about so many species as we walked through the pathways of ferns and little white flowers awakening after the winter's dormancy. The largest poplar tree in the world is a strictly kept secret, and only a few park rangers know where it is, so we did not see that but felt privileged to see the historic log cabin of the John Oliver family, early pioneers of the Cades Cove area.

When I was a child growing up about two hours from there, my family came each year for a weekend in autumn to thrill at the beautiful colored leaves, and I especially remember the little restaurants that featured yummy pancakes with mountain-made syrup. Gatlinburg was our favorite little sleepy mountain village, but how it had changed in about four decades! It is still a wonderful mountain location with so many attractions, but the traffic on the only main road, which also traverses Pigeon Forge and Sevierville, is a nightmare of long-stop-and-brief-go traffic. But some things are worth waiting for. We were looking for the little pancake house I remembered but found instead Crockett's Breakfast Camp, well-named because we had to "camp out" in a long line to get a table. The enormous and delicious breakfast kept us going all day, and we even brought the huge cinnamon rolls back to our RV.

We found several locally owned RV parks in this popular area of Tennessee, and we camped beside a stream for the destination wedding of our nephew at the little Wedding Chapel in the Glades. It was a perfect setting for the vows, and the bride and groom spent their honeymoon in a beautiful little mountain cabin.

Later we drove to Knoxville. I had been to the impressive zoo there. But this time, we were witness to a heartbreaking scene. A baby elephant had recently been weaned from its mother and placed in a fenced area next to her habitat, but they could not be together. We watched as the baby elephant reached his trunk through the wire fence to be able to barely touch his mom's leg. With tears rolling from her eyes, the mother reached over the tall fence with her long trunk and stroked her baby! In the past, I had read a book about Africa, which stated that elephants truly do have tear ducts beside their eyes, and tears of distress can be seen when an elephant feels threatened. As a mother myself, I felt such sorrow for that mama elephant as her baby was moved away.

The next time I returned to Gatlinburg and Pigeon Forge was in December for a four-generation girls' weekend. Bill was not invited, so taking the RV was out of the question. I do not like driving other people through mountains (and as it turned out, in the rain), but my niece volunteered, and then the day before we left home, she broke her gas pedal foot! But her doc agreed she could drive safely with her boot cast, and she insisted we not cancel the trip because her eight-year-old daughter would celebrate her birthday there at Dollywood. All of us were eager and excited to have the weekend together, and we arrived in time for the Country Tonite's Smoky Mountain Christmas performance at Pigeon Forge. We only had time to leave our suitcases in the motel I had reserved online, the last room I could find anywhere in the area for that holiday weekend (also one of the cheapest). We had a fun evening really getting into the spirit of Christmas and returned to the motel singing carols and giggling.

Our room was the last one on the bottom floor and next to a dark vacant gravel area with large trash receptacles and backed by woods. None of us mentioned the creepy possibilities that vacant area held, but we were quite dismayed to learn we could simply push our locked door open at the sidewalk without using our key! I was embarrassed since I had booked the room, but no one voiced dismay and alarm; however, our driver, with cast on her foot, placed a chair and all our luggage against our door, then she took her sanitizing spray and towelettes and cleaned all surfaces, while the eight-year-old called loudly from the bathroom, "Oooh! Hair and smushed candy and chewing gum are on the floor in here!"

We were afraid to pull back the worn bedspreads, but no crawly things were evident, and our hero driver had brought bedbug spray! If we had found any of those monsters, we didn't know what we would have done in the heavy rain at nearly midnight with no more rooms available in the entire area and three hours of winding mountainous highway between us and home. We had a good laugh about our situation, and we were so tired we fell to sleep right away, wishing for my comfortable RV!

Limping around Dollywood in the cold rain was not anyone's choice of fun, but we refused to disappoint the birthday girl, so we pulled on raincoats, grabbed umbrellas and water bottles, and we had a glorious day getting into the Christmas spirit, although it was just before Thanksgiving. At night in the dark, we took a ride on the Dollywood Express, the coal-fired, steam-powered locomotive train. At each curve in the track, we could look out to see the other rail cars passing through Dollywood shining with thousands of colored lights for the festive season. We got home safely the next day with many tales to tell and the broken foot to heal.

Close Encounters...
I *Wish!*

ALONG UTAH STATE Route 211, we were delighted to find Newspaper Rock State Historic Monument in Indian Creek State Park, twenty miles south of Canyonlands. We hiked to see the ancient boulders and were fascinated as we stood in wonderment studying the hundreds of petroglyphs on one of the largest, best-preserved, and most easily accessible petroglyph sites in the world. In 1976, this incredible site was added to the National Register of Historic Places. This two-hundred-square-foot rock is a large sandstone cliff with hundreds of carved primitive pictures of people and animals.

During our explorations of the southwestern part of the United States, we have pondered many petroglyphs from *Anasazi*, the prehistoric Native Americans. For many years, ever since the movies *ET* and *Close Encounters of the Third Kind*, my hobby had been reading articles and watching TV programs about alien beings from outer space. I interpreted many of these pictographs and petroglyphs as documented proof of aliens descending to this land from spaceships in the sky, some flying saucers with lightning or fire emitted, and other shapes with wings. The large humanoid figures in the carvings are clearly shown in helmets and what could be interpreted as the space suits we see depicted today. Although no one knows for sure what these petroglyph stories are telling, I, along with thousands of other people who have been to these places, could not help interpreting many petroglyphs as the history of aliens coming to earth in eons past. My family all tease me about my favorite

TV show, *Ancient Aliens*, which shows archeological finds around the world. The narrator tells the archeologists' interpretation of the sites and then asks, "What if these were created by aliens?"

Of course, as we were driving through Nevada, I *had* to go in search of some aliens on the officially named Extraterrestrial Highway, State Route 375. Bill chuckled as he drove us along. The first thing I spotted, which really spooked me in a delightful way, was a sudden and mysterious whirling activity that began on the flat red sandy field dotted with cacti. It began on the ground and grew skyward, furiously spinning red dust like a tornado. Had it come from above and gone downward, I would have been certain it was from an invisible alien being. But Bill, who grew up in a desert in Texas, laughed at my excited fear and said, "That's just a *dust devil*. It's like a tornado of sand caused by the wind."

My mind comprehended, but my imagination was disappointed. After all, we were traveling Nevada State Route 375, officially named "Extraterrestrial Highway," where countless numbers of people have reported hundreds of sightings of unidentified flying objects.

Soon we were passing a very, very high fence that ran for miles with signs warning severely Keep Out! It was the Nevada Test and Training Range, and in the far distance, we could see buildings that are part of the infamous Area 51, purported to have a hangar that contains the remains of a spacecraft that crashed near here in the past. Although the United States did not admit until 2013 that Area 51 even truly existed, stories persist that those aliens, rescued alive from a spaceship, work there and helped advance our NASA space program far more rapidly than would otherwise have been accomplished. I wanted to climb the enormous fence and to see the hangar, but of course, that was just a pipe dream! I had seen photographs of one of the buildings in Area 51 that has an enormous statue of an alien creature and an official sign, Alien Research Center!

Instead, Bill pulled into the parking lot of the Little A'Le' Inn, a small inn with a unique cafe and bar where we had a sandwich and spent several fascinating hours studying the many newspapers and magazines and photos of sightings. Also, there were news articles, especially those about the spacecraft that crashed into the desert in 1947 near Roswell, New Mexico. I told Bill I *had* to go there. Along the Extraterrestrial Highway, I kept my eyes peeled, but we did not have any stupendous sightings. We could not stay overnight in this magical place where dry air and no light pollution made perfect viewing of starry heavens. There is only one town of fifty people within about a hundred miles of this straight stretch of lonely highway, which averages only two hundred cars a day.

When we drove through New Mexico, my dear driver did take me to Roswell, and we went through the fascinating little local museum that featured many reports about the spaceship crash there in 1947. The surgical operation on an alien depicted with mannequin doctors and nurses was in a large display behind glass as we entered the museum. It was just for fun but was almost real looking, if hokey! After a while, Bill decided to return to the RV to read while I took my time studying all the photos, drawings, and testimonies of sightings by famous people, including US presidents and astronauts.

To me, the most convincing story in the museum was the handwritten report made by the coroner who was called to bring child-sized caskets to the place of the crash in 1947 to take the bodies of the "alien beings." There was the report of a nurse who was witness at the medical treatment and operation on the "alien" who survived the crash. I was hooked to read more and more about this exciting subject, which captured millions of imaginations and sparked reports of real sightings around the world. I *knew* similar sightings were what the ancient petroglyphs I saw in Utah were reporting!

Our first RV visit to Roswell, New Mexico, was in the 1990s, and we have returned several times. In 2021 we discovered the little museum describing the crash of 1947 has been transformed into a large, very modern International UFO Museum and Research Center, to which thousands come for a UFOlogist convention each July. The displays now are state of the art, with history from many countries of actual sightings and encounters of first, second, and third, and fourth kinds displayed in many ways. There are touch-screen features, and the most fun is a display in the center of the large museum with the spaceship landing and blinking with moving alien space creatures. The official testimonies in the library there are very convincing. And it was a fun stop on our travels.

Driving through Memory Lane

A FEW YEARS LATER, we took Bill's trip down memory lane through Texas and New Mexico for me to hear the fun stories of his childhood. We traveled Highway I-40 through Texas, and just before the New Mexico border, we came to a friend's huge ranch, where Bill spent many teenage weeks riding horses across the flat plateau with hundreds of thorny mesquite trees and rattlesnakes. He explained that leather chaps cowboys wear are necessary to cover blue-jean legs to protect from the thorns of the trees and cacti. Bill loved staying in the plain concrete block ranch house, drinking water from the windmill-pumped tank, helping "cowboy" roundups, and branding and working cattle.

I had ridden a horse only a few times in my life. The horses at this ranch knew the terrain well, and it was a good thing because when we stayed there once, I was enjoying riding along this flat plain with our six-year-old Tommy on his horse. Our horses suddenly stopped still and refused to budge. We looked a short distance ahead and saw the deep cliff we knew nothing about, but these horses knew, and they were not about to attempt that death dive.

Every time we visited James at this ranch in the desert, it rained, and we were in our RV and sometimes got stranded until the flash flood would clear. James said he wanted us to come often because in this dry land, they always needed the rain, which we seemed to bring. Often as we passed through flat desert lands in the Southwest, we loved seeing sudden huge rain clouds, perhaps twenty miles distant, burst to a torrent of rain and watching the heavy gray downpour move slowly across the vast landscape. It was truly the land of the big sky. With no trees for scores of miles, the sky touches the earth like an enormous inverted bowl. Cloud formations, sunrises and sunsets, and cool starry nights are magnificent!

All the children adored James and thought this ranch was fun to experience, so very different from ours, which had trees, grass, and gardens in East Texas. James and Bill took Blake one day across the very rough terrain, and as they bumped along Blake fell asleep sitting upright in the front middle seat of the Chevy pickup. It was a very hot day in the desert sun.

When Blake awoke, he asked, "James, why don't you have a radio and air-conditioning in this truck?"

James, who could have well afforded those items that Blake considered necessities, laughed and responded, "You see over there my employees who work this land? When I get a new truck, they get this one to use when they are working. How many hours of a work-day do you think they would spend listening to the radio in the cool if my truck had those things?"

Our children loved searching the ranch ground for arrowheads and other treasures left behind a century before, with Pamela, the oldest and the one who was responsible for the other two, carefully watching for rattlesnakes. She was thrilled when she found a large rattle that had either broken off the snake or been shed. Many years later, she proudly keeps this real souvenir of fun RV trips there.

Since the forty-five-square-miles of James's ranch was seven miles from the highway, and his western property line was the border of Texas and New Mexico, he loved to tell the story of the time he had to house an outlaw who was trying to make it across that border so the Texas Rangers would not find him. James was rounding up cattle in the upper part of the ranch, and a man came walking toward him from the highway. James's wife, Betty, was waiting in a pickup truck, and the man came to her. James knew something was wrong, so he told the man to get into the back of the truck and drove him to the New Mexico border and let him out to protect Betty. Later they learned the man had robbed a small store and shot the manager and was trying to escape, but James could never find out any more about the incident.

Cloudcroft Memories

WHENEVER OUR FAMILY entered New Mexico in our RV all of us wanted to see Cloudcroft, where Bill and his family had spent many happy summers. Our kids loved hearing stories of their dad's childhood in this area. No one had home air-conditioning in those days, and the Midlanders liked to rent houses in this mountain town where it was naturally cool all year. Bill's mother and her four other friends and all the children went to spend the summer at the mountain house during the weeks, and the dads came for weekends.

One day the women were playing a game, and the children were entertaining themselves in other rooms. The three young teens, Bill, Andy, and Tevis, went outside, and the women thought nothing of it until Bill's mom smelled smoke. She quietly came out and saw smoke rising through the wooden staircase and peered down at the three boys hiding below to smoke a cigarette, feeling very big. Instead of scolding them, she wisely went back inside. The boys thought they were in the clear, so they snuffed the cigarettes, hid their evidence, went back inside acting innocent.

Later, Mrs. Neely said, "Boys, let's go get milkshakes at the drugstore."

They were happy, anticipating the treat on that summer day. They all enjoyed the large chocolate milkshakes, and on the way back to the cabin, they returned Andy to the one his family was in. But upon reaching their cabin, Bill and Tevis began to feel ill. Their stomachs rebelled, and they began throwing up! (Of course, Bill's mom knew this would happen.) Fortunately, lesson learned, Bill and Tevis never wanted to smoke again.

During the time at Cloudcroft, the boys would walk to the stables in town, where visitors rented horses for trail rides. The three teens had ranch backgrounds and some experience, so they volunteered to help the horse wrangler during these holidays just to have something to do. One day the wrangler commented on what good work the boys did and asked if their families had horses. They replied yes and then told the story Bill's dad had repeated about how he met Bill's mother. Mr. Neely loved to juggle apples for kids who visited in their home and told the tall tale that he had once been a circus juggler and had met Mrs. Neely, who was a bareback rider on the circus white horse. All the kids believed the tales.

One beautiful Cloudcroft day, Bill's mom, who was raised on a farm, volunteered to be the grown-up in charge and took all the eight children to rent horses for a trail ride. When the trail master asked what their riding skills were to determine which horses were suitable, Mrs. Neely responded, "Beginners all."

She had no idea the boys had told the trainer the bareback rider story (which was not true). The kids who were to ride the horses were ages eleven to five, and their gentle horses proved suitable, with the teen boys having slightly livelier horses. Mrs. Neely rode the horse assigned to her with the two-year-old boy sitting in the saddle in front of her.

All the children's horses went in front of Mrs. Neely so she could keep a watchful eye, but it was soon evident that her horse was very high spirited and eager to run. She was having a hard time controlling him and wondered why she had been assigned this horse because she knew there were others available. She was quite uneasy trying to control this horse while holding the toddler and watching the other children. The older boys galloped far ahead and then back several times.

Andy boasted, "We are just keeping up with everyone for you, Mrs. Neely."

Of course, they were just loving to prove themselves good riders and independent! At dinner that night Mrs. Neely was relating to the other mothers about her spirited horse and the difficulties she had, and the teenage boys began to laugh and confessed, "We told the trail master you used to ride the circus horses bareback!"

Ghost Stories and History Tales

O UR NEXT STOP for the night was at a delightful surprise
Bill had planned. We set up camp at the Alamogordo, New
Mexico, near the White Sands Proving Grounds. Bill told
the children his family and the others at Cloudcroft always loved to
bring picnic lunches here and have races rolling down the high sand
dunes. Our three kids were delighted! Bill told me he had carefully
researched this to be sure it was safe, although it was close to the place
where the atomic bombs were tested for World War II. The kids
loved running barefoot through the sand. They climbed the dunes
with sleds we rented at the visitor center and slid down the hills,
pretending they were in snow.

It was a fun afternoon and a beautiful cool evening when the
stars came out by the millions while we sat around our campfire
making s'mores. Bill told them the ghost story one of the dads had
told when he was a child at the Cloudcroft cottage: Years ago, when
children played in these huge, ancient, pure white sand dunes, giant
ghost white lizards would come up from their hiding places deep
within and chase the kids. Our children became very cautious and
occasionally squealed when they "saw" a ghost lizard.

Our last fun stop in New Mexico on that trip was for Bill to
relive with our children his fun cowboy fantasies in Lincoln, where
the notorious outlaw, Billy the Kid, was apprehended and placed
in handcuffs in the jail there. The kids were fascinated to learn that

Billy the Kid not only had their dad's name (he was "Billy" as a kid) but also *my* name, because his real name was William Bonney. What a fun coincidence when we were in this place, but we hated to be associated in any way with such an infamous wild west character. Bill and I had grown up watching cowboy TV shows: *Gene Autry, Hopalong Cassidy, Roy Rogers, The Lone Ranger,* and *Gunsmoke,* and reading books such as *Pecos Bill,* about the fabled Texas cowboy. Our children were very familiar with these also.

Blake interjected, "Remember when I was about four and loved to play with my Lone Ranger figure? We went to the state fair in our RV, and Mom had a press appointment to interview the Lone Ranger after his show there, because she knew it would thrill me. I had my paper and pen ready to get his autograph, and Mom pushed the curtain back to go for the appointment, but the Lone Ranger had forgotten about it. He had taken his mask and hat off and was just a man sitting there in a chair. I was so disappointed because he didn't look like the Lone Ranger to me!"

We chuckled, and Bill had a similar story. "When I was about six, I adored Gene Autry, who came to Midland on a promotion for his TV show. My dad was the mayor then, so we went together to meet Gene Autry's plane. I was in the backseat peering over the front seat at my favorite hero, and that cowboy never even spoke to me! I was so hurt!"

I then told my true tale: "When I was growing up, my favorite song was 'Red River Valley,' and my favorite story was *Pecos Bill,* which my grandmother read to me over and over. And when I was nineteen, I married my Pecos Bill, a real cowboy, and he moved me to his ranch on the Red River! And *that* is all true!"

In Lincoln, the little jailhouse where the Kid was handcuffed and jailed did not look very secure by today's standards, so we were not surprised to learn he had been able to slip a gun from the jailer's pocket and kill the two jailers in charge. Then he stole a horse to make his getaway. He was notorious as a member of the vigilante gang called Regulators, who fought and killed various other vigilantes over land disputes, and the Kid claimed to have killed scores of men, although only nine were documented. Finally, after eluding the law many times, the Kid was twenty-one years old when he had been camping outside Lincoln, his hometown, and slipped into Sheriff Pat Garrett's house at night to get a slice of beef. But in the dark, he surprised the sheriff, who pulled his gun and killed Billy the Kid just before his gun would have killed the sheriff.

Not for Everyone

WHEN OUR DAUGHTER'S family with children, ages three, six, and seven, came for a visit at home in Texas, we all looked forward to time at Pat Mayse Lake. Bill set up the RV at the campground there before they arrived. This would be a perfect surprise for our daughter and her husband, who seldom had getaway opportunities. We thought they would love to have a night alone in the motor home under the stars, and we knew having the grandkids at our house would be fun for everyone. When they arrived, we had lunch at home and then headed to the lake.

We launched our outboard motorboat, and the children thought fishing was great! We had a bucket of minnows in the boat, which our grandsons were delighted to play with. The preschool boys would lift a minnow from the bucket of water and squeal in glee, "I caught one!" while three-year-old Erica sat on Granddad's lap to drive the boat. When we stopped in the small cove, the little toy fishing poles were a useless novelty that the boys would dangle in the water without the minnow, but it was all fun! We persuaded them that with life jackets, they could jump into the water safely with us and paddle around, which they did, overcoming their fear of the large lake. The adults skied and took kids on the big tow raft for lots of laughter.

Arriving at the RV, the men built a campfire and roasted hot dogs on sticks and made s'mores. Little Erica ate three hot dogs, one for each of her years! Everyone had campfire tales to tell, and then we said good night and drove the kids to our home about twelve miles away, while the parents, we hoped, would have a very happy restful night alone. However, when they drove their car back to our house the next day, their tales were somewhat reminiscent of Pamela's disgust with camping when she was a college student. Eric seemed equally unenthusiastic about RV life. We did not understand why they didn't like their night alone by the lake in our very comfortable RV, but RVing is not for everyone. We and the grandchildren had had a blast!

We were not sure we could ever get Pamela to go in the RV with us again, but the next year, the children persuaded her it would be fun. So we drove our RV to New Jersey to stay in their driveway a few days and then packed Pamela and the kids in to go to see our South Carolina family at a beach house for a week. Everyone was excited! The first night we stopped at Candy Hill Campground in Winchester, Virginia. The park was decorated with candy canes, and the playground had a real red caboose the kids could play in. They loved this fun place. We drove on next day to stop in North Carolina at an antique car museum for young Nicolas, who already loved race cars. He was enthralled with the many kinds of cars.

When we reached Greenville, South Carolina, little Erica knocked on her great-grandmother's door. A very happy Honey opened it and welcomed us into her apartment at the retirement center. We spent awhile on her porch with cookies and lemonade and then walked around the duck pond, and the boys could spot little fish in the clear water. After lunch, we packed Honey into the RV also and drove all afternoon to the beach house at Harbor Island in the lower part of the state known as the Deep South.

Our daughter-in-law Beth and our other two grandchildren, Jordan and Jacob, flew in the next day, and the time on the quiet, environmentally protected beach was delightful. Bill and I slept in our RV at a campground about two miles away on the South Carolina State Park campground at Huntington Beach. The next day, my sister and her husband arrived. She is an environmentalist and teacher at a science center and came here often and could show us fun, educational outdoor things to do. We went first to the little science activity center at the South Carolina Visitor Center for Hunting Island, where we all loved watching the big alligator in his outdoor pond surrounded by thick ferns and the palmetto state trees. We took a boat ride to Monkey Island, where no one is allowed to land because it is a science research center, but we saw scores of monkeys in the trees as we circled the little island.

Returning to the house in late afternoon, we took the children on a walk in the sand down to the pond where bird viewing is rewarding. A large flock of white egrets was nesting in the trees surrounding the little pond. Thick jungle-like vegetation surrounded the pond, and we were outside the gated enclosure, thankful no kid could fall in. We looked carefully for the big turtles and more alligators known to live in this pond, and sure enough some of each did surface near us. The kids squealed in delight and a little fear.

On our final day, my brother's family arrived. He took his young daughter and our five grandchildren to the little bridge where they could try to catch crabs. We followed along to help and also to learn how to go crabbing. He gave the kids wood poles with a string attached and bated their hooks with pieces of raw chicken. (Since chicken is not on the watery habitat natural menu, I wondered how people had decided it would attract crabs!) The boys, with careful supervision, dropped their lines into the water beneath the little bridge and very quickly were pulling in big blue crabs. Alex, who loves all outdoor life, was ecstatic as Aunt Pam instructed him how to be careful not to have his fingers grabbed by the sharp pincers of the crab's legs. She showed us how to tickle the crab's under shell to soothe the animal so that he stops striking! Sure enough, Alex got to hold the peaceful crab. The youngsters continued joyfully until we had ten large crabs.

Returning to the house, we felt it was time for lunch and naps. While they slept, Uncle Jim boiled the crabs to make crab cakes for dinner, but I knew Alex would be heartbroken to know we had killed his crabs. But thankfully, when the boiled crabs were removed from the water, they had turned from blue to red, so Alex never realized these were the same ones he had played with. Jim made a delicious dinner feast, but we did not tell the kids what they were eating.

The day before, we had taken them on a horse-drawn carriage tour in Beaufort, and they saw the home of their great-great-great-great-grandparents, now on the National Register of Historic Places, beside the Broad River in Beaufort. As we were gathered around the dinner table, Honey told her great-grandchildren about their ancestors, who had owned a large plantation here two hundred years before. The kids were thrilled that even the alligators and snakes, birds, and waterways had been part of the family history.

I interjected the exciting part of the story Mother left out: "When Honey, Pam, my cousin Bettye, and I were here to look up family history, someone told us to go to Fripp Island because that was the last name of the great-great-great-great-grandfather she told you about. He was called Good William Fripp. His father, Johann Fripp, had been sent by the king of England to fight the Spanish men who were trying to take this land. Johann defeated the Spanish in a big battle, and the king gave him this land as a thank-you reward. The big sign on Fripp Island had a picture of a pirate and the words that said, 'Johann Fripp, the bloodiest pirate ever known in these parts. He saved this island for the British King.'"

The kids were so excited about having a real pirate for their great-great-great-great-great-grandfather. They could hardly sleep and couldn't wait to tell their friends at home!

We had loaded our RV with rubber rafts, sand buckets, and shovels for beach fun, and everyone played and built sandcastles. When we took three of the kids out a little way in the quiet water, it was only knee-deep on Bill and me, but the tide started coming in, and water started rising quickly. Pamela was screaming from the shore in terror that her children would drown because she could not tell we were in less than two feet of water, but we hurriedly got them all back to safety.

We hated for our week to end, and everyone had to go their separate ways. Our daughters and grandchildren flew to their homes because we were headed farther south. However, as we were driving away from the airport, I received an angry-sounding phone call from Pamela.

She asked, "Mom, how could you do that to me?"

I asked, "What?"

She told me that it was difficult enough to travel alone with three children, but the airport officials had checked all their luggage and found within Alex's little suitcase a dead moth and another pretty beetle he had wanted to keep for his nature collection. I had not known these were illegal to transport by air, nor had I realized he was trying to take them home. I apologized, and Pamela admitted they had still been permitted to board the plane. We were all thankful he had not secreted away a little sea turtle we had watched make its way to the ocean from the nest far ashore. Aunt Pam had carefully instructed him these animals are protected as an endangered species, and it was illegal for anyone to capture one.

Playing Astronauts

O N A LATER visit when we had come from Texas to the Carolinas, we took a detour to Florida. Often when Bill and I thought of a place we wanted to see, we said to each other, "Well, it's on this side of the United States, so why not?"

We did the same this time. We had always wanted to go to the Everglades, and we were now on the east side of the country, so we pointed our RV to Florida. It was a longer drive than we had estimated, and we got near Orlando and decided to make a special alternate route, stopping at Kennedy Space Center Visitor Complex on Merritt Island.

We found a nice RV park with space for us and checked in for two nights. What a thrill it was to see what the NASA program had developed in our lifetime! This was better than any theme park we had ever been to. We were able to see the engineers working on the shuttle to Mars and even ride the simulated shuttle launch experience. We loved the two giant screen IMAX films about the moon landing and other ventures into outer space and the historic rockets and so much more. Our favorite experience was to put on big gloves and use the instruments provided to experience what it is like to be in space, floating outside the spaceship and trying to put a screw in for a repair. We found it impossibly fun.

It was informative and interesting to take the bus tour throughout the working area, where engineers were building a huge rocket destined to go to Mars in the future. We wished we had been able to time our visit for an actual launch. Even though visitors see if from afar, it is an unforgettable experience, as many people told us.

Traveling farther down through Florida, we reached the northernmost part of the Everglades, having no idea that the national park RV campground was many more miles away. We found the unimaginably gorgeous Everglades Isle, a motor coach retreat restricted to Class A motor homes only, so ours was permitted. We registered for two nights at this, the most expensive we had ever booked. Everglades Isle had permanent RV pads you could buy for a half million dollars! The lighthouse visitor center and clubhouse was quite ritzy. Many of the permanent pads had barbecue pits, lanais, patios, and their own yachts tied up to their site. We felt like we were shabby guests in an RV palace! But the people there were very nice to us.

We had saved several hundred miles of driving because our reservations were at Flamingo RV Park in the south end of Everglades National Park, and we didn't want to drive that much farther. This RV park was perfect except for the loud and constant daytime noise from Captain Jack's Airboat Tours across the narrow water inlet from the RV sites. We took a narrated airboat ride all around the cove and through some of the Everglades' waters with red mangrove forest all around us. We wore the earphones provided so we could hear the excellent narration. It was fun, but I worried about the noise pollution and the detriment to the environment that these boats caused.

The dense jungle of mangrove trees had long stilt-like roots in which numerous species of wildlife hid. This network of roots provides a nursery for crustaceans and invertebrates. There was Spanish moss hanging from some of the trees, large ferns, bromeliads, and many pond lilies. We laughed when the guide told us about the "tourist trees" (gumbo limbo) in the Everglades forest, whose red bark peels, much like the sunburned tourists.

Living in the Everglades are many kinds of animals including American alligators and American crocodiles. We learned how to distinguish one from the other: crocodiles have pointed noses and visible rows of teeth. We saw parrots, lizards, turtles, and all kinds of wildlife that the captain told us about, but thankfully, we never saw the panthers, black bears, or enormous Burmese pythons, and invasive species that have taken over many of the waters of the Everglades. Several decades ago, pythons were sold as pets, but when they grew too large or people tired of them, they were released into waters that flowed into the Everglades. Some have grown to be over thirty feet long! We knew they are not venomous, but we had seen one squeeze a monkey to death and devour it when we were in South America. We did not want to topple into that water!

Boy Scout Memories

F OR YEARS, BILL had wanted to take me to Guadalupe Mountains National Park in Van Horn, Texas, so I could see where he and his Boy Scout Troop had a memorable camping trip when he was a young teen. Along with the group of boys and their two scout leaders, Bill's dad went as chaperone helper and drove an old Studebaker pickup truck carrying all the bedrolls and tents. When they arrived at the camping spot on the side of Guadalupe Mountain, Mr. Neely parked the truck facing up the incline and began helping set up camp. When he started back to unload some more items, the truck was rolling backward down the steep incline. He ran to stop it in time to save it from rolling off the ledge. Since the emergency brake did not work, he had to use rocks to chock the wheels.

That night, everyone had sleeping bags in their tents, including the scout leaders in a separate tent, but no one had thought to bring one for Mr. Neely, who spent a sleepless, uncomfortable night stretched out on the ground. Guadalupe Peak, at around 8,750 feet, is the tallest mountain in Texas and close by is El Capitan at 8,085 feet, the tenth highest peak in Texas. The next day, the boys had a great time exploring the area, and they persuaded Mr. Neely to climb to the top of Guadalupe with them (while the scout leaders stayed behind to relax in their tent). This became a favorite tale at the family table after that. It gave me a window into the childhood world in which my husband had grown up, with parents so willing to give time, energy, and money for anyone.

I had expected this place to be a Texas desert landscape, but when Bill and I arrived, I was very surprised to find streams, green grass, beautiful forests, and many wildflowers. It was lovely! We stayed in the luxury of our RV at the very nice campground there, instead of on the bare ground with or without tents. I was glad he did not want to totally relive that childhood memory! We climbed as high as we felt we should, and it was invigorating but kept us panting.

Nearby is the Permian Basin, a place where rocks of the earth's crust dropped into a fault about twenty-six million years ago and lifted and moved the Guadalupe Mountains about two miles. In those ancient times, a lake was here from 18 to 37 feet deep, but the climate became drier, and the lake disappeared. With summer rains, sometimes a very shallow lake re-forms here. Walking through these various areas of the landscape made us comprehend the powerful forces of time and wind and rain.

Later, we moved our RV to Monahans Sandhills State Park with its huge sand dunes. We camped near the Pecos River. Bill had another favorite childhood experience here that he loved to tell me and the children. He, at ten years old, and his sister, just five, were near here wading in the river and hoping to catch a minnow in their buckets while their parents set up a picnic not far away. There was an oil rig nearby, not an uncommon sight in West Texas, and the kids were not paying much attention to the work going on there. Suddenly, someone shouted, "Watch out! Here she comes!"

They felt the earth tremble and looked back. They were a little frightened, not knowing what was happening. They ran back to their parents, who explained workers had struck oil, which was about to shoot up from the ground. Then it came—the gusher of legends! They all watched in awe as the black oil shot high in the air while the men on the rig scrambled to close the valve. Other men saw an oncoming truck in the distance and ran toward it, waving and demanding it to stop because the friction of it could ignite a raging fire in the oil rig. What an exciting picnic they had with this show in progress!

Chopra and Chocolate

WE WERE HEADING west again and wanted to stop in Las Vegas, where we had been invited to come as travel journalists to write about the new plans the city had to bring more tourism there. We eagerly anticipated hearing the keynote speaker for the convention, one of our favorite writers, Deepak Chopra. We drove our RV and stayed again in Oasis RV Park, so aptly named for its lush environment in the middle of this sparse desert landscape. At this time in Las Vegas, homeowners were given the incentive of high pay to dig up grassy lawns and replace them with landscape gravel to preserve water, which was at great shortage at that time of drought.

We had tickets to go to the Blue Man Group performance on our arrival night, but first we were invited to the governor's reception. We had thought that would be quite boring, so we just intended to stay about fifteen minutes and leave in time to have dinner and make the performance. But we had not thought about *where* we were! The reception was at Caesars Palace, and everyone was dressed to the nines. We were greeted warmly at the entrance to the ballroom by George Burns, who shook our hands and invited us in.

Puzzled, I asked, "But aren't you *dead*?"

He laughed and shook his head, and we moved on. His costume and makeup, even up close, were completely convincing! Of course, show business thrives there. Anyone can be anyone!

The food was a large buffet instead of just drinks and chips, as we had thought. I wanted to eat quickly, so we wouldn't be in a long line and could leave after our buffet. I got a plate while Bill, who is the photographer for our articles, wandered to the back of the long ballroom to take pictures. I sat down with my plate of elaborate and sumptuous food to reserve our table and just glanced at one of the large decorations beside us: a huge golden claw-foot bathtub.

I thought, *That's an odd decoration*, but I was too short to see over the top of the tub and gave it no more notice.

Bill returned and sat down with his plate of food and was exploding with laughter over what I missed at the back of the room. On each of many pedestals around the room, I had noticed the colorful decorations. From the distance, we had thought they were bouquets of flowers.

"No!" Bill said breathlessly. "They are completely nude live women painted to look like different kinds of animals like tigers, etc."

Well, we *were* in Vegas! Then Bill pointed for me to look up as his eyes nearly bugged out of his head. A very tall man dressed as Caesar in his toga began pouring pitchers of melted chocolate over the nude woman casually seated in the big tub! We could not believe we had to leave this show to go to the next one!

Although no one in the Blue Man Group was nude, the show was so fun. Since we were representatives of the press, we were given front-row seats and supplied with raincoats! We didn't know why, but the raincoats proved necessary, as paint was sometimes squirted from the stage. The show was fantastic! The Blue Men, with painted blue hands and faces, made funny facial expressions as they pantomimed silliness and played amazing percussion music on PVC pipes!

The next day we attended the Chopra lecture, and I was thrilled to meet him in person at the small press conference that followed. I had read so many of his books and followed his teachings for years, and no other journalists there seemed to know his work. I gave him my card listing the places my articles were published and thanked him for his writing, which had greatly inspired me. When we were leaving

Las Vegas, I told Bill how much I wished I could sometime go to the Chopra Center in Carlsbad, California, to one of his workshops.

A few weeks later, back in our Texas home one afternoon, I was on the phone with my sister. I was again telling her about the inspiring talk Chopra had given in Vegas and expressing my hope that I could go to one of his retreats someday, and my doorbell rang. I asked Sis to wait while I answered the door. It was a special delivery letter, and when I opened it I almost fainted! It was a personal invitation from Deepak Chopra to come for a week to his Carlsbad Center to write about the spa/retreat/educational work there! Genie? Guardian Angel? Fairy godmother? My wish was granted!

Playing beside the Pacific

WE DROVE OUR trusty RV again to California so that we could be with our children and grandchildren in Los Angeles before Bill and I journeyed down the coast for him to leave me at the Chopra Center. Our kids introduced us to the terrific paved walkway along the beach from Malibu to Venice Beach and farther. We rented roller blades, bikes, and the kids had their own little three-wheelers. It was our first time to see Venice Beach, and we were astounded at the talent of the graffiti artist, whom we and many others watched as he illegally spray-painted an intricate picture on the sidewalk. The picture was so pretty, we all crossed our fingers that he would not be arrested.

This was all a part of the Los Angeles area scene on a weekend afternoon! No other place in the world was like it! The stimulating exercise along the sidewalk with the Pacific Ocean waves on one side and the numerous shops and restaurants on the other was so entertaining we wanted to repeat it each time we returned to Los Angeles. At Santa Monica's wide sandy beach, we stopped for the kids to build sandcastles and play in the cold water before we made our way back to the parking lot.

Later when we were there at Christmastime, the park by the beach in the city of Santa Monica had a quite large homeless community gathered. They seemed peaceful, and we could understand why they had chosen this warm climate in which to congregate, although this was a big problem for the city. A little farther up the sidewalk, we enjoyed the life-sized figures in several dioramas depicting the Bible story of the birth of Jesus. The displays were stunningly real looking.

We find the Pacific Ocean too cold for us at any time of year, but not for our little elementary-age grands. We thought we could count the chill bumps on the kids' arms as they ran into the water to ride little boogie boards on their stomachs. We walked with them a bit farther down the beach, and the kids begged to stop so they could have a sword fight with treasures they had spotted. We watched as they delightedly picked up the huge green slimy-looking sea things that were washing onto the shore in great numbers. They told us these new playthings were kelp from an underwater kelp forest far from the shore, growing deep within the ocean. We watched as their little imaginations turned these tall stalks into swords, then building pieces for a tent, ticklers, and finally floats, which refused to go out with the waves but kept coming back. What an education we gained from our little ones since we live in midcontinent, nowhere near an ocean. We had never seen kelp and were quite impressed they could name it and tell us where it grew.

On that visit, we were staying near the beach at one of our favorite RV parks. We so hoped the two grandchildren would spend a few nights with us and learn firsthand the joys we had in RV life. But our son and daughter-in-law would not permit it. We were so disappointed and asked why. There had been a recent report of a big drug arrest within that RV park, of which we were totally unaware. We were glad our children were being so careful, and after that trip, we did not stay at that place again.

Various Kinds of Overnights

BEING PART-TIME NOMADS has opened our eyes to many ways of living and many kinds of people. We have learned not ever to judge a book by its cover! Experiences with people vary from terrific to scary, and it does not matter how swanky or how run-down a place to park our RV is. What we have learned is that a lighted, guarded place to sleep overnight in an RV is, by far, the safest choice! Walmarts and other big box stores have lighted parking lots that are large enough to park easily. Usually this is permitted, and these lots are guarded by security people driving through or by video. But we prefer not to be the only RV in the lot. It feels like there is safety in numbers, or at least other people in RVs or semitrucks nearby who understand the predicaments that can occur during long or brief stays.

Once when we were traveling through the crowded East Coast, we were exhausted and needed to find rest for the night. There were no RV parks on our route, and no state parks that allowed overnight stays that we could find. Then I spotted a mobile home park just outside a small town. We asked if we could stay overnight, and the manager said, "Yes, we do have one vacant place, but no hookups."

We agreed and finally bedded down. We noticed some loud noise in the night but thought nothing of it. The next morning on the radio, we learned as we drove away, police had arrested two men charged with murder who were hiding there at the same mobile home park. Of course, this was a rare case, but made us more careful of our choices.

By contrast, we have stayed in some utterly fabulous RV parks such as the ones described in other chapters: Flamingo RV Resort at Everglades City in Florida, the Oasis RV Park in Las Vegas, and an elite KOA Resort just west of Glacier National Park. In these more expensive RV parks, we saw numerous RVs, some forty feet long, costing around a half million dollars. At RV showrooms and sales events, we have inspected some that have large, built-in wet bars indoors, and the additional outdoor kitchens in the side of the coach have a large screen TV also. Often these expensive nomadic homes have washer and dryer and dishwasher within. Some RVs are built for lakeside parties, others for full-time living. But having seen the scarcity of parking places for large rigs at national parks or state parks, we would not want the added difficulties of one of these elaborate and expensive coaches on our long hauls. On the high mountainous roads we love, they would be very difficult to handle. As for the convenience of laundry and dishwashers, it would be great not to have to use a laundromat or wash dishes by hand when wanting to head for bed. However, water weighs heavily, and the extra water use would require more regular hookups than we want to find. We have learned to conserve water in ways that enable us to shower every day but stay without hookups up to five nights. But for full-time RV life, a luxurious big one would be great because most full-timers rent one site for months or years and don't move around as we do!

Years ago, we were staying in a New Jersey RV park and arrived late at night. When we set up, we looked around in dismay to see the trashy appearance of most of the sites, which also had many items outside pushed to the back of each RV. A few others had potted plants, a little fence, and a Welcome sign with the family's name and a flag. A little later, as we were checking out, we asked the owner about the condition of the various sites. She replied that many people from an adjoining state could not afford the very high taxes at their former homes and had moved their families to live in this RV park. This was a rare experience in all our travels. Most parks had a two-week limit, unless a site was purchased or leased for a long time.

But when jobs are plentiful in an area, many companies bring in temporary workers to supply the demand, knowing the work will not last long. Some RV parks encourage these blue-collar workers to stay for long periods, as it is good income for the park. We saw this in West Texas when oil was booming, and many oil rig workers were needed. RV parks jacked their prices up very high, as did motels for a hundred-mile radius. And reservations had to be made far in advance. Some vacant, unpaved areas on roadsides were turned into places for RVs to stay. Instead of hookups, these had water trucks and sewage disposal trucks that came through regularly. We never stayed in an RV park in West Texas during that time since we had friends and family who would let us park in their wide driveways. But the next year, when the oil boom had died, we drove through West Texas and saw oil rigs piled up in parking lots, out of business. Those temporary RV lots had vanished, and prices and availability had returned to normal.

The Beautiful Snake

WE HAVE A small inflatable boat and paddles we carry in the storage compartment under our RV. Our first time to use it was on a small lake in a state park in California. It took us a long time to inflate the little raft with only our foot pump, but we had fun paddling around in the small lake. When we returned to our RV parked by the water, we tried valiantly to deflate our raft. With it flat on the ground, we took turns walking on it, pushing with our hands, lying down on it, and finally lifted it to the picnic table where we tried rolling the stubborn piece of plastic to deflate it! Exasperated and exhausted, we sat on the bench with our backs against the table, unintentionally gazing in the direction of our next-door neighbors, who had a car instead of an RV. We looked toward the water where we heard giggles and splashes, and there they were on their raft enjoying the sun with their whole bodies, in the nude! We hid our laughter, averted our eyes, and finally got our raft deflated.

Before we tried the raft again, we purchased an inflator machine that used our car battery, so we spared ourselves the pumping action. For deflating, we found another automatic machine, and then we could really enjoy ourselves on the water. At an RV park in Pennsylvania, we found a site by the river and loved putting our little raft in to float downstream. At the park's end, we were able to drag it out and together take it back upstream.

In Idaho was our most daring adventure with our little inflatable boat. We put in at a part of the Snake River, which had formed a quiet lake at the park where we found lots of families enjoying

Sunday afternoon swims, picnics, canoeing, and ball sports on the wide green grass. We asked if we could park overnight to catch the narrated boat tour early the following morning, and the park attendant said we could. We were paddling around in the peaceful river and observing a lovely, brilliantly colored sunset. Suddenly we realized it was quickly growing dark, and we heard no voices.

We paddled swiftly to the shore where we had left our RV and discovered that everyone else had vanished, checked out for their workweek ahead. We were alone in this beautiful now-deserted park. We deflated our raft, thankfully now with the help of machines, so it did not take much time. Then we locked ourselves into our RV, checking to be sure our cell phones had reception here and nearly full batteries. We spent an unsettlingly too-quiet, lovely night. Next day before it was light, we drove a few miles north along the Snake River to cross the bridge from Idaho to the Oregon side for our 8:00 a.m. boat tour. After anxiously awaiting daylight and the tour group, we realized we had arrived an hour early for our tour because the river was the line for changing to Pacific Time Zone.

Next, we went on to Seattle where we planned to stay for two weeks and have several couples fly in at separate times to stay a few days with us at our favorite national park: Mount Rainier. To me, this is one of the most beautiful places in North America since I love mountains. The hikes there are among wildflowers, or on snow fields, or on enormous rocky mountainsides crossing the remains of an avalanche. The visitor center and science research areas are beautiful and remind me of buildings in the Swiss Alps. We spent time with these various friends and family climbing some of the steep mountain trails, taking hundreds of pictures, feeding little marmots, and looking for elk, deer, moose, and bears.

The enormous trees in the Olympic Peninsula stretch so tall we could not see the tops. And hikes in the Northern Pacific Coast forests are mythically haunting in their beauty with the enormous fronds of fern along the forest floor trail and weeping from trees. At the visitor center, we walked through a field of blue wildflowers and were able to take pictures of bighorn sheep contentedly grazing the beautiful bounty. The winding road back, with the play of light and shadow constantly through our windows, did not help our carsick passenger.

The next day, when we had returned our friends to the airport in Seattle, we were making a left turn across traffic on the Main Street when suddenly our RV stopped dead still. With traffic alert enough to divert around us, Bill frantically tried everything he knew to do and was finally able to get it started. He drove slowly with the engine cutting in and out on the busy I-5 Highway to the nearest garage for trucks and motor homes.

*****

A few days later, our son was meeting us at Death Valley, California. Even in this autumn, the temperatures were well over a hundred degrees in daytime. None of us could imagine, as we gazed from the top of the mountains into this famous well-named valley 282 feet *below* sea level, how terrified pioneers reaching the mountain ridges must have felt when they looked out at the landscape they had to cross on wood-rimmed wheels of covered wagons! This is one of the hottest, driest places on earth, but with modern conveniences of air-conditioning, we were comfortable in our RV, and many visitors were enjoying good accommodations in rental apartments and cottages there.

We hiked into Badwater Basin, wondering from a distance how this mysterious place had snow in early fall. But when we started out across the visitor pathway, the guide encouraged us to feel the "snow," which is sodium chloride, or table salt, many inches deep, covering almost two hundred square miles of the lowest place in North America. We learned that the name "bad water" was given because a mule pulling a wagon through here in early days refused to drink from the natural spring, which is extremely salty. Ads for 20 Mule Team Borax originated there, where the Borax was first mined. Amazingly, scientists have discovered organisms living in the basin. Some plants like the pigweed around the edges and an endemic snail are found only here. While we were on the boardwalk, our guide pointed out to our west the Panamint Mountain Range, where the gigantic Telescope Peak towered over two miles above us, the most dramatic straight-up view in America. To the east, where pioneers must have been overcome with fear, we saw the high cliffs of the Black Mountains with a sign signifying sea level far above us.

We particularly delighted in exploring one of the mountainous trails leading to the rim of the valley with our son Tom, a professional artist in Los Angeles. These areas of rocky deposits are called Painters Palette Mountain because the rocks contain many different minerals, each presenting a different color. The rocks are naturally beautiful, and the rainbow shades of their color range change with the sunrays' direction, a true wonder of nature.

Ancestor Legends

A
FTER OUR SON returned home to his work, we decided to go to Mount Shasta. I enjoy reading about unprovable things that possibly could be, so I was eager to see this mountain where native cultures believed their far distant ancestors emerged from underground by way of the navel of this mountain. In Northern California, at the southern end of the Cascade Mountain Range, Shasta, 14,179 feet high, is a potentially active volcano. This is the most voluminous stratovolcano in the Cascade Volcanic Arc and is part of the Shasta-Trinity National Forest.

The earliest discovered relics of civilization reveal that it was inhabited over seven thousand years ago. This area was part of the massive Gold Rush in the 1850s, and explorers reported various Native American Tribes living within the area. These included Shasta, Okwanuchu, Modoc, Achomawi, Atsugewi, Karuk, Klamath, Wintu, and Yana. By 1887, explorers had written poems and books about the beauty and wonder of Shasta, so the Central Pacific Railroad built along the path of the Siskiyou Trail from Oregon to California. This meant hotels were built and large numbers of tourists began to come. In the early twentieth century, the Pacific Highway system was built along the base of the huge mountain, and today Interstate 5 is the way most people get to Mount Shasta.

The little town, Mount Shasta, is 3,586 feet above sea level, and now its population almost equals its elevation. With the beautiful Shasta River, it attracts artists and people of alternative lifestyle. Curious tourists come here to work and play. I loved browsing in the unique shops that contain weird and wonderful works of art, esoteric books, incense, crystals, and more.

We hiked up a challenging distance on the huge mountainside. Many local legends tell that the ones who first lived here included angels, aliens, and survivors of Lemuria (an island that legend says sank twelve thousand years ago into the Pacific). Shasta is considered a magical, mystical mountain with energies that can be absorbed by one who visits there, and many spiritual retreats are held there each year. We found a sacred labyrinth made of hand-placed stones in the ground in concentric spirals, where spiritual seekers reverently walk to the center for a deeply spiritual experience. In the 1980s, New Age believers declared this place to be part of the harmonic convergence, which is the grid of "power centers" throughout the world. We did experience great peace walking the labyrinth as we stared out at the vast Pacific Ocean and pondered this place dedicated to world peace.

RV on Ferries

W E HAD STOPPED for a couple of days in Oxnard, California, where we had contemplated moving permanently. We loved this town just outside of Los Angeles and enjoyed our walks on the wide sandy public beach bordered by palm trees. We took a narrated tour of the city, and the most interesting place to us was the public golf course. This course was green and beautiful, with sprinklers watering many places. The guide explained the course was built atop a hill of recycled waste. The golf course was maintained entirely through composted vegetation, and wastewater was purified to keep the golf greens thriving. We had become environmentally conscious through our travels, and this gave hope for what cities could do to save our planet and prevent us from burying ourselves in our own waste. The next day, we were to take a ferry near Oxnard to the Channel Islands in the Pacific.

When we first encountered the need to drive our RV onto a small ferry, we were crossing a river in Guatemala to enter El Salvador. It was early evening, and this was the last crossing of the day. The very small ferry could only carry a few vehicles, and we hoped it could accommodate the size and weight of ours. We were the first in line, and we drove on with no difficulty. It seemed miraculous that a little boat could hold vehicles as well as people. We made the crossing with no problems and loved the experience.

Years later, we had driven our RV across the Yukon Territory en route to Alaska and came to a similar river crossing by ferry at Dawson City. Traversing the Yukon River into Alaska was not a long crossing and was the only way to get back into the United States at this northern area of the Yukon Territory. We drove onto the small ferry holding our breath. But it was fun, and we got out of our RV to enjoy the river scenery and breathe the fresh, cool air.

On a later trip for a ferry crossing in Eastern Canada, we were allowed to park and sleep in our RV overnight at the ferry parking lot in North Sydney, Nova Scotia. We planned to drive onto the ferry that goes to Port aux Basques in Newfoundland the next morning and continue our Canadian motor coach experiences in that far-out province. However, the weather was threatening, and the finger of the Atlantic Ocean for the crossing was rough that next day, so we canceled our trip.

Going by ferry from Tadoussac to Quebec City was a brief but beautiful transit across the Saguenay River near its mouth, where it flowed into the Saint Lawrence River. We searched the water for the seals and beluga whales, purported to be lively there at that time of year. We saw quite a few large seals and a group of more than ninety pairs of belugas leaping from the water and arching back in. It was very exciting! This water crossing saved us many miles of highways, but we still had plenty to see along this Canadian fjord.

Fearing they might run out of space, we had lined up quite early in our RV for the early morning ferry from Seattle to the San Juan Islands. Our friend Jeff was staying with us, and the men were determined to rent motorbikes for the day to see Friday town and the island area, while I would enjoy a shopping spree there. I wished I were brave enough to ride a motorbike with them, but I was never even a good bicycle rider! The line to board the ferry was about to start moving when Bill suddenly realized he had left his cell phone at the restaurant in the very back of the parking lot, a long walk back. He must retrieve it to be safe, so he gave Jeff the RV keys and ran back as quickly as he could and found the phone. Thank goodness, he just did make it back as the ferry gates were about to close. It was a fun ride to the San Juan Islands and back, and the men had a blast on the bikes.

*****

Our greatest ferry ride thrill was just South of Oxnard in Ventura, California, where we left our RV in the parking lot and boarded the Island Packers Ferry on foot to go to the Channel Islands National Park. The five islands of this archipelago lie a three-hour ferry ride from the mainland. One of the islands allows camping, but visitors must bring in food and water. No concessions are allowed on any of the islands. These wonderful places are protected for wildlife. We went to Anacapa Island where we had magical walks along a pathway amongst the ground nests of seagulls protecting their eggs. We loved the beautifully wild place and learned a lot from the ranger guide. However, the highlight was on the return ferry trip.

According to our captain, what we were able to witness was a very rare and wondrous sighting in nature. He stopped the boat about an hour from the Islands when he saw a large flock of birds circling above the water. He knew this signaled a bubble-net feeding event, where a pod of humpback whales was rounding up their prey. These whales use their blowholes to create bubbles in the water near the surface, which seem to stun the krill or small fish. This enables the whales to catch their meal.

These, the largest mammals on earth, began jumping high in the air, then returning to their fishing expedition in the sea. They flapped their flukes at us as if waving goodbye. This was repeated with a pod of beautiful black-and-white orca whales joining them, recognizing that food was near and an easy meal below them. The ocean flurry was frantic, and we watched in awe as the captain explained what was happening. Having seen the signal of the gulls and other flocks of seabirds circling above the water frenzy, scores of dolphins swam past us, surfacing and diving in pairs. The captain, who knew what a significant, unusual, and special this sighting was, kept our ferry stopped for almost an hour as we watched with fascination nature's grand display.

Whale Adventures and Lessons

W E HAVE STOPPED in many places to go on guided whale-watching excursions. After a few of these unfruitful excursions, we learned that whales migrate in spring from warm southern oceans, where they mate and breed, to colder oceans in the north where they feed during summer. Humpbacks migrate over three thousand to five thousand miles, so we walked out on many Pacific Coast piers hoping to glimpse some during migration. Most whale-watching tours do not take visitors when there is slim possibility of whale sightings in the wrong time of year, but we have been on a few disappointing small boat rides which advertised whale watching but was just one fisherman trying to boost his income.

When we were on an RV trip to many places along the huge Saint Lawrence River, we learned so much in the Marine Mammals Interpretation Centre (Centre D'Interprétation des Mammifères Marins) of Tadoussac, Quebec, Canada. With many species of whales displayed in mannequin form, photos, skeletons, and films, we could see the difference between baleen whales and toothed whales. There are twelve species of baleen whales (including blue, white, fin, and humpback whales). Instead of teeth, baleen whales have up to six hundred plates of baleens with hairs in their upper jaw, like our fingernails. The hairs help capture small fish and plankton, which the whale sucks in and filters through these baleens, and then the ocean water flows back out of its mouth. This amazing process feeds larger whales up to a ton of food each day, so to us it was easy to understand why baleen whales were near extinction. Amazingly, they have two blowholes on top of their heads. These mammals do not fall into an unconscious state when they sleep, as we do. Because their breathing is not autonomic, they can only sleep with half their brain and one eye closed at a time, so the other half remembers to breathe!

At the museum, we could see the difference between the mouth types of baleens and toothed whales. It was easy to see why the orcas (the beautiful whales in tuxedos at SeaWorld) are called *killer whales* for a reason. Toothed whales are predators that capture their prey, such as seals and sea lions, or even other whales, and kill it with their teeth but swallow it whole! This kind of whale also includes belugas, bottlenose dolphins, and even common dolphins! How could these mammals living in the ocean be, like us, warm-blooded, have live births, and nurse their young with milk?

After learning so much about whales, we couldn't wait to take the boat tour into the wide Saint Lawrence River and see these up close. We signed up for a guided trip on a big orange Zodiac raft, which held about ten people. We were instructed to put on big waterproof suits, and we all looked like astronauts in this sturdy gear, which floats. The guide motored us far away from shore. The magnificent river looked as big as the ocean. Only a few other rafts were where he stopped our motor, but that signaled whales in the area. We did not have to wait long before a gray whale, perhaps three times the size of our raft, swam up beside us in friendly greeting and acknowledged us by blowing through his blowhole and showering us! What a thrill; however, my mind said, *What if he decides to submerge under our raft?* (We had just learned about whale's teeth!)

I frantically tried to remember whether he had blown from one or two blowholes. It really wouldn't put my mind at ease anyway because I could not remember whether it was one or two blowholes that indicated whether or not a whale had the gigantic teeth. It was like trying to remember whether to act big, wave arms, talk loudly, or be quiet and still and roll into a ball, depending on whether the bear you encountered was a brown or grizzly bear. In a panic, who could remember? And if I did remember, what could I do about it!

After this gigantic friend swam peacefully away before submerging, we all were excited about seeing it up close. Then we began looking for more. We did not have to search for long because our guide soon pointed out a huge humpback swimming toward us, and when he got near, he breached and waved his flukes (tail) at us! Our guide explained humpbacks stayed closer to the surface and spent longer times in view. We were lucky to see it breach and show its unique markings. These, like our fingerprints, enabled scientists to identify each whale by the different pattern on its underside and part of its flukes.

Next, the smaller *minke whales* appeared nearby. They seemed docile enough, and we could clearly see the differences in the three species we had excitedly observed. The last whales we saw before we had to return to shore were fat, round *right whales*. Our guide explained that these were named *right* because in the early days, whale fishermen named the species because they were the right type to try to catch because they had the most and best blubber and meat. At last, I thought quite belatedly, the guide explained that all the species we had seen on the excursion were baleens, *Mysticetes*, with no teeth to fear. However, I still wonder how many times small watercraft are overturned by whales as they resurface from beneath a boat. This orange Zodiac ride was the most exciting and rewarding water trip we had ever had!

A few days later, we booked another guided water adventure: a guided sea-kayaking tour. We had a brief lesson and good instructions from the guide, who would follow the four kayaks on our tour, each of which held two passengers with paddles. It was near sunset, and the tour around the shores of the Saguenay Fjord seemed easy because the water was not too deep, and we stayed close to shore. The scenery of vast water, colorful sunset, and lush greenery behind the rocky shore was lovely. We thrilled at this unique first experience for us. Neither of us had grown up near water nor experienced many water sports. We even had to learn how to get into and out of the kayak. Our only other kayak adventure was in a small lake, where we tipped it over several times while getting in or out. The sea kayaks were longer and did not tip quite as easily.

As we paddled along, the guide came up to our kayak and warned us to watch out for seals. It was mating season, when they were very aggressive and dangerous. He told us they are large enough to turn over the kayaks and attack us! (And *now* he tells us this instead of when we booked the tour and could have turned back and cancelled!) We became aware and watchful, and just before we were back safely to the dock to end our excursion, sure enough, a very large seal was swimming behind us. We had only a few more paddle strokes to safety, and we fiercely attacked the water with our paddles, both to hurry and to scare away this now beastly instead of cute mammal.

I remembered the first time I saw a small dolphin in an aquarium at the beach when I was a child. I loved its smile and begged my dad to buy one and let me take it home for a pet! He asked where I would keep it, and I innocently replied, "In my bottom chest drawer or my sandbox!"

Now, at the museum, I could hardly believe these adorable permanent smiles on dolphins, a species of whales that kill other mammals, are their deceptive masks, perhaps to trick and attract unsuspecting prey!

Asleep at the Wheel

L EAVING OUR RELATIVES in Estes Park, Colorado, after a wonderful time hiking the challenging trails of the Rocky Mountain National Park there, we headed northward. We stopped for gas in Rock Springs, Wyoming, and were just leaving when a girl about twenty years old came running up to our RV. She was wearing a peasant blouse and a full skirt. She gave us a pitiful story about being stranded and needing some gas money. We have been instructed often by our close friends who run a homeless shelter in Atlanta, Georgia, never to give a beggar cash but to take them for a meal, lest the cash be used for alcohol or drugs. Unfortunately, we could not take time for a meal, so kindhearted Bill gave her a $20 bill. She was overjoyed and appreciative and danced away. As we were entering the highway, I looked back and saw her showing the money to her very hippie, druggie-appearing friends, and we knew we had been duped. But we guess it was better to err that way than to refuse to help someone who was starving or truly stranded. After all, many times strangers have helped us in need, especially in foreign countries, where people do not seem so afraid for their own safety when confronted by strangers. Perhaps it is because guns and drugs and crime rate are so high in the USA. Our laws grant us the most freedom of personal choice of any in the world. We need to teach children from a very young age that freedom means taking responsible actions and never infringing on anyone else's rights or causing anyone harm. And we must stop being entertained by watching killing and violence on TV, films, online, video games, and news. To me, it seems like the Romans in the Coliseum cheering as the Christians were slaughtered by lions.

Driving north in Montana, we saw an interesting sign in the middle of a lonely expanse of land. The Dinosaur Research sign beckoned us to stop. In the little stone building, we discovered a dinosaur artifacts store called Trex Agate Shop, a rock shop managed by an elderly couple who owned the property nearby. In Bynum, Montana, in 1977, Marion Brandvold, who invited us into her shop, discovered remains of juvenile dinosaurs in a formation south of Choteau, Montana, which is now known as Egg Mountain. She showed her find to a paleontologist she knew, Jack Horner. He and his team, excited over the amazing find, excavated the area Marion indicated and discovered more juvenile bones and fourteen nests of dinosaur eggs! Paleontologists credit Marion with proving dinosaur mothers took care of their babies instead of abandoning the eggs as scientists had previously thought. These dinosaurs were classified as *Maiasaura*, which were a duck-billed form of hadrosaurs, hatched at about 2.2 pounds, and in eight to ten years, one had grown to about 4,400 pounds! Marion told us of her exciting find and declared that dinosaur remains were best discovered where the layers of geology in exposed rock mountainsides are green, white, and red in color. She told us she had donated her find to the Bozeman, Montana, Museum of the Rockies at the Montana State University.

Our son, Tom, had always loved studying about dinosaurs, so we were quite interested ourselves and made our way to the museum to see the display there, which was quite impressive. The discoveries on Egg Mountain helped scientists determine that these dinosaurs had colonial nesting behaviors. They nested in groups, and as the herd grew, they would migrate to find food and later return to their same nests to hatch the next sets of eggs. We were so thrilled to have met Marion, who had made the first dinosaur egg discovery in this section of Two Medicine Formation.

We love traveling through Montana with the magnificent high mountains, usually covered in snow along highway I-90, which ran through a large valley. Bill had grown tired, so I told him to take a nap and I would drive, since the highway was wide, straight, and had almost no traffic. I drove about a hundred miles before I needed to get gas. The first station I found was across the highway on the other side, so when I stopped to fill up. Bill awoke and then took over the driving. We were going along enjoying the beautiful mountains in the distance and the river beside the highway, which is the same beautiful scenery for miles with snow-capped mountains too far distant to distinguish unique landmarks, but all lovely. After he had driven for about an hour, we passed a statue of a large rabbit, and I squealed, "Bill, I passed that statue when I was driving!"

Then I realized I had failed to tell him I had crossed the highway to get gas at the only station I had seen while I was driving. Unaware, he had now driven fifty miles in the wrong direction, back where we had been before. The lovely scenery seems to be all the same for many miles!

Calgary Stampede
Rodeo Times

A T THE AIRPORT in Calgary, Alberta, Canada, we met my brother Jim and his five-year-old daughter, Bryann, who loves music. When they got off the plane, a Western band of four young men in cowboy hats were singing and strumming to welcome visitors arriving for the Calgary Stampede, an enormous annual rodeo. She was overwhelmed and delighted and began to do a little dance around them. We all happily headed for our RV, which we set up at the Fairgrounds for the two nights. We had tickets to attend the Stampede, advertised as "The Greatest Outdoor Show on Earth." Bryann loved seeing the horses and all the animal care going on at the barns. I prepared our dinner in the RV, so we could go to the opening night show in Rodeo Arena. It was such a fun evening. Bryann was so excited to see all the calf roping, bronc riding, and barrel racing. She sat on her dad's knee and pretended she was holding reins and bouncing in her saddle.

On our second happy day, we ate cotton candy, drank sodas, walked through the show stables, and Bryann was allowed to pet some of the animals. To our delight, the evening rodeo performance began with cowboys and clowns. Next was the rough wagon-coach race, with teams of horses pulling large chuck wagons. They raced wildly around the rodeo arena, and it was a bit scary to watch as we feared for the horses. If one tripped, it could be disastrous. Then there was an elaborate parade with horses and costumes and impressive native dances by First Peoples. All went well, and everyone left happy.

The next day, we drove to Lake Louise Lodge, where we had planned a beautiful day at this castle-like setting, keeping Bryann especially in mind. Unfortunately, it seemed all the hundreds attending the Stampede had decided on the same plan, and Bill had to let Bryann and me out at the lodge and drive nearly a mile away to find a parking place. While the men were trudging back up the hill in the high altitude, Bryann and I were having a delightful time.

In the lodge dining area, she discovered a "princess" in a queen's dress playing a harp. Our little niece was totally enthralled and stood watching the talented musician for a long time. The harpist talked to Bryann between pieces and asked if she had a favorite song to request. Bryann asked for a Disney favorite, and the harpist knew it and willingly played for Bryann a personal serenade. The men returned while Bryann was watching the princess's hands move over the strings and render her favorite song. This became a very special memory for all of us. We tried to buy a recording of the artist, but she had none.

After our lunch in the elegant dining room, we decided to walk around Lake Louise to hike up to the teahouse at the mountaintop. This lake is known as one of the most beautiful in Canada, and we agreed. We began the hike having no idea how long or steep the trail was. Surely, afternoon was a normal naptime for little Bryann, but she hiked like a trooper. When she complained a few times about being tired, I said, "Bryann, let's pretend we are Hansel and Gretel, who dropped breadcrumbs to find their way back. We can drop these little white pebbles to find our way back."

She enjoyed the game, and it took her mind off her tired feet. We finally made it to the top and had a delightful tea party, with cake and milk for her. We revived, and the walk back seemed less daunting. The views all along the way were spectacular!

When we left Lake Louise, we found a nice campground just off the road leading to Glacier Parkway and stopped overnight. It had a big swing set and jungle gym, which Bryann enjoyed. Jim prepared us hamburgers on the grill. After a good night's sleep, we drove the spectacular Icefields Parkway (Highway 93), the highest road in Canada. We saw tall glaciers as backdrops all along the smooth paved highway leading to the Ice Explorer Boarding Station at the Columbia Icefields Discovery Center on the way to the Athabasca Glacier, then nearly seven thousand feet above sea level. Before it was our turn to board the Ice Explorer, we walked out on the foot of the glacier, an awesome experience. The guide told us we could sample the snow if we wanted to taste its purity since it was frozen eons ago. I declined, but Bryann and Jim sampled a little. We were informed the glacier is a tongue of ice about three and a half miles long and a half mile wide. Since it has been melting for the past century, there are dangerous crevasses, hidden cracks in the surface, where occasionally people have died. We were warned to be extremely careful. We boarded the enormous vehicle with huge wheels and sat in the comfortable enclosure as we rolled out onto the glacier to see it up close while the narration told us all the facts of this wondrous glacier, which is a river frozen in motion. Icefields Parkway has to be one of the most beautiful scenic drives in the world! We were glad we had gotten here in time before the roads close for winter.

Years later, when our grandchildren in New Jersey were ages eight, eleven, and twelve, they wanted to go to the Stampede. Our time at this event years before had been so much fun, we had retold it often, and we were delighted they wanted to go. However, the Stampede ticket prices had really increased! We had driven our RV there, but we thought the six of us would be too cramped, so for the two nights at the rodeo, we rented a hotel suite. Bill found an RV park that had no hookups, so it was inexpensive to leave our RV there while we stayed in the hotel. However, as RVers know, it is much easier and more comfortable to sleep in the RV, even when staying in the driveway of friends or family. In an RV, there is no convenient compartment in which to place a suitcase, so moving into a home or hotel to sleep requires packing clothes and toiletries in a sack and looking weird to check into a nice hotel, hoping you have left nothing important behind!

We met our daughter's plane in Calgary and welcomed them with big white cowboy hats, which matched the ones of the Western band greeting them in the airport with cowboy songs. Everyone was in festive spirits.

As we walked through the downtown area of Calgary, Pamela was reminded of Fort Worth, a truly Western city that honored cattlemen's traditions. The kids loved spending their souvenir money on some Western items. The boys wanted to buy toy cowboy pistols, but Pamela told them the story of our plane flight when Blake was four years old and always played cowboy and literally lived in his cowboy hat and wore holster and toy pistols and cowboy boots every day. When we were checking in for the plane, the attendant made Blake relinquish his holster and pistols and told him they would save these accessories for him for when we returned. Reluctantly, he relinquished them, but when we returned a week later, they were not to be found. Erica chose a little plastic horse, and the boys wanted toy spurs, which they learned back at the room, too late, do not fit on tennis shoes!

At lunchtime, we stopped at a popular barbecue restaurant with outdoor seating. The waitress was dressed as a cowgirl with a short skirt and, of course, boots. Both boys thought she was adorable, and they felt old enough to flirt. Pamela, Bill, and I surreptitiously watched the innocently awkward flirting taking place, and the waitress, probably twice their age, led them on in a sweet way. For us, it was a special glimpse of the future and a realization these boys were quickly growing up.

That afternoon at the hotel, we rested before the big night at the Stampede. The kids loved the games we had brought from the RV and challenged us to Rummikub. It was very special to be all together again.

We arrived at the rodeo a couple of hours early so that we could walk around the barns and stables. Pamela, a cowgirl at heart, fondly remembered as a child going to cattle conventions and state fairs with Bill. Seeing the animals in the show barns was always her favorite. The children were able to pet some of the livestock. We were all in high spirits for the big rodeo's grand entry parade. All the show events were exciting, and Bill told the kids these activities that comprise a rodeo are really practicing and demonstrating the skills a real cowboy must learn to do his work.

Knowing their granddad had been a real cowboy, they were very impressed and kept asking, "Did you do that?" with each of the events.

For bull riding, Bill answered, "No, it is too dangerous!"

For the bucking bronco events, Bill said, "Yes, I had to learn to break horses to be able to place a saddle on them and ride."

When the bronc-rider cowboy hit the ground, Nicolas asked, "Did you ever get thrown like that?"

Bill responded, "Yes, and it really hurts, but it is part of teaching a horse to mind the rider and wear a saddle obediently."

The kids were very impressed. The calf-roping event was next, and all three children wanted to know if their granddaddy could rope a calf. The impressive answer was, "Yes." They later begged him to buy a rope and teach them to lasso. Bill said he would happily teach them when they came see us in Texas, where he had the ropes and a place a friend would let him demonstrate with their cattle since we no longer owned the farm/ranch.

When the cutting-horse event started, I told the kids their grandfather had been in this event in rodeos when he was a teen. They were excited and wanted to hear all about it. First, Erica wanted to know if the cowboy had a knife to move the cow out of the herd. Bill explained no knife or actual cutting happened. The term *cutting horse* meant the cowboy would ride his horse to divert or *cut out* a cow from a herd so that cow could be sold, doctored, branded, or whatever the cowboy needed to do to it. He explained that Western horses were trained to do that and could even do it without anyone in the saddle. He told them about the thrill of riding in a few rodeos when he had just learned how to perform the cutting-horse maneuvers. I think their grandfather grew hugely in the eyes of these three children as they imagined him performing the rodeo scene in front of them.

The next day, we left our car in the hotel parking building, and Bill walked very early in the morning to rent a van for our day at Lake Louise, a part of Canada that is memorably beautiful, and we knew Pamela would love it. We had a special lunch in the Lake Louise Lodge, but no harpist was there then. We hiked around the famous, exquisite lake, and we told the children that when we were here to ski nearby in the winter, we saw people sledding on the frozen lake. We had walked across it on the ice, and the hotel had amazing ice sculptures in several places on the lawn. Another time in summer, Bill and I had rented a canoe and paddled this beautiful lake, but we had been warned of the ice-cold water and that if we tipped over, it only took ten minutes to become hypothermic, when your body temperature gets so low your organs cannot function well. We did not want to chance this with the children. The scenery is spectacular, and we got some picturesque backgrounds of mountains and water for our family pictures, which other visitors were happy to snap for us with our camera.

We returned to Calgary for our last night and played games in the room after dinner. But there was a huge problem—the toilet would not work! It was a very nice hotel, but it was completely over-crowded with the Stampede crowd, and the manager could not find a worker to fix it for us so late at night. I was furious, but Bill, who can fix almost anything, got to work and literally rebuilt that toilet, so we made it through the night. But I was happy to check out the next day, although sad to say goodbye to our loved ones as they boarded their plane home.

We drove our car to the RV to connect it so we could tow it again. But we were in for a dreadful surprise. Several nights it had rained, but since it was not in daytime and did not bother our activities, we thought nothing of it. However, we found the RV had begun to sink in the mud of the open, unpaved field. Bill saw the backend was deeply mired in the mud, and he could not back it out of the space.

The automatic levelers of our Winnebago were stuck tight in the dried mud, and our tires had sunk about a fourth of their height! It was like we were glued in place. Bill got his foldaway army shovel from his tool kit and got beneath the RV and slowly dug all the mud from one of the lifts and raised it. Then he repeated this tiring process for the other back "leg" and pushed it up. Finally, he was able to dig around the tires until he could shove a piece of board under each back tire. The front end had not sunk, so we could drive away with no real damage, just a tired, muddy husband!

Jasper Glaciers

ALTHOUGH WE HAD been to this part of Canada several times, it is one of our favorites, so we decided we must drive again to Jasper Provincial Park. We were in luck to find an RV spot open, so we checked in for three nights. What an exquisite place in nature to relax after our city activity. Jasper surely must be one of the most picturesque places in Canada. At the large Maligne Lake, poorly named because it is so beautiful, we took a boat tour for several hours in the gorgeous scenery. There were coves and inlets not visible from the main part of the lake, which people normally see. This excursion was well worth the price. We learned from another tourist about a hike we must take the next day.

At Annette Loop Trailhead, we found other hikers tempted by the promise of five exquisite but unusual lakes. The long hike was mostly level and always lovely. The five lakes, Edith, Annette, Mildred, and two Trefoil Lakes, were indeed worth the hours of hiking! Each lake was a different brilliant hue of aqua, deep blue, green, lavender, and deep purple. The minerals in each lake and the reflections of the sun rendered all these different natural colors, yet the lakes were not far apart. We were so glad we had learned about this hike. The lakes are truly beautiful!

The next day, we drove to see the Edith Cavell glacier, not far from the road so we could hike to the base of the mountainous glacier. It was here that I finally understood the concept of a glacier being a moving giant, a river that froze during the Eemian Glacial Ice Age, about 130,000 years ago to 115,000 years ago. Our RV has taken us to places where we saw huge shiny, smooth rock, which our hiking guide told us had been the path of a glacier moving through and polishing the bedrock on its way. Often we have driven past deep valleys where glaciers had moved through, pushing everything in its path to each side, thus creating the mountains.

We have camped in Rainier in the rocky moraine rubble rock broken up by a glacier's movements. When we were in Alaska in our RV, we took a boat tour to see an enormous glacier calving, as it had started melting and was dropping enormous chunks of ice into the river because of global warming. But I had never understood how an enormous mountain that looked like it was still and covered with thick snow could be an actual moving block of frozen river. At Edith Cavell, we could carefully walk through the rocky creek bed up to the huge glacier and beneath see the water dripping out, and finally, I understood it was returning to its original form as a flowing river. Glaciers are known to move a few inches most years as they melt.

To Tow or Not?

THROUGHOUT OUR FIRST two decades of travels in our RVs, we did not tow a car. It was quite a nuisance to have to unhook from all the connections at a motor-home park to go sightseeing, especially if we wanted to go into a town. Some of the campgrounds had bus service to town, and we always were happy to use that. But most places did not have that service, so we found as many places as we could just to stop overnight without hooking up, and we learned how to conserve water and electricity. Some gas stations or highway rest stops had sanitary dump stations, which we greatly appreciated, and we had a book listing those places.

One spring, Bill said, "Let's get mountain bikes and attach them to the back of the RV, and we won't need to tow a car."

I had not ridden a bicycle in years, but the myth that the skills always come back reassured me. We bought two nice ones, but the hand brakes and gears were difficult for me. My bikes had always had foot brakes and no gears. I had won a snazzy Schwinn bicycle in a coloring contest when I was twelve years old, and it was presented to me on television. It was quite a thrill, but I never spent much time on it because my childhood neighborhood was very hilly.

With our new bikes, we began riding around our Texas neighborhood, which was flat. I made an effort but found bike riding difficult. But Bill attached them to the RV when summer came, and off we went, headed for the northeast to see our children but also to find some of the well-publicized rails-to-trails places to enjoy our bikes. One of these trails was just beginning to be constructed in the woods near our home. We could have good exercise and lots of fun with our bikes at home, if only I could feel comfortable riding mine.

Near an RV park in Columbus, Ohio, we found one of these trails and took our bikes out for the first exciting adventure. We had a new video camera that was small, and Bill wore it around his neck to film the pretty scenery. My bike was in front, and we were doing well on the trail at first because it was smooth and flat. However, I soon came to a difficult stretch on a downhill slope with some tree roots and rocks exposed. I made my way slowly but then heard a loud, painful cry. I looked back to see Bill on the ground with his video camera in the dirt. He lay there for a minute while all kinds of "What am I going to do to get him back?" thoughts raced through my head as I let my bike drop and ran back to him. But he was getting up and assuring me that he was fine. The "oh no!" cry was about our new camera, which he was sure he must have broken. But later we found out the video was good. The camera had withstood the impact and was okay after it was cleaned and checked at the professional camera shop in Columbus.

Although the bikes were a great idea to use around campgrounds as transportation or for exercise, we did not try to take an excursion with them for a while. Later, when we were in Glacier National Park, we had parked overnight in the gravel parking lot near the lake. It seemed flat and a very nice place to get our bikes out again to head to the paved walkways nearby. Bill went ahead of me, and I had to make a wide circle in the gravel lot, but I had never experienced the terrible combination of a bicycle and gravel, and I promptly fell over and badly scraped and bruised my knee. It was over a year before I wanted to try a bicycle again.

Our last RV biking excursion was wonderful. I had practiced more at home, and Bill enjoyed riding with other men who were regular bikers in Paris. We attached our bikes to the back of the RV and drove about a week before arriving in Astoria, Washington, at the mouth of the Columbia River. We found a great campground on the Oregon side of the river at a former army camp. There were long flat sandy trails from our campsite to the Pacific Ocean, and even I found these trails and those within the camp to be fun. I had nearly gotten used to the bike, but it was still an endurance test for me with the difficult hand brakes. I was glad when we sold that motor home a little later and bought one that Bill had fitted to tow a car. He bought a GMC car that required no changes to brakes or steering to be towed. From then on, the campground stops were much easier since we could stay a week at a time without having to unhook for quick overnight stops on long travels. As we drove we were never conscious of the tow car behind us, unless turning or parking or backing, when only Bill could manage these maneuvers safely. At a campground, we could unhook the tow car and make easy trips in that to restaurants, museums, shopping, or visits away from the RV park.

The main difficulty with a larger RV and a tow car is that it is only possible to park in large parking lots, such as malls or grocery stores, so if we wanted to enter a city, I looked for those. And when we were visiting our families or friends, we no longer had to crowd their driveways with our RV, since we could easily drive only our car to their house from the RV park.

More Utah Explorations

I N SALT LAKE City, we spent some time at the visitor center, where we watched the film about Mormon heritage and beliefs. I like to learn all I can about a place we visit, so I went to the main desk and asked a lot of questions about the founders, Joseph Smith and Brigham Young, the Church of the Latter-day Saints, Mormon beliefs, and the city.

Finally, the woman at the desk said, "You are so interested. It may be time for you to talk to our elder and consider converting to become a Mormon."

I laughed and said, "Thank you, no. I'm a journalist here to write about Salt Lake City."

She told us when and where to go to hear the famous Mormon Tabernacle Choir at the Temple Square. We were able to attend a service at the gorgeous tabernacle to hear this world-famous choir in the perfect acoustics of the building. The moving experience was unforgettable.

We love the many diverse national parks of Utah, and we drove down to stay at the Zion Campground beside the rushing Virgin River. Hiking in and around Zion National Park was awe-inspiring, and we gazed up at the majestic rock mountain walls. On our third day, we walked around the little town of Springdale at the main park entrance, where we found delicious healthy meals at various restaurants. At the outfitters shop, we inquired about guided excursions nearby. They recommended the experience of rappelling into a deep canyon. At first, it sounded too dangerous and challenging for our strength, but I had climbed a thirty-foot-high rock wall in a gym a couple of times and loved the feeling of rappelling. The shopkeeper explained that we would have an experienced guide and all the protective gear and harnesses and ropes. We decided to try it.

Our guide drove us about forty-five minutes away to a canyon in the red mountains. The hike to the top of the hundred-foot cliff was steep but doable slowly, and we had sturdy boots. The air temperature was just over a hundred degrees, but since it was so dry, we hardly felt the heat. When we reached the top, Bill wanted to go first in case he felt I should abandon the leap. The guide, Charlie, tightly attached himself to a metal eye hook permanently embedded in the top of the mountain and harnessed himself. Then he helped Bill to securely tighten his helmet and harness. When the young man gave the signal, Bill stepped off the ledge as instructed and was slowly rappelled by the guide down the sheer hundred-foot precipice. My heart fluttered as I watched and then photographed Bill waving from far below. When it was next my turn, I was ready and even eager because when I had previously rock climbed, the rappel was my favorite part. After Charlie again made all security checks, I took the first scary step to leap off the ledge. I whooshed down and loved every minute and have wished for years since that we could do it again.

Back at Charlie's vehicle, we asked him if he was Mormon, and he replied, "No," so we felt it would be okay to ask a few questions we were afraid might be rude to ask a member of the Church of Latter-day Saints. I asked if it were true about some Mormon men having multiple wives.

He said, "Yes, and we can drive past the main place they live, at Colorado City, Arizona, just across our state line. You know, this is a practice frowned upon by most Mormons nowadays, and it is actually illegal in Utah."

We were passing a little creek where we saw a man and seven little boys dressed in overalls and long flannel shirts, even though it was a hot summer day. Then a woman and five little girls, all dressed in long pioneer-looking dresses, emerged from the woods. We asked

Charlie, and he assured us this was probably a Mormon man with one of his wives and all his children.

Charlie drove his car slowly past a community of houses blocked off by a very high chain-link fence. He explained a man might have four wives, but each would live in a different house with her children, and he would visit each often. We were intrigued when we stopped at a restaurant and enjoyed a delicious meal where the women who were preparing the food were also dressed in pioneer-type of dresses. Men would come and go barely speaking to the women. A curious sight to us!

RV Stories Exchanged in Campgrounds

OUR NEXT STOP on our way back to Texas was Durango, Colorado, where our son Tom was to meet us for a few days. He and Bill had spent a weekend the year before in a little cabin he wanted to rent again, but it was not available, so we checked in to an RV park that also had a cabin for him. We had a wonderful, rare visit with him for two nights, sitting around our campfire reliving family RV fun in past years. Since he had been an infant when we first started our RV escapades, he could not believe some of our antics we related to him.

We told him about the time Pamela and Eric brought their boys to stay a few days in Colorado with us in our RV so they could attend a conference before Erica was born. The little boys loved camping in our RV playhouse and fishing in the creek. Nicolas was really into trains at that three-year-old stage, and he was thrilled when we suggested taking a ride in the mountains on the old steam engine train in Silverton. The ride around those mountains was exciting for the kids, and the coal smoke did not bother me as I had thought it would. With the little ones, we had roasted hot dogs and marshmallows over the fire. With Tom, we chose to eat healthily and roast veggie dogs, since he is a vegan!

*****

That night, a friendly couple came over from their site next to ours, and we shared RV stories around our campfire. When he was introduced to our son Tom, he said he had a good story of his son Rick renting an RV, his first RV venture, which lasted only a day. Since Rick's alma mater was playing in a bowl game in his city, he and his best friend rented a party-type RV and parked near the entrance gate to entertain out-of-town friends who were coming to see the game. They set up drinks and snacks for their guests. All the friends had a great time coming and going from the RV, and when the word "party!" got out, some friends of friends and a few strangers lined up at the door. These guys did not have the heart to turn anyone away. However, they had not thought of one important thing: beer overworks bladders, so the RV bathroom also got overworked and overfull. They realized what had happened and had to end the celebration!

Next day, they found the RV reeking. After cleaning what they could and getting rid of trash, they were not about to try to hook up to a sewer, so they carefully drove, with all windows open, to return it to the rental agency.

"We didn't know where or how to empty the black water," they said, with great apologies.

The kind rental agent said, "It happens all the time!"

The man telling us the story said, "I thought to myself, 'Yuck! What a job!'"

Bill thought Tom would enjoy the mountain drive to Silverton and on up the Animas River to the old mining town, which is now a ghost town. He took his sketch pad and pen and delighted in drawing the old mining camp buildings still in good condition. The Animas River, down in the gulch it has created, is picturesque but polluted by the chemical sludge the miners dumped into it decades ago. We took lots of photos, and when we got back, we could all see the ghost in the second-story window of the largest cabin! Tom drew some wonderful pictures from our experience.

We three went to Telluride, another beautiful place in the mountains. The day was rainy and cold, but it didn't dampen our spirits. We took a hike up at the end of the box canyon to the top of the magnificent waterfall. A tale of Butch Cassidy claims he robbed the bank of Telluride and escaped on the trail through the mountains where we stood. Tom is a good hiker and helped me when I found a trail difficult. When Tom had to return to work in Los Angeles, we took a route through Albuquerque, New Mexico, to return to our Texas home.

Snow Thrills

COLORADO HAS SO many majestic mountains reaching for the sky, and we have friends who live there and are trying to get notches on their belts for climbing each of the highest peaks. One, a photographer, is always searching for the perfect bird image to capture. Photography is also our hobby, but for us, *just* a hobby. In Rocky Mountain National Park, we love to search for wildlife, and the best sightings of moose we ever had was when we were hiking and saw a pair calmly chewing on willow bark, which is also the natural source of salicylic acid, the main component of aspirin. Maybe that's why they seemed so calm!

Our first RV experience of snow skiing was at Santa Fe, New Mexico, where we and our close friends set up our little RVs at a campground, and we took ski lessons at Ruidoso. Bill and I were still beginners, although we had had a week of lessons a year before. But Pamela, eleven, and Blake, five, had never tried it, so they had beginner ski school on the baby slope at first. Since kids seem to catch on quickly, they wanted to ski with us on the medium slopes on our last day. Our friends had a thirteen-year-old boy who was with us, and Pamela had a crush on him and wanted to impress him, but she just about froze in her consternation and self-doubt. However, fearless Blake, in his Snoopy snowplow position, barreled down the slope, waving to all of us as he zoomed past! We held our breaths mentally until we reached him at the bottom of the slope. He was still fine and grinning in pride, but we knew the expert slope crossed the easy slope near the bottom, and we were so relieved that no one had run into him. When we finally caught up with our little daredevil, we carefully cautioned him that on his next ski run, he must stop before crossing that dangerous path.

Several times, we have skied in the Rockies, and their high altitude makes us so tired from shortness of breath. By the time we have struggled into our boots and carried skis and poles to the lift, we are almost too tired to move! But snow sports are wonderful. Once while there at Winter Park, we took a horse-drawn sleigh ride beneath blankets to a restaurant in a cabin far out in the woods. It was magical and seemed like the movie setting in *Dr. Zhivago*. The horse even had bells on his festive harness! But most RV parks are closed in winter because pipes could freeze.

Once we found an RV place open in winter. The manager educated us about all the precautions we must take to prevent our water pipes from freezing. We could only connect to the on-site water faucet to fill our tank. If we did not disconnect, the freeze would burst our pipes. We were also glad we had a heater that could be engaged in the RV "basement" storage compartments to prevent freezing of pipes. Had we not had this heater below, Bill would have had to wrap our waterline within the RV with an electric coil he would plug into electricity. These were all new instructions for us, and we were thankful for them.

The only problem we had there in this snowy season was with our little dog, who could not figure out where she was supposed to do her business because she had only been on grass before. We had to walk her for so long we were afraid her little paws might get frostbite, so Bill bought her some little boots for puppies to protect her feet, but she promptly pulled them off with her teeth!

Perhaps our most special memory of snow in the Rockies was on a Christmas Eve when some friends lent us snowshoes and showed us how to walk in them. Then we followed three locals in the moonlight to warm up with hot chocolate from a Thermos in an ice cave they made. Then we snowshoed down the mountain in the soft light of the full moon reflected on the white snow beneath the evergreen forest. We were even able to walk on the frozen stream bed and go right up to the incredibly beautiful frozen waterfall. We trusted the trio to lead us safely because they were experienced with winters in the Rockies.

They told about one of their friends who had had an amazing life-or-death experience when he was ice climbing with an instrument like an ice ax. He was unaccompanied but had a cell phone. At a very high precipice, he slipped into a downward death fall. He had the quick presence of mind to drive his Black Diamond Cobra ice tool's sharp point into the ice with a mighty blow and was able to hang there for a long while until search and rescue found him and helicoptered him to the hospital.

At Winter Park ski area, we saw an amazing teacher who was instructing people with all kinds of handicaps to learn to ski. We met brave men and women and even young boys and girls who were paraplegic, quadriplegic, blind, had Down syndrome, or had other difficulties in their bodies. Their instructor invited us to watch them ski and enjoy the special thrills of wind in their faces as they zoomed down the white hills. Special skis had been designed for each of these kinds of infirmities. The blind skiers were tethered to a sighted person. People without arms or legs were strapped into a sled-type seat attached to skis. They had to be so brave to learn how to ski. We loved seeing the joy on their faces with their great thrill and accomplishments. We were greatly inspired by their spirits of trust and determination.

Grand Canyon of Mexico

BILL AND I really wanted to see the Grand Canyon of Mexico, so we flew to Chihuahua, Mexico, and took the very nice train with first-class service through the high Sierra Madre Mountains to Los Mochis, Mexico, and on to Copper Canyon, which is 5,214 feet deep, compared to our Grand Canyon, 6,001 feet, at their deepest parts. We were so surprised that the train also ferried RVs on railcars especially designed to carry them. RVs can travel about four hundred miles on this train from the Sea of Cortez to Chihuahua or Los Mochis. In the town, we talked to several Americans who had RVs on board, and they loved the experience. Had we known that, perhaps we would have taken our RV on this rail ferry also.

At Los Mochis, we spent the night in a lovely hotel and enjoyed a tasty authentic Mexican meal in the nice dining room overlooking the canyon. When we walked out onto our room's private balcony, we peered over the only two-foot-high wooden rail and looked straight down into the vast canyon! We were glad we are not sleepwalkers!

The next day, we hired an experienced chauffer/guide to drive us down to Batopilas, the ancient town at the bottom of the canyon. The drive of about forty-five miles was on the narrowest, most twisting road we had ever encountered, and it required almost seven hours of expert driving to arrive safely. Our driver stopped at several spots on the way where there were places to park and sights to see. Our experiences in the canyon were material for another book and created such happy memories.

Because the town is small and is one of the oldest towns in Mexico, we stayed in a home B and B whose owner rented out two rooms. For our meals, we ate on porches of various homes that served as cafes and had a few tables for tourists to enjoy a meal with their family. We watched many women take their family laundry to the Batopilas River in the base of the canyon and dunk the clothing in the river, rub it with soap, scrub each piece on the rocks to get them clean, rinse in the river, and then wring them by hand. The women, who knew no other way, seemed to enjoy this time of socializing with each other. The population is composed largely of Tarahumara native tribe people, most of whom never leave this canyon in their lifetime. Such a fascinating place to visit and see how functional and cooperative their more primitive culture is.

Some of the local men of the valley are such amazing runners, they can run straight up the mountains in handcrafted straw flip-flop sandals for supplies someone needs. These are such expert runners they competed and sometimes won long cross-country competitive races in the USA. Our return drive on the daring road seemed a little less frightful.

Holidays in Los Angeles

AFTER WONDERFUL HOLIDAYS with our Los Angeles family, we hugged sad goodbyes on New Year's Eve morning. We had a long RV drive ahead. The Rose Bowl would be the next day in Los Angeles, and we went to see the floats being constructed. We looked forward to the amazing floral creations each year on TV. We purchased tickets to go inside the large barn-looking buildings where hundreds of volunteers were frantically putting finishing touches on the floats. It was incredible to watch the intricate details that untrained people could achieve using only fresh natural flowers and greenery. The floats were enormous, and we could not imagine how many millions of flowers had to be flown in from all over the world to achieve the beautiful designs, which would perish within a week. We had never seen the parade in person, but we, like most of the world, faithfully watched it on TV every New Year's Day.

We wanted to return via a route we had not done in years, so we drove to Lake Havasu City, Arizona, near the California line. The lake was formed by Parker Dam on the Colorado River and provides the perfect place in this vast desert for water sports and all kinds of fun. We stopped early to avoid the holiday traffic and inebriated drivers celebrating New Year's Eve. We parked near the lake and intended to celebrate and buy tickets for the elaborate buffet at the best restaurant in town, which advertised a band and dancing. We almost never go out for this celebration evening in our little hometown,

323

so this sounded like fun until we saw the $100-per-person ticket price. No thanks! We couldn't pay that, so after walking around the pretty lake and exploring its island, we returned to cook our dinner in the RV. When we finished our meal, we went out to sit by the lake and watch the spectacular orange sunset in the western sky. A young man approached us and asked if we knew that the bridge nearby was the actual London Bridge, which had recently been purchased and moved to this state park. We did not and were so glad to learn this. We asked if walking across it is permitted.

He replied, "Yes, ma'am, but there is a much better way."

We asked what he meant, and he pointed to his gondola tied beneath the bridge. "Let me serenade you on this beautiful New Year's Eve, while I oar you around the lake and we go under the London Bridge."

We jumped at this unusual and very romantic way to end the year. It seemed as if we were mixing the United States, Italy, and England, together as we floated along beside the Native American land of the Chemehuevi Indians of the Southern Paiute people. The moon came out brightly, and the singer's voice, in a serenade, was indeed a memorable way to welcome the New Year while we reminisced our happy time in Los Angeles.

Nomadland for Real

THE NEW YEAR began with us heading toward the strange place we had heard lots about from other RVers who lived in homes in the north most of the year. Winter is the peak time for these human snowbirds who migrate to winter in the warm desert at Quartzsite, Arizona. It was a little town of about five hundred people, but somehow they coped with about two million visitors each winter, all arriving in different kinds of homes on wheels: from old beat-up vans, converted buses, to old RVs, and large luxury coaches. Quartzsite has 52 RV Parks, but the most popular place is the free Bureau of Land Management, which offers miles of hot, dusty, flat, dry camping (which means no hookups, water, or electric). Sewer trucks, garbage trucks, and water trucks come through frequently to keep the place sanitary, with so many people living there.

The rule is you can stay for two weeks, then you must move at least twenty-five miles away for several weeks before returning. The camaraderie is inviting, no one is pretentious, and these are a collection of over two million *individuals* who love their freedom. It was winter, so we just had to see it for ourselves, since summer temperatures average 120 degrees there and they have no hookups for air-conditioning and almost no nomads then. We knew we would not want to experience that summer heat again in the desert, as we had the previous summer when we arrived at Joshua Tree and our RV engine died in the heat. At that time, we had had no air-conditioning as we waited for hours before the AAA men arrived to rescue us. January was the perfect time of year to experience this place, now immortalized in the 2021 Academy Award winner film *Nomadland.*

We only stayed that one January night in the mass of humanity but found everyone very welcoming, orderly, and law-abiding. The very hard rock quartzite is mined in this area. It has a grainy, sand-paper-like glassy surface composed predominantly of an interlocking mosaic of quartz crystals. Rockhounds flock to this area, so I wanted to visit a rock shop, and we found many interesting stones that our grandson would love. The next day as we were leaving, we saw the sewage truck making its round to clean out RV waste tanks, not a job we would choose, but everyone here was glad someone was making a living that way.

Going through Arizona, we veered a little off our highway to go through the famous Petrified Forest National Park; however, we were very disappointed because the specimens were few and far between. The park ranger told us that through the years, souvenir seekers had stolen many of the petrified pieces before laws were established to protect this unusual place. The few pieces of petrified wood we saw there were beautiful rocks of several brilliant reds, greens, purple, and yellow, with diamond-like sparkles in the sunlight. The rocks are all granite crystal, composed of different minerals: iron, carbon, and manganese. These had once been trees, which over two hundred million years ago had sunk quickly and deeply into an ancient river system. They were so quickly buried by the sediment that oxygen was cut off and the decay process slowed. As minerals seeped into the porous wood, they had solidified into stone of many colors, and we could clearly see the trees' cadmium rings in some of these beautiful slabs.

Farther along this Highway I-40 going toward Texas, we stopped near Winslow to see the Meteor Crater Natural Landmark, which is the best-preserved meteorite impact site on earth. The pieces that broke off the meteor are known as the Canyon Diablo meteorite. The diameter of the big hole is about three-fourths of a mile, and the depth is 560 feet. The iron meteorite hit the earth at about twenty-nine thousand miles per hour here about fifty thousand years ago. Most of it was vaporized by the high impact, but some fragments remained, from which scientists have gleaned valuable information. At the visitor center, we learned a lot about meteors and saw one of the biggest meteor chunks on display. The crater is on privately owned land of the Barringer family and therefore cannot be protected as public land by the USA government laws.

Lots of Laughs

O UR ADULT SONS, who now appreciate more our fond RV memories from their childhood, had kept us laughing when they related their funny adventures when they rented an RV. For Tom's bachelor party, the two brothers decided to rent an RV for a couple of days. They set off together for Yosemite, just a few hours away, knowing that would be more fun than a typical bachelor party. Blake had recently composed some of the music for a comedy movie, *RV*, and the hilarious predicaments in the film had piqued his interest after years of not traveling in an RV. However, he vividly remembered the scene about twenty seconds long, which he had to watch over and over to time the music exactly right. It was a scene of the RV sewer connection at a campsite turning into a horrible fountain of mess! He told Tom, "We can have a great trip, but I am *not* hooking up to the sewer!"

Tom agreed and they made a pact to time their bathroom needs to stop at gas stations, or visitor center, or hiking trail restrooms.

Since *real ventures* always have lots of good stories after the travelers overcome the stressful difficulties, Blake told us about one eventful day near Yellowstone. He was traveling with a college friend and their sons. They stopped to investigate a point of interest they saw advertised. They parked and were ready to step out. Blake pulled the handle of the only door of this rented RV, and it would not open. It was not locked. The boys began laughing at the predicament, and the dads searched through the RV and manual to see how to solve the problem, but there were no solutions. Bewildered, they realized they were trapped! They were angry that a rental RV would not be reliable. They tried and tried, but the door would not budge. Then Blake remembered from his childhood motor-home experiences that RVs have a back window that is for emergency escape. He quickly pushed it and climbed out to discover it was a big jump to the ground! He made it, but the key would not unlock the door from the outside either. There was no way to open it, so he tried to climb back in to call for a locksmith, but it was entirely too high to reach the wide opening in the rear. No one was nearby to lend a ladder or to give him a boost upward, so the other three inside grabbed hold of Blake and tugged and tugged until he could scramble back in.

The driver said, "Let's drive on into Yellowstone and find a gas station or garage."

Blake laughed and replied, "There are no services within a national park!"

There was no way to close the emergency window, so everyone strapped in as tightly as possible and they drove to a garage, where the mechanic had to use a ladder to climb into the back opening, and with a lot of work, he found the bolt of the door latch had come loose. When it was replaced, the four travelers made their way on to Yellowstone and home. With a house on wheels, anything can and *will* happen, but the fun is worth it, and the difficulties become funny memories and terrific stories to tell.

COVID Pandemic
RV Travels

DURING THE FIRST year of the COVID-19 pandemic, RV sales and rentals skyrocketed because thousands of people realized camping was the way to get outside and feel free and safe for a few days. Campgrounds, which were closed for a while, opened in new ways. Management was taking great care to enforce protections for everyone: social distancing at each site and on trails. Playgrounds and public restrooms were closed. Even the check-in and checkout procedures were outside and touchless, and campground stores were closed. All park officials wore masks and gloves and admonished campers to do so. Parties at campsites were forbidden, and picnic grounds were blocked off. Seasoned campers in tents, trailers, and recreational vehicles kept hoping for camp spaces, which remained fully booked throughout the season. With schools and many jobs being virtual, if the park had Wi-Fi, it was much in demand since that meant families could travel at times of year not possible during normal schooltime. Parents could work by computer Wi-Fi from the RV campsites, and kids could attend virtual school on ZOOM.

Even knowing all these restrictions, by September, we were ready to try the challenge. We drove to our daughter's home in New Jersey and returned to the closest RV park we had found there in preceding years. We made the drive slowly, spending two nights in campgrounds during the eight-hundred-mile trip each way. All the

COVID-19 safety precautions were being strictly required in each place we stayed, and campers were complying.

We settled in the RV park at the border of New Jersey and Pennsylvania and invited our family to come for a picnic. Only three of the five who live there were willing to risk it, as we had all been isolated since February. Fear was a big factor for each of us. We all wore masks. And we stayed six feet apart, so thankful to be together, but longing to hug our loved ones whom we had not seen in nearly a year. We had brought our own folding table, and I covered the campsite picnic table with a disposable tablecloth. I had new paper products and disposable utensils to open in front of them, and even new bags of hamburger buns with tongs for each person to lift out his or her own bun. And we had brought our own little hibachi. We all felt as comfortable as possible with these arrangements and sat six feet apart and enjoyed a wonderful several hours together. What a relief to be let out of our cages for fresh air! In the next couple of days of continued very careful precautions, we all felt the great joy of being together safely.

After a few weeks back home in South Carolina to rest and restock our RV, we bravely set out to cross the entire continent to see our California family in October. During the seven days, we leisurely drove to Colorado, only stopping and wearing gloves to refill our gas tank and to sleep at night with no hookups except one time. We never talked to anyone along the way nor went in any building, nor ate anything but the food we prepared in our RV. It was a challenge but gave us great peace of mind.

We had expected RV parks to be emptier since it was growing late in the year, so we had not reserved a campsite, but we failed to realize Colorado was at the peak of exquisite fall color, with especially gorgeous gold aspens and red maples. We were fortunate to get the last RV site in all of Durango. We stayed for several nights and loved walking whatever empty trails we could find and driving through the mountains in our tow car. We went to Mesa Verde National Park and were surprised but happy to see all the trails, restrooms, and buildings were closed and had signs reminding all visitors to observe safety precautions and wear masks. We were glad we had been there a few years before and had gone through the ancient pueblo settlement on the mountainside along with scores of tourists and many guides. Now everyone had to peer across the valley to see the ancient pueblo dwelling.

We were ready to complete our cross-continent drive to Los Angeles to our favorite RV park there and see our sons and two adult grandchildren. When we called to tell them we would arrive in about four days, they reluctantly said, "We hate to tell you, but you can't come. Today our mayor issued new, tighter restrictions because COVID has spiked very high. We cannot have outside gatherings of more than six people and then for only two hours. And the forest fires are raging. Our air quality is terrible. Please don't come. For your own safety."

Our disappointment was enormous, but we were glad they were being so careful and were considering our safety. We sadly pointed our motor coach east instead of west and started homeward. When several days later we reached New Mexico, we knew we could park overnight in the casino parking lots, so we found a small one on an

Indian reservation with lots of cars parked. We thought it was lighted and guarded for the night, and the guard assured us we could stay. We bedded down, but shortly after midnight, when neither of us was asleep, we realized the lights were off, all but a couple of cars were gone, and we saw no guard. We were both feeling very unsafe. Thankfully, we had not unhooked our tow car, so we could just drive away, and Bill did. He remembered a huge all-night casino somewhere along this highway and set out to find it, now 1:30 a.m.

After about twenty miles, the big, bright casino hotel came into view. It had hundreds of cars still in the brightly lighted parking lot. Guards were in several places, both on foot and in security vehicles, and they nodded for us to park overnight in the lane with other RVs. Finally, after 2:00 a.m. we fell asleep, certain that we were guarded and safe. But a little after 3:00 a.m. I was awakened by the rocking back and forth of our RV. I knew we had not been hit by another vehicle, but I was puzzled. Then I realized we were in storm country, and it must be a big rainstorm.

Bill woke up suddenly and after looking out the window, announced, "We are in a dust storm!"

The wind was ferocious and continued to rock us from side to side while the raging sand pelted our RV hard for about an hour. I had heard of dust storms but never witnessed one. To Bill, this brought back memories of his childhood in West Texas, where dust storms were frequent.

After this sleepless night, we got out to inspect the damage to our vehicles but found none, so we drove on uneventfully the rest of the way to our home in South Carolina. Although we were tired, we were very happy to know that even though we are in our late seventies, we are still able to drive so far safely. We hope to do it again when the pandemic is finally ended. I told Bill I have always been grateful he bought that first little RV so many years ago and convinced me to try it. RVs have given us so many incredibly happy experiences and adventures and enabled us to see our faraway children frequently, considering the distance.

One night, we had stopped late but wanted to grill burgers on our little hibachi. As Bill lit the charcoal, I went inside to prepare the rest of the meal. I wanted to quickly heat a pot of baked beans and a pot of corn, so I turned two burners of our RV kitchen's gas stove on high. Something didn't look quite right, and I smelled a weirdly unfamiliar odor, but I was tired and hurrying. After a couple of minutes, Bill entered the RV. I looked over at him, and it saved me! As I stepped toward him, the clear glass stove top, which served as counter space and stayed closed except when we were cooking, exploded! I had forgotten to open the glass cover! The safety glass broke into a million little blue pieces, and we were glad they were not big jagged slivers, but it was over an hour before we were able to get most of the glass gathered into the trash.

The stove top was replaceable when we returned to our home. I had made a stupid, expensive error! Bill gave me loving consolation, never casting blame. Later, the RV dealer in South Carolina fixed everything, but it was a $500 expense that could have been avoided. Our trip had provided the change of scene and lifestyle, which was a nice break from the months of staying to ourselves and worrying over the distressing COVID-19 news broadcasts. Our RV had really made a great difference in our lives again!

Emergency and Miracles

O UR MOST RECENT RV venture was the most amazing and memorable of any. We headed home after three weeks of marveling at brilliant New England fall leaves and visiting our New Jersey family. Bill is a confident driver, but I'm not. Bill had reserved an RV park for our first night on return, close to Highway I-81 near Harrisburg, Pennsylvania. We kept our car attached and used only the hookup for electricity because we intended to depart early the next morning. I prepared a simple, bland dinner, and we watched TV until about 11:00 p.m., and then we headed for bed.

Suddenly, Bill started burping nonstop and complained of stomach pain. In the past, he had had a few less severe bouts like this, which stopped in about an hour. I had forgotten his doctor suspected an allergy to pork, and tonight's dinner was ham. We went on to bed, assuming all would be okay with sleep. But this time was quite different. As the sleepless night wore on, he was in more and more pain and still burping constantly. By about six on Monday morning, he was doubled over in agony and groaned, "I need to get to the emergency room."

I had never heard him say that in sixty years together. We quickly dressed, and I walked our little dog while calling for a taxi since our car was attached to the RV, and I was not strong enough to detach it. I was informed that we were not in Harrisburg, taxis were over thirty miles away, and there was no Uber service. The campground office was still closed, but finally the taxi receptionist gave me a number for a local car service, which arrived at about 7:45 a.m. and drove us to the nearby urgent care just as it was opening for the day. When the doctor there examined Bill, he told the nurse, "Call the ambulance. He is going straight to the hospital ER."

We were stunned!

We knew nobody and had to ask which town we were near, and we had no idea where a hospital was. The kind and careful paramedic and EMT attendants examined Bill and loaded him into the ambulance. I asked about the intended hospital and explained I had no car, so the empathetic paramedic driver said she would break the rules, and I could ride in front with her because the hospital was only a few blocks away. This was our first ambulance experience, and the gratitude and relief I felt was enormous.

We were admitted to the emergency waiting room, where everyone wore masks. Bill was doubled over in pain in a wheelchair. I was immensely grateful that I was allowed to stay with him. People with COVID symptoms were at the other end of a huge waiting room, and everyone inside the hospital wore masks. Many hospitals in the United States, including those in our hometown, were so overwhelmed with the pandemic patients that they allowed *only* unaccompanied patients inside and were turning away many severely ill people because all beds were full. Most hospitals were severely understaffed and had supply shortages. We were relieved to learn that we were at a premiere hospital, the University of Pittsburgh Medical Center, in Carlisle, Pennsylvania, a place we will never forget because of so many kind and caring people and such skilled, compassionate medical staff.

We waited as hours went by with Bill in enormous pain. At noon, the car service drove me back to Western Village RV Park to walk our little dog and pay for another night. I realized the park was less than a mile from the hospital! The compassionate driver waited for me and drove me back to the ER waiting room, where I waited with Bill another five hours before I had to return by car service again to care for Angel and again hurry back to Bill. By about 8:00 p.m., he was given the last bed in the emergency room and a shot of morphine for his pain. There were no beds in the hospital available, so he would stay there for the night. When his pain eased and he slept, I talked to the doctors and attendants. They assured me he was safe and would be carefully monitored throughout the night. Carlisle Transport Service again drove me back to the RV at about 10:00 p.m., where I grabbed a sandwich, walked the dog, and fell into bed.

I felt Bill was in the best care possible. Normally, I would be scared to stay alone overnight. Also, I have always been directionally challenged, yet we were only a straight three-fourths mile from the hospital, and our RV site was near the entrance and office, so I could not get lost within this large RV park. I felt God was protecting us, and I was amazingly at peace. In our hometown, I would have been about ten miles of heavy traffic from the hospital, and I had been lost several times trying to get there for medical appointments. I would have been unable to return every few hours to care for our little dog, and my fears would have loomed in the empty house at night. Surely, God had gone before us, even as Bill reserved this RV site a month ahead, completely unaware. Although our reservation had been for one night only and the RV park was fully booked, the very kind, empathetic campsite staff made it possible for me to keep our RV in the same place, since I was unable to move it.

When Carlisle Transport returned me to the hospital early Tuesday morning, the driver suggested I get my car unhooked so I could drive myself, but he picked me up for the return trip at noon and waited on me again. Bill was still in the ER, sleeping through the pain thanks to the morphine and caring nurses. There was still no vacant room in the hospital, and he was taken for a CT scan in the afternoon, which showed the culprit was his gallbladder full of stones. Later, he was taken for an MRI to determine what the doctors should do. The hope was that by night, there would be a hospital bed for him, and he would be officially admitted.

This time when the car service returned me in the late afternoon to the RV, two of the campground men asked what kind of help I needed. They attached all the hookups necessary and assured me they would make sure my site was available for me to stay as long as needed. They detached my car, so I could now drive back and forth. As I thanked them profusely, one of them said, "In a campground when there is a need, there will be up to about ten volunteers ready to help, but in a town, it is hard to locate even one!" Ironically, the campground managers were also named Bonnie and Billy, just like us!

In the early evening, Bill had been taken to his room on the presurgical floor. He was attached to more monitors, given morphine, and soon was asleep. I stayed awhile, and nurses assured me he would be cared for all night, so I returned about 8:30 p.m. to the RV. I had not called our children yet since I had no official news to tell them. I fell instantly asleep for about ten hours, emotionally and physically exhausted. I could not believe that I, who was usually a worrier where health issues were at stake, felt totally peaceful and unafraid. I could feel heavenly protection surrounding Bill and me and giving us strength and peace, answering my prayers even before our need!

I returned to the hospital early Wednesday hoping to be there for the doctors' rounds. Entering before visiting hours, I had to pass through the ER waiting area, where I felt great empathy and said silent prayers for the many ill people and the workers, since I now knew, all too well, how the frightened patients and their loved ones felt and how exhausted the kind attendants were. A few of the patients with less urgent needs had been waiting thirty-two hours for admittance and were on the floor with a blanket and pillow. I arrived in Bill's room just after the doctors' visits. He was in bed and had been treated for his pain but was not allowed anything to drink or eat but ice chips.

The nurse told us he would go for an MRI as soon as they could get him in. I called our sons in California and told them their dad was in the hospital and we expected surgery but would not know until morning. I did not want to call our daughter, who was about five hours' drive away, because I knew she would strain herself to come. I did not want that because she was recovering from a serious *long-haul* COVID. I asked her brothers not to tell her yet, but they both thought this was a bad decision. I assured them I would call everyone when I had something official to report.

Bill drowsed all morning. At midday, I returned to our quiet, patient little dog, ate a quick sandwich, returned to the hospital, and found Bill's room empty because he had been taken for an MRI. By midafternoon, he was returned, and we spent hours hoping for a report. However, we would not know anything until morning. We were so grateful he was in good care, and I was allowed to stay with him.

I had to leave when visiting hours were over at 9:00 p.m. I fell asleep quickly in the RV. At about 2:00 a.m., our daughter awoke me with a phone call and said she just wanted to ask how we are.

I said, "Fine, but we were sleeping soundly."

She asked, "Are you sure you don't have anything to tell me?"

I responded, "No, we were asleep, and you need to be also."

Pamela has always had a strong sixth sense, and I could tell she *knew* something was up, but I had answered her questions honestly. I did not feel it was safe for her to drive down, and I knew she would want to, but the hospital could not let her in, and I needed to stay with Bill. I stayed awake the rest of the night praying for the doctors and Bill's healing. I got to the hospital again very early Wednesday morning. After a few hours, the MRI results were reported, and Bill was listed for afternoon surgery to remove his gallbladder, which was necessary due to infection. At lunchtime, I drove back for the dog. I cleaned the entire RV, not knowing what was ahead. I paid for two more nights at the campsite and made a grocery list.

I returned to the hospital at about 1:45 p.m., and Bill had just been taken for surgery. Of course, I knew nothing about the doctors, but I had requested an anesthesiologist instead of a nurse anesthetist. I had no knowledge or any control of the situation. I could only trust, and miraculously I felt deep peace. For over three hours in the surgical waiting room with others, I read and watched TV. On an electronic screen, the progress of each operation appeared regularly. When Bill went into the recovery area, the staff called me to say all had gone well. About forty-five minutes later, I was the last one in the OR waiting area and growing a little nervous since his board message had not changed. Finally, the surgeon came out to talk to me.

Dr. Saad was from the Middle East and had the kindest eyes and most caring manner. I was quickly at ease with him, and he assured me all had gone perfectly, and the gallbladder had been removed laparoscopically, which was the best way he had hoped for. The doctor had received his advanced residency in robotic surgery training in Greenville, South Carolina, known as the best place in the world to train for this, and he had lived just a half mile from our home! We bonded heart to heart, and I felt he was relating to me as a caring friend. He told me what to watch for after surgery, but he assured me all had gone very well, and the blood tests the next day would determine if any further procedures were necessary. He explained to me all about the gallbladder-liver-pancreas relationship and positions in our bodies. I was so grateful for all the time he spent with me.

A little later, Bill was returned to his hospital room, and I stayed with him for a while, although he was sleeping. By early evening, I drove to the nearby grocery store, bank, and gas station, so I was prepared for whatever happened. I returned to the hospital for a while, but I was exhausted physically and emotionally. I was not allowed to stay all night with Bill. He would sleep and be monitored constantly.

Although I knew this was best for both of us, I left a bit uneasy but thankful all was well, and we both could sleep.

On Thursday morning, I returned early again and found Bill alert and sitting in bed watching TV, vastly different than the previous four days! The doctors had already been in and declared he was doing well, took the blood for the tests, and said he would perhaps be dismissed later in the day. I objected because I did not feel capable of taking care of him so soon after surgery. However, the nurses said the blood tests would be the deciding factor. Glad that I had prepared everything the day before to be ready, I stayed all morning and saw he was greatly improved. Before he could be dismissed, Bill was required to break the fast of only water for the past three days and nights, eat a bit of scrambled eggs and toast, and be sure his body was functioning properly. At noon, nurses had orders that he must eat lunch, so he requested baked salmon, mashed sweet potato, and green beans and ate a good bit of each while the nurses schooled me on what he could and could not ingest after the ordeal he had been through. Without a gallbladder, he must have no alcohol or carbonated drinks and very limited greasy foods for a month and drink lots of water. He must walk as much as possible to get rid of the gas pains that follow abdominal surgery. Enduring this gas is very painful and lasts over a week. He was given directions about taking Tylenol and Gas-X or Pepcid. No other medications were necessary, as he had been given injections of antibiotics.

At my insistence, the nurses helped him bathe and dress in case we were forced to leave the RV park. About 1:00 p.m., a very cross elderly doctor we had not seen came in, sat on Bill's bed, and ordered us to evacuate. I begged him not to dismiss us till tomorrow, explaining we are from out of town and alone. He was rudely insistent and said the blood test results indicated he was well enough to leave. I begged again, and he said, "We must have the room for others who are waiting."

We understood this all too well, and we both just felt so thankful that they had had a room for Bill in his great need. I was so tired and frightened of the responsibility of caring for him so soon after surgery, but I went for the car and first drove to the RV to walk

Angel, leave our belongings from the hospital, and do the last preparations so that I could stay beside Bill 24-7. When I returned, just outside the hospital, I saw Bill waiting for me with the nurse who had pushed him in a wheelchair.

The short drive to the RV was no problem, and Bill was able to go up the two steps without much pain. Angel was wagging her tail in glee and welcoming him. I got him settled in the recliner in front of the TV and gave him water. Next, I called the children to tell them all we had gone through, and Bill assured each that he was okay. Our daughter confessed the boys had told her on Monday night, despite my request for them not to do so. She had called all the hospitals in that area of Pennsylvania until she found the right one and was told she could not visit there.

The worst was over! I went to the wonderful RV office staff and paid for two more nights. They were happy all had gone well. By late afternoon, we made a brief walk in the campground, ate soup, and headed for bed, both totally wiped out! The prescribed OTC meds got us through the night. The next morning, Pamela called to say she was on her way, although she and I, having had several surgeries ourselves, remembered the second day after surgery is the worst.

She said, "Mom, Daddy will probably be sleeping, and I know he will feel terrible today, but I am coming mainly for *you*!"

Oh, the timely and much-needed comfort of our caring daughter. She had mapped a way that took a little over two hours instead of five, as I had thought. While Bill slept in pain, her visit gave me the caring encouragement and strength I needed as we talked and snacked on the brownies and sweet bread she and our granddaughter had made for us from the fresh pumpkin we had picked at the patch the week before. At the end of the day, she insisted I go for Bill's necessities of Ensure, Gatorade, and more before she left us. That was wise because I was afraid to leave Bill alone. I could return before dark, and she could get home before too late. She had been such a joy and relief for me, and her wisdom, caring, and strength always amaze everyone. She had been so ill herself for months recovering from COVID-19.

On Friday night, I turned on the shower to get myself ready for bed, but there was *no water*. After studying the situation in his mind, Bill said, "The pump is broken."

We knew instantly this meant we would have to use public restrooms on the way home and *had* to stop in RV parks and attach water and sewer, but he was not able to do this, and I could not maneuver the backing and parking in a campground. I physically do not have the strength to lift the bars that were attached to the car, and Bill was not allowed to because of their weight. We were too tired to worry about it, and there was no one in the office to call for help. Bill showed me how to connect to city water, and we were able to make the night.

Saturday, Bill slept very late while I went to the office to ask who could come out to install a new pump. I called the numbers they gave me, and after nearly an hour, I found one dear soul who had the right type of new pump and came out to install it at our site. Expensive, but we were so relieved and appreciative because now we would need no hookups during the journey home. Bill was awake and watched football much of the day. He could eat a little more than yesterday, and he surprised me by feeling like walking around the edge of the large campground.

It was a shame Pamela had to teach horse training lessons and could not come on this day when Bill could have enjoyed her visit. He was so much improved it was miraculous. I called Dr. Saad that afternoon to ask his advice about heading homeward. He assured me the blood tests were good and we could do a follow-up with our doctor at home. Although we did not know it, he had come on Friday to the RV park to make a house call and check on Bill, but he did not find us. Bill talked to him and was instructed again to walk and drink lots of water to prevent blood clots and to pass the gas. We were so very impressed with this wonderful, caring doctor, and we hope he will come to Greenville and bring his family to visit us. He promised to do this someday.

On Sunday, Bill awoke feeling good and insisted we start homeward. It would be necessary for me to drive, and I was *really* scared of the responsibility and of getting on the road with my husband fragile so soon after his ordeal. Billie, one of the RV park managers, came to help unhook, fill with water, and reattach the car. Bill gratefully accepted the help while I got the RV inside ready to travel and took care of Angel. I prepared snacks and water bottles for the front seats, knowing he could not get up en route. Bill promised we would stop every hour for me to rest, and we planned to spend the night in Lexington, Virginia, at a large truck stop where we had stayed several times before when we did not need hookups. It was three hundred miles away.

We set out midmorning on Sunday, knowing the traffic would be lighter than weekdays. Highway I-81 South is a favorite route for truckers, and all highways in the northeast are very busy. Our route included steep mountains, and the wind was high. I drove the first hour with blue knuckles and a grip on the steering wheel so tight it made my shoulder muscles cramp. I inwardly kept repeating the Bible verse, "I can do all things through Christ, who strengthens me." I deliberately blocked fearful thoughts and kept also saying a motto from *The Little Engine That Could*, one of my favorite childhood picture books, "I think I can, I think I can, I think I can!"

Bill told me what to do in the strong gusts of wind, and on the winding mountain highway, I learned when and how to use engine brakes for steep descents. After about an hour, I pulled into the first rest stop, and we walked, rested, got snacks, and I started to relax, realizing I truly could do it.

Through all this, I learned I can do *anything* I *have* to do. Bill was fully alert, and if he were in pain, he did not indicate it. We found places to stop where I could drive in and drive out without having to back or turn the RV/car around, which was the length of a semitruck and fully loaded. At each highway rest stop, we walked, thankful our highways were so well planned for safety. Since we had the RV bathroom, we did not have to find facilities at stops, and that was very good because the pandemic was still in high force. Our little dog was happy to stop and walk frequently, and it helped Bill's gas pains. Our overnight at Lee-Hi Travel Plaza was uneventful and easy, and the huge noisy trucks alongside us with generators running served as our sleep sounds and sort of hypnotized us.

We pulled out early Monday morning, and I was more relaxed. I could even listen to our audiobook, which I had barely followed the day before. I drove to Charlotte, North Carolina, where we had planned to stay in the KOA, but we decided not to do so since it was only a hundred miles from home, and we were eager for the trip to be over. Because of highway construction and very heavy traffic, Bill said he could take over the driving through Charlotte area and into Greenville. I was relieved but hoped and silently prayed it was not the wrong decision for his midsection recovery. But he seemed fine, and he is an excellent driver and loves to be at the steering wheel. We had a two-hour standstill because of two accidents far ahead, but we finally got through Charlotte and two hours later, arrived in Greenville at our RV storage place, where he pulled in and the owner unhooked the car for us. At last, we were home Monday by early evening!

We both fell into bed right after we ate a quick supper from the freezer. I had told Bill I would only consent to drive if he promised not to try to help with unpacking the RV since he was not supposed to lift it. He agreed, and for the next three days, to my amazement, he slept and put up no argument about helping. I worked about two hours and then rested an hour throughout those days of unloading and transporting the RV contents a mile home by car. Because of COVID, we had not used any laundromats in the four weeks away, so I washed fourteen loads of clothes, towels, and bedding over the next two days. By Thursday, I had completed all the unloading, cleaned the RV, and put away all the items. Then I was the one resting for hours through the weekend.

Epilogue

Rolling On and On

S EVERAL OF OUR friends have asked through the years, "What do you recommend if we get an RV?" We have worn out eight different RVs of various sizes, types, and manufacturers. Our first response is, "Watch the movie *RV*," a hilarious film of novices having a holiday in an RV, for which our son, Blake, composed additional music. "We have experienced nearly everything that happens in that movie, and anyone who takes a house on the road will have many unexpected occurrences!" But we *love* RV life for adventure and exploration, for going to see our children on the two opposite ends of the USA, and for short excursions just to get away from the normal daily grind or boredom.

The most important answer is Bill's sage advice, "You *must* rent an RV before you buy one. Try it for a weekend at a nearby campground and see what you think. It will give you a chance to learn how RV's operate, test your ability to drive, park it, and learn how to hook up to facilities."

I add, "You will either *love* it, or you will *hate* it! And be forewarned, an RV is a tough test of your marriage! I loudly protested our first RV trip."

After all, our track record speaks for itself. After forty-seven years of holidays and long trips in an RV, we still *love* it and still enjoy each other's company. I think our *real ventures* have "bonded us at the hips," as our kids describe us with a smile.

After our emergency ordeal, the scary necessity for me to drive the RV towing our car home, and the exhaustion of unpacking and moving everything to our home, I vowed silently in my mind as I locked the RV, *I never want to get in this thing again!*

Of course, I did not say this to Bill, as I had very loudly when he bought our first RV. A few weeks later when he was fully recovered, he excitedly said, "Now since you can drive the RV, I think we will go to Texas next month. It is only a thousand miles to see our old friends!"

I gasped in reply, "Nope! You've got it all wrong! I am *never* choosing to drive the RV again!"

Although we are getting older and it is more difficult to drive across the country, we are hopeful of being able to continue, at least until our total mileage equals the earth's equator at least one more time! We will just limit our drives to no more than 300 miles a day instead of the 750 miles we have sometimes made in one day in earlier years when vacation time was running out. After all, now is the time of our lives! We hope to roll on and on and have many more *Real Ventures*. The problems along the way make the best stories!

When asked why we love it, we reply, "We can go places it is not possible to go any other way and enjoy nature and all the out-of-doors and spectacular scenery. It is truly a blessed time of togetherness with each other, with family, or friends, creating a bond that lasts forever, and having…

REAL VENTURES OF WONDER AND JOY!"

About the Author

BONNIE BURGESS NEELY has been known for four decades as a professional travel writer and founded the first and longest-running travel features site on the web, RealTravelAdventures. com. She was a scriptwriter and project coordinator in the 1980s for *Children of Portugal on Hawaii Educational TV* and *Ageless Arts of Portugal on Discovery TV*. She has been published hundreds of times in every form of media, including her book *ParenTips: Quality Time with Children*. In the 1980s and 1990s, she used the name Beth Stone for her syndicated column, Formulas for Fun, and for a child's self-help book, *Do You Have a Secret?* by Russel and Stone about child abuse. Search engines will direct you to many current travel adventures by Bonnie and Bill Neely.

Thanks to my intrepid driver, my partner for life!